on file

192   630
Donation

THE BRITISH PEOPLE
1760–1902

COLLEGE BR

THE
BRITISH PEOPLE
1760–1902

by

Dorothy Thompson

HEINEMANN EDUCATIONAL BOOKS
LONDON

Heinemann Educational Books Ltd
22 Bedford Square, London WC1B 3HH
LONDON   EDINBURGH   MELBOURNE   AUCKLAND
HONG KONG   SINGAPORE   KUALA LUMPUR   NEW DELHI
IBADAN   NAIROBI   JOHANNESBURG
EXETER(NH)   KINGSTON   PORT OF SPAIN

ISBN 0 435 31890 X

Printed in Great Britain by
Butler & Tanner Ltd, Frome and London

Contents

The British People

General Editors: Peter Mauger and Diana St John

The British People is a series of social, economic and political histories of Britain for Secondary Schools, and in particular for C.S.E. and G.C.E. work.

Titles in the series:

Preface

This is a short book describing about a century and a half of the life of a nation. In these years occurred some of the most profound and far-reaching changes that have happened in the whole of human history. It is inevitable, therefore, that a very great deal has had to be left out. Readers who know a good deal of history will find things missing which they think are important. I am sure they will be right, for many very important events and processes are missing from this description. The full story can only be told in hundreds of volumes, most of them not yet written. In this book I have tried to follow a few of the strands which move through the history of the people of England in the century and a half before the present one.

What I have tried to show is some of the ways in which historical change takes place. In particular, to show that history is not something that happens to people, but something which they have a hand in making themselves.

Dorothy Thompson

Acknowledgements

The author and publishers would like to thank the following for permission to reproduce photographs:

Radio Times Hulton Picture Library: 3, 7a and b, 8, 9, 10, 11, 12, 13, 17, 18, 19, 20, 21, 22, 23, 26, 29, 30, 31a and b and c, 35, 36, 39, 41, 44, 45, 46, 49, 52, 53, 54, 60–68, 71, 72, 73, 76, 78–89, 93a and b, 95, 97a and b, 109, 112, 113–119, 130–132, 133b, 134–140, 142–145.

Mansell Collection: 5, 16, 28, 40, 74, 69, 75, 77, 91, 93b, 110, 120–127, 129, 133a, 141.

National Portrait Gallery: 6, 14, 38, 42, 50, 57, 70, 92, 94, 111, 128.

National Martime Museum: 1, 51.

Aerofilms and Aero Pictorial Ltd: 37.

Hull Museums: 43.

Photographie Bulloa: 47.

A.C.K. Ware Photographs Ltd: 58.

Punch: 96.

Science Museum: 24, 25a and b, 27, 32.

Chapter 1

England in 1760

When George III came to the throne of England in 1760, he ruled over an island with rather fewer than eight million people living in it. It was an island whose people were known throughout the world as skilful sailors, and wild and rebellious citizens.

English Sailors

The sea was for England a protection – in spite of many foreign wars, it had been nearly two hundred years since an enemy had actually landed on English soil. It was also a very important part of the lives of the people. Many of them made their living directly by the sea, as sailors, merchants, fishermen, whalers, even smugglers, or as shipbuilders. The Merchant Marine was essential to the rapidly growing trade which England was exchanging with every part of the world. The Royal Navy helped to protect the sea routes, and was the most important part of the nation's armed force.

English seamen, however, were not keen to serve in the Navy. In spite of its importance to the country, pay and conditions were so bad that crews had often to be "pressed" into service. All around the coast, people went in fear of press gangs who, armed with cutlasses and headed by naval officers, patrolled the streets, looking for sailors to force into service in the Navy. Of course they often took men who were not seamen at all, and if they could not get enough men from the ships and dockyards, they collected the rest from the alehouses. Many a young man found himself aboard ship when he awoke after a heavy night out.

Once aboard, he soon discovered why the Navy lacked volunteers. Food was scarce and bad (it was supplied to the ships by "contractors" who would agree to victual a ship for a certain price, and then, by supplying cheaper goods, pocket the difference as profit), pay was only about half the pay on a merchant ship, and was very irregular, discipline was harsh, often vicious, and no attention was paid to the health or well-being of the men.

James Silk Buckingham, who joined the navy as a lad, tells in his *Autobiography* of the flogging to death of a deserter which he witnessed. The deserter, a young pressed man who had been dragged from his wife and family, and had tried to escape back to them, was sentenced to be "flogged around the fleet". He was taken in a launch and flogged in turn within sight of each ship of the fleet. In this case he was dead after visiting ten or twelve ships. The men aboard were forced to witness this cruelty; "The rest of the crew" Buckingham wrote, "pressed their lips closely and ground their teeth, and not a man among them all but seemed ripe for mutiny". Before the end of the eighteenth century there were to be actual mutinies in the Navy, after which things gradually improved.

The officers in the service, although they too suffered from the cramped quarters and bad conditions in some of the ships, were in general a good deal better off. They were mostly the sons of gentlemen, and entered the service as very young men or boys, getting much of their training and general education at sea.

1. "The Liberty of the subject", a young tailor with his scissors and tape in his pocket being captured by a press gang in spite of the rescue efforts of some of the local women.

The Countryside

Inland a great many of the people of England were engaged in producing the country's food. In 1760 Britain was still a grain-exporting country, and not much food was imported from abroad. Grain of various kinds formed the most important item of food – barley, oats, and rye as well as wheat. Fruit and vegetables of many kinds were grown and hops for making beer. There were stock animals for food – cattle, pigs, sheep and poultry. In addition to food crops, there were forests, whose wood was used for building and for ships, and flax for linen weaving was grown in several parts of the country. We shall be looking at the means by which these crops were grown and stock was raised in a later chapter.

Towns and Villages

Eighteenth-century towns were small by our standards. There were about 8,000,000 people living in England and Wales in 1750. 900,000 of them lived in London. In Bristol there were about 90,000 people. Nowhere else had more than 50,000. Many more people lived in the country than in the towns. But this does not mean that they all lived in agricultural villages. A great deal of the country's industry was carried on in villages and small settlements. There were mining villages – not only around coal mines, but tin, lead, iron, alum and silver in different parts of the country. There were iron works where the iron was smelted; weaving villages in the cloth areas of East Anglia, the West Country, Lancashire and Yorkshire, centres around Sheffield where knives and other tools were made, and areas in which knitting, by hand and machine, lace-making, rope-making, nail-making, quarrying, pottery, and very many more trades were carried on, all outside the large towns. Even in the mainly agricultural districts, the wives and children of farm workers, and sometimes the farm workers themselves, might do some work at home,

2

preparing wool or cotton for spinning, spinning it at a hand wheel, knitting, or some other craft connected with a manufacturing industry. Although in 1760 there were a few places in which goods were manufactured in large factories, by far the greater part of all work was done in the home, or in small workshops employing only a few people.

The Artisan

The second half of the eighteenth century was the great age of the *artisans*. These were skilled workmen who had served an apprenticeship in their trade. There were no technical schools to teach them, so that the skills of each trade had to be taught by master to apprentice, or sometimes by father to son. Machinery driven by power was hardly in use at all by 1760, so that it was the skilled artisan, working with his hands, who made possible the great expansion of trade and production which was already taking place before industry became mechanised. These people also made an important contribution to the social life of the country. When foreign visitors spoke with astonishment of the "independence" of the English workman, it was the artisan they were speaking of. An Irish visitor to London in 1760 was astonished to see, in a well-known coffee house:

> a specimen of English freedom, viz, a whitesmith in his apron and some of his saws under his arm, came in, sat down and called for his glass of punch and the paper, both of which he used with as much ease as a lord. Such a man in Ireland (and I suppose in France, too, or almost any other country) would not have shown himself with his hat on, nor any other way, unless sent for by some gentleman.

The artisans often had to travel, both in the course of their work and in search of work in their own trade; they often needed to be able to read and write, to understand plans and drawings and to be able to experiment with new materials and new ideas. So they were a mixture of the old and the new – inheriting the old practices of their trades, but bene-

fiting from the exchange of ideas which came from travelling and meeting people in different parts of the country. Their pride in their trade, and their importance in the growing manufacturing industries, gave them a feeling of independence. This set them apart from the agricultural workers, who tended to be tied to one place and one employer, to whom they had to show a proper deference.

1760 is sometimes given by historians as the year which marked the beginning of the *industrial revolution*. We shall be looking at this whole process in a later chapter. Looking back, we can see that an important start had been made by 1760, particularly in the understanding of the possible uses of steam power, but neither George III, who became king that year, nor the artisan in the

2.   A handloom weaver in the early nineteenth century.

workshop would have had much idea of the great changes that were going to take place in industry during the next forty years.

The Domestic System

The most important industry in England was still, as it had been since the Middle Ages, the manufacture of cloth, especially of woollen cloth. The industry was organised on what was known as the *Domestic System*. This system worked in various ways, but the important thing about it was that the work was done in the home. Sometimes a weaver, for example, would buy yarn, weave it into a piece of cloth, take his cloth to the market, sell it and buy more yarn and so on. But by 1760 it was more usual for the yarn to belong to a merchant, who would "put it out" to a weaver, and then pay him for his work when it was finished. In this case the merchant might actually own the loom on which the cloth was woven, even though it stood in the weaver's cottage. As you can see, there is a considerable difference between these two methods. A man who owned his own loom and bought his own yarn to weave was a small independent manufacturer, while the man who wove for the merchant was really not so very different from a factory worker, except that he was still in his own home. The trend was away from the small independent craftsman in the late eighteenth century. An important part of the domestic system was that it supplied work for whole families. Apart from the main processes like spinning and weaving, there were a great many other jobs concerned with the making of cloth, some of which needed little skill, and could be done by children. George, son of Samuel Crompton, inventor of one of the most important cotton spinning machines, tells how he used to help prepare the raw cotton "soon after he was able to walk":

> My mother used to bat the cotton on a wire riddle. It was then put into a deep brown mug with a strong ley of soap suds. My mother then tucked up my petticoats about my waist, and put me into the tub to tread upon the cotton at the bottom ... this process was continued until the mug became so full that I could no longer safely stand in it, when a chair was placed beside it and I held on to the back ...

Little George obviously enjoyed splashing about in the soapsuds. But the jobs were not all so pleasant. Sometimes little children wound bobbins for the loom until their fingers bled from the harsh yarn; then there was the revolting job of "sinking" the bobbins, when they had to be soaked in foul-smelling liquid, and the air sucked out of them through a hollow pipe. Another job done by children was the setting of wire teeth into cloth or leather for carding raw wool, a boring and often painful occupation, in which fingers must have got very sore and eyes very tired. Nevertheless, the children worked under the eyes of their parents, and the fact that they were able to work without going away from home was regarded as a great good fortune for the people in the woollen districts. Daniel Defoe wrote a famous description of the cloth industry in the West Riding, in which he commented with pleasure on the way in which whole families were at work:

> We saw the houses full of lusty fellows, some at the dye-vat, some at the loom, others dressing the cloths; the women and children carding or spinning; all employed from the youngest to the oldest; scarce any thing above four years old, but its hands are sufficient for its own support. Not a beggar to be seen, not an idle person.

This family employment was available to the home worker, whether or not he owned his own loom and yarn. In fact, as long as the work was done by hand, there were more small jobs to be done by women and children than there were the main jobs of weaving and finishing the cloth. This meant work for wives and children of men in other trades, particularly agricultural labourers, so that the centres of thriving textile trade were in general the centres of highest living-standards and fullest employ-

3. Hand combers.

ment for working people. The position of the great majority of these hand-workers was something between that of an independent craftsman, like a blacksmith or a shoemaker, and that of a modern factory worker. Although they worked at home, and could plan their working hours, they had to work to a time-plan, as the merchant would come round for his spun yarn, or his woven cloth on a certain day. The weaver who was late with his piece was in some ways in the same position as the worker who is late at the factory, but he did not work all the time within sight of an overseer or charge hand.

The Cloth Merchants

Their employers were the merchants who put out the raw wool to be spun and the yarn to be woven. Long before the invention of machinery which had to be used in factories, these merchants carried on very extensive businesses. Some of them had buildings in which spinning wheels and hand-looms were worked, some had "finishing shops" in which cloth which had been made in the homes of the weavers was dyed, brushed and finished under the eye of the merchant. But most, in the second half of the eighteenth century, still left the actual work to be done in the workers' homes. Many of the merchants came from farming families, like John Clough, whose story is told by a Yorkshire historian:

Mr John Clough, . . . a yeoman or gentleman farmer, in the latter half of the eighteenth century was engaged in business as a manufacturer of stuff pieces, such as calimancos, plain-backs and wildbores, employing hand combers and hand loom weavers, and having his yarn spun by the hand spinning wheel one thread at a time. He was in the habit of taking his tops [raw wool] into the dales on horseback, and delivering them out in small quantities to hand spinners, or, like other manufacturers of that day, leaving a bag of tops with a village shopkeeper, and allowing a small commission for his trouble, and the shopkeepers were generally ready to undertake this business as it brought additional custom to the shop. There is a tradition in the family that Mr Clough was the first to set up a pot-of-four (round which four combers could work) in Sutton, where it appears he had his warehouse for sorting and storing his wool, and for delivering out work to his combers and weavers. . . .

Here we have a picture of a typical man of this class. Well before there are any power-driven machines, he is gradually building up something very like a factory industry, controlling each stage of the production of the cloth, introducing new ideas to improve and concentrate the work. It is easy to see how the new inventions which developed in the later part of the century, and which we shall be looking at in more detail in Chapter 3 would be taken up eagerly by such men. They had the knowledge of the industry, the money to build mills and try out machinery, and the need, if their businesses were to grow, to bring in new and more efficient methods of production.

Domestic Servants

In country districts of England in which there was no textile industry, there was not as much chance of the wives and children of labourers getting work to do in their own homes. For the girls especially the best chance of earning a living was to go to work as a domestic servant. The number of people, men and women, who worked as servants of various kinds was very high, and during the next hundred years the number increased considerably.

The main occupations, then, of the ordinary people of England when George III came to the throne were as servants, outworkers – skilled or unskilled –, labourers, artisans, farm workers and sailors. In the cities, and especially in London, there were also many people who lived very precariously by begging, stealing or a mixture of both.

The Nobility

As in the other countries of Europe, a large part of the land in Britain was owned by a small number of noble families. These were the families with great titles and great estates. They lived on the rents from their property, farming land in the country, and houses and shops in the towns and cities. Most of these great landowners were peers – that is they were members of the House of Lords, and they or members of their families held most of the important positions in the Government. Because of their wealth and their ownership of land, they also had a great deal of control over who was elected to the House of Commons, as we shall see in Chapter 4. In 1760 there were about 170 peers. By the end of the century the number had gone up to nearly three hundred, as many wealthy families were given new titles in this period. These rich and powerful people made up only a very small proportion of the total population, which at the end of the century was about 9 millions.

The Gentry

Below the great families of the nobility came the lesser landowners, usually called the gentry. Of these, perhaps a thousand or more were people with titles, baronets or knights, and a far greater number, possibly around ten thousand, were landowning gentlemen without a title. Some of the "upper gentry" were probably a good deal richer than some of the nobility, for fortunes could be lost and estates run down even by peers. But in general the gentry belong to a class with less power and property than the nobility. They were, nevertheless, extremely important people. The very great houses were spread thinly over England, but the houses of the gentry were to be found in every village. They were the richest people in their own districts, the members of the upper classes with whom most ordinary people would come into contact. They provided Members of Parliament, magistrates, army officers, nearly all the positions of authority and power in the country below the very highest. They had a very direct effect on the life of the country. The quality of life in a village depended very much on the personality of the local squire.

If the squire was a good man, who wanted to make life easier for the people of his village, there was a lot he could do. Some provided schools and almshouses, and helped with gifts of food and fuel in periods of unemployment or severe weather. In many villages feasts and sporting events were provided by the big house, and occasions such as the weddings of the squire's children were celebrated by the whole village. Richard Oastler recalled the days during the late eighteenth century when Fixby Hall, in Yorkshire, was well-known for its hospitality. In a letter to the son of the former squire, he wrote:

> It is your father's wont to meet the saunterers in the grounds – not to discharge them, but kindly to ask them inwards. According to their ranks, the servants' hall, the housekeeper's room, or his own table, afforded refreshment to their need.
> He was the only very rich man in the place; and he was careful to prevent any from being *very* poor.

There are many such instances of hospitality and generosity by squires who kept a friendly and kindly eye on their tenants and their families.

There are also, of course, many examples of cruel and thoughtless men, who forced their own views on the village, who were ruthless in their enforcement of the game laws, and who made themselves thoroughly hated.

The Clergy

The Church of England clergyman at this time could be classed with the gentry. In the country in particular, he lived very much as they lived, indeed many clergy came from noble and landowning families. Most country vicars were farmers as well, and many of them landowners. Many were men of considerable education, and some became known as writers, or as scientists – especially as naturalists. The one thing they were not as a whole outstanding for was their work in their parishes. It was a widespread custom for clergymen to serve several parishes so as to have the income from them all. This made for greater comfort, but usually it meant that some at least of the parishes were very neglected. A hard-working parson, and his wife, could find a lot to do in an eighteenth-century village, and there is no doubt that some did take their work seriously, and worked hard to make life better for the people they served. In some places the vicar and his wife and daughters taught in village schools, visited people who were sick, and generally helped and advised those who were in need. But in many more parishes this sort of work was left to a poorly-paid curate, while the vicar and his family lived the life of country gentlemen. If a young man from a wealthy family wanted money he could go into trade or become a lawyer. If he wanted adventure there was the East India Company, or a career in politics, but if he wanted a quiet and comfortable life, with no effort involved, the Church was for him.

Merchants and Bankers

Land was the most important kind of property in the mid-eighteenth century, because it carried power with it. The landowners controlled Parliament and the Government. They were the class that ruled the country. But there were other kinds of property-owners in Britain at this time. We have already seen how the clothing trade was organised by merchants who put out work and sold the finished cloth. In the towns

4. A small country inn, around 1800.

and cities there were many other merchants, some buying and selling goods made in England, some engaged in trade all through the world. Some of them were owners of great shipping fleets, and many of them, having made fortunes in trade, had become bankers, and made further fortunes by lending money and handling money for other merchants. In many European countries, trade was considered rather a disgraceful occupation. In England, although owning money or goods did not give political power, as the ownership of land did, there was nothing disgraceful about trading. Members of many noble families went in for it — especially younger sons who would not expect to inherit land. People who made their money by trading were often able to buy land, and so become part of the politically powerful ruling class. The daughters of rich merchants married the sons of lords, and brought some of their fathers' money into the countryside to build huge country houses or lay out elaborate parks. It was a period when money was flowing into the country, and much of it went to increase the fortunes of the landowning classes.

But there were plenty of families, especially in the towns, who had made their money in trade, who had no particular interest in becoming country gentlemen. Their sons might become doctors or lawyers, or go into business on their own account. They were comfortably off, and in some of the older boroughs they might have votes, and take part to some extent in the affairs of the town. But on the whole such men, especially if they were not members of the Church of England, and many were non-conformists of various kinds, played very little part in the government of the country, or of their own district.

Innkeepers and Shopkeepers

Below the merchants came the shopkeepers and innkeepers. There were a surprisingly

8

5. A London coffee house in the late eighteenth century.

large number of innkeepers, for in those days of slow travel, before the coming of the railways, people of all classes were often in need of meals and a room. Inns ranged from large comfortable places with plenty of servants and splendid meals, to cottages where the poorest sort of people, including beggars and thieves, slept several to a room. Inns or beershops provided then, as now, a centre for social activity in towns and villages. There were also coffee shops in most towns where people could meet, read newspapers and discuss the news. Coffee-house keepers and shoemakers were great sources of news, local and national, and their shops were centres for gossip and discussion.

Shopkeepers varied from the pedlar, with his pack of ribbons and pins, who travelled through the country districts selling to farmers' wives and maidservants in districts which were out of reach of town shops, to the city merchant. More substantial pedlars, selling pots and pans and other household goods, travelled by cart, making regular tours of country fairs and markets and apothecaries or herbalists filled the rôle of doctor in many districts.

To give a picture of all the different sorts of people who lived and worked in George III's England would take a whole book in itself. London alone, the greatest city in the world, held a tremendous variety of people of every trade and profession. It was a great age for English painters, writers, actors and architects. There is no room here to do more than mention a few names, but one of the best ways of getting a picture of the life of the times is to look at some of the books that were written at the time, or at some of the pictures which were painted. Portrait painters like Sir Joshua Reynolds, Thomas Gainsborough and George Romney painted the aristocrats, gentlemen and merchants and their families, and the portraits were hung in the town or country houses of their

6. David Garrick, one of the greatest actors in the history of the English theatre: a pupil and friend of Dr Johnson, he was painted in this portrait by Sir Joshua Reynolds.

subjects. These houses, designed by some of the greatest British architects of all times, were also being decorated with the work of artists and craftsmen whose names we do not know – wood-carvers, casters of lead or plaster statues and ornaments, smiths who made the grates, stoves, gateways and palisades of wrought iron, gilders and painters who decorated buildings and coaches.

London was a lively centre for writers and journalists. The novelists Samuel Richardson, Tobias Smollett and Laurence Sterne were all alive and writing in 1760, and their books describe many aspects of the life of the times. The London theatre was flourishing with the great actor-manager, David Garrick, at the height of his career. Altogether, it was an age in which creative arts of every kind seemed to be being produced and being appreciated by growing audiences.

George III

George III, who came to rule over Britain at the age of twenty-two, was the third king of the House of Hanover. Like his predecessors, he ruled also over the small German State of Hanover, but unlike them he had grown up in England, and saw his chief work as king of England. He came to the throne at a time when the monarchy was not at all popular. His father, Frederick Prince of Wales, had died in 1751; a rhyme written at that time gives an idea of some peoples' attitude to the Hanoverians:

> Here lies Fred,
> Who was alive and is dead.
> Had it been his father,
> I had much rather.
> Had it been his brother,
> Still better than another.
> Had it been his sister,
> No one would have missed her,
> Had it been the whole generation.
> Still better for the nation,
> But since 'tis only Fred
> Who was alive and is dead,
> There's no more to be said.

The young king brought to the throne a seriousness and devotion which had been lacking at the time of his grandfather and great-grandfather. But although he was to rule for sixty years, he never achieved great popularity with the English people. It was not until the reign of his grand-daughter, Victoria, that a new respect for the monarchy was to emerge. George's own life was to be shadowed by illness – he was for years subject to fits of apparent madness, which became permanent in the last ten years of his life, when he was blind and deaf as well. He had a large family, but for all his own piety and the high moral tone of his court, his sons brought little but disrepute to the monarchy.

In 1760, Britain was still at war with France. The Seven Years' War lasted another three years, and ended with a victory which established Britain as one of the great powers of Europe. Above all, it established her as a great trading and colonising power; her possessions and trading rights in India, in

7a.   George III in 1760.

7b.   George III in 1820.

North America and in the West Indies had been strengthened, and her fighting strength had been proved.

George III became king at the beginning of a period of English history when the country was just beginning to change very rapidly. The story of the next 150 years is the story of these changes. At home the old ways of farming and of manufacturing goods were to be replaced with quite different methods – new people were coming into control and new ideas coming into use. These changes were to affect Britain's place in the world, as well as the life of her people at home.

Chapter 2

The Changing Countryside

By far the greatest number of English people in the eighteenth century lived in villages. Some of them were craftsmen, or worked in country industries, but the majority worked on the land.

If you were to go back two hundred years into the English countryside, the thing which would strike you at once would be the un-hedged fields. We are used now to farms which have a farmhouse and farm buildings, surrounded by fields, fenced or hedged. In some of the fields we expect to see crops growing, in others animals feeding. But in eighteenth-century England, most of the good farming country was being farmed quite differently, on what was known as the *open field system*. The change from open to enclosed fields was one of the most important things which happened in the English countryside in the last two hundred years. To understand how it happened, we must first have a look at the open fields.

An Open Field Village

If you look on page 14 you will see a plan of the small Lincolnshire town of Barton. The shaded bits near the top of the plan are the houses and gardens of the township itself, and the land around is divided into several large pieces. The three largest are labelled West Field, South Field and East Field. The other divisions have names – Horse Pasture, Cow Pasture, Marsh, The Ings and Common Wold. At the very bottom is a shaded area called Warren Farm. This was the only farm at the time which was fenced in in the modern way. At some time its owner had fenced in part of the old common, and turned it into a farm. But the rest of the district was still farmed as it had been for centuries.

Each of the three great fields was divided into strips, probably of about an acre each. You will see that there will have been hundreds of these strips in each field. Every farmer in the village had some strips in each of the fields. The rich farmers would have a great many strips, but scattered about in the fields, not all in one lump. In this way, each man would have a share of the good and poor land in each field. Many hundreds of years ago the earliest farmers had discovered that land gets tired if the same crop is grown on it year after year. This was the reason for the three fields. On each field crops would be grown for two years – sometimes different ones, wheat, then barley or oats, and then the third year the land would be allowed to rest, or lie fallow as it is called. In that fallow year, animals would graze on it, and the land would be rested and manured ready for planting again. And as each farmer had some land in each of the fields, he would never be in the position of having all his land resting at once, even if he only owned a few acres. Some villages had only two fields— one under wheat and one fallow each year, and a few had four, but probably the great-est part of England's best farmlands were farmed like Barton, with a three field system.

As well as the three great fields, Barton had its pastures and commons. The Ings was the meadowland, where hay was grown, and the Common Wold and Marsh, were stretches of land which was not good enough to grow crops. On these pastures and commons each farmer would have the right to graze his animals – horses which were very important to him in those days when all carrying as well as ploughing had to be done by horses; cows – probably only enough to provide milk for his own family; pigs – very valuable for salting and putting away for meat during the winter; and perhaps a donkey or a few geese, although these would probably have to scratch around on the poorer common land, and would not be allowed on the good pastures. There were rights, too, of turning his animals to graze on the big fields after the corn had been cut, rights of taking hay from the Ings for winter feed for the horses, perhaps the right to take a certain amount of bracken from the commons for his animals' bedding, and wood for his fire.

You can see from this that the farmers of Barton would have had a pretty good idea of how their farming would go each year. They would know which field was going to be planted, when the harvest would be and the time to turn the animals out to graze. These things were done year by year, as they had been done for centuries.

The Parson and his Tithes

There were other people in the village who had a place in the year's activities as well as the farmers. At one end of the scale was the parson, who, as in many districts, had the right to a tithe, that is one tenth of all that the farmers produced. In Barton he also had a few strips and he farmed this land (called the glebe) and was still allowed his tenth share of his neighbours' farm produce. As you can imagine, this was not at all popular with the farmers. A Lincolnshire paper

8. A small farm in the eighteenth century. Notice the hay and straw stacks, and the plough and cart. The horse, essential for all farming activity, has the best building apart from the farmer's own family.

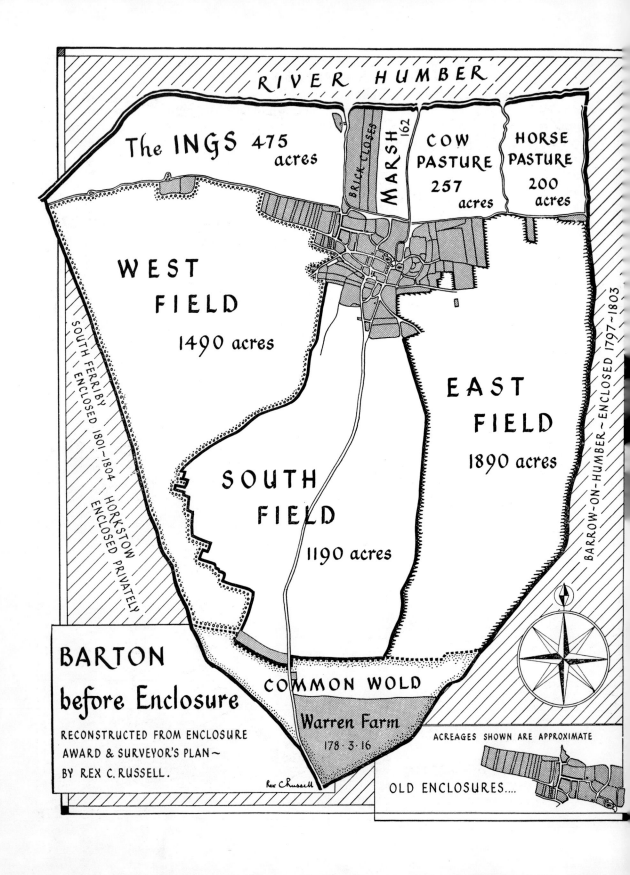

RIVER HUMBER

The INGS 475 acres

BRICK CLOSES

MARSH 162

COW PASTURE 257 acres

HORSE PASTURE 200 acres

WEST FIELD 1490 acres

SOUTH FERRIBY · ENCLOSED 1801–1804

HORKSTOW ENCLOSED PRIVATELY

EAST FIELD 1890 acres

BARROW-ON-HUMBER ~ ENCLOSED 1797~1803

SOUTH FIELD 1190 acres

COMMON WOLD

Warren Farm 178·3·16

BARTON before Enclosure

RECONSTRUCTED FROM ENCLOSURE AWARD & SURVEYOR'S PLAN ~ BY REX C. RUSSELL.

Rex C Russell

ACREAGES SHOWN ARE APPROXIMATE

OLD ENCLOSURES....

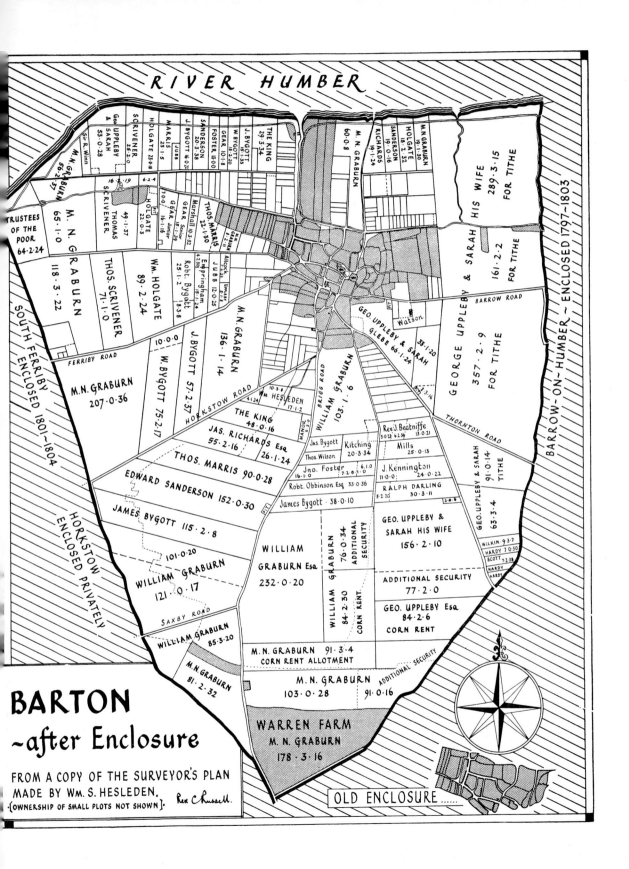

BARTON ~after Enclosure

FROM A COPY OF THE SURVEYOR'S PLAN MADE BY WM. S. HESLEDEN. Rex C Russell. [OWNERSHIP OF SMALL PLOTS NOT SHOWN].

OLD ENCLOSURE

9. "The Tithe Pig."

10. "The Ghost of Small Tythes."

published some rhymes about the parson and his tithes which no doubt caused some chuckles on market day . . .

There's not a joy the Parson gives like that he
takes away,
When he eyes a tenth of all the land and claims
it for his prey.
There's not a pig the Parson takes from out the
farmer's sty,
But grunts to leave his native home, and heaves
a bitter sigh.
There's not a cow the farmer hath that grazes
in the field,
That doth not low and swing her tail whene'er
the pig is killed.
There's not a turkey in the yard but gobbles
more and more
Whene'er he sees the parson enter at the farmhouse door.
There's not a goose the farmer hath that swims
upon the pond
That doth not stretch his neck and hiss to see
his master wronged.
There's not a thing upon the farm but shows
some kind of fear
Whene'er he hears the name of Tithes, and
finds the parson near.

The rhyme goes on to tell how the animals pull the parson into the duck pond and drown him, after which they all sleep more soundly.

The Cottagers

At the other end of the scale from the parson, were the cottagers or squatters. These were usually poor people who had built small houses on or near the common, and had come to have certain common rights. They might keep a couple of geese, or a pig, on the common, even though they had no share in the open fields. They perhaps gathered firewood, berries and mushrooms, and managed to make some sort of livelihood by working at harvest time, by begging a bit if times were very hard, and poaching when they got the chance.

The Rest of the Village

Between the parson and the cottagers were a number of people like the parish clerk, who owned a few strips, and in return looked after matters like the keeping of records, seeing to the election of the Parish constable and the Parish overseer of the poor. In some places the schoolmaster was also paid by the gift of some strips of land which he farmed in his spare time. Then there were always some craftsmen – the miller, the cobbler, the harness maker, the blacksmith and others, who did work which had to be done in the village, and were paid by the farmers.

Even the smallest farmer would get a certain amount of money by taking some of

16

11. A parson in difficulties with the collection of his tithes.

his produce to market. With this he would buy the things which he did not grow himself. There were not many shops in the villages, apart from the inn, but there were travelling pedlars, and fairs which came on holidays, at which it was possible to buy necessaries like pots and pans, and luxuries like hair-ribbons and lace.

So, in our open field village, we have the houses standing together along the main street of the village, with the fields and commons spread out around them, and everyone in the village knowing his place in the life and work that went on. Some of the customs were written down, like the list of the vicar's tithes. Some of them were never written – like the right of some poor cottagers to put their geese on the common. But since everyone in the village knew of these customary rights, there was not usually any argument about them.

The open field system had gone on for centuries. Why, then, did the changes come?

The Population Increase

The chief reason for change was that the number of people living in England was beginning to get very much greater. In the hundred years between 1750 and 1851, the population of England and Wales nearly trebled. From around 6,250,000 in 1750, it grew to 18,109,410 in 1851. People did not realise exactly what was happening until after 1801, when the first census – that is a Government count of all the people in the country – was held. After that, there was a census every ten years, and although these early ones were not very accurate,

17

they soon showed clearly that the population was steadily increasing. No one knows exactly why this happened at this time. It was happening especially in the countryside. People in the towns were living in such over-crowded and insanitary conditions at the end of the eighteenth and beginning of the nine-teenth centuries, that more children died and the death rates generally went up, but in the country as a whole more people were being born, and they were living longer.

This increase in the number of people to be fed put strains on the old ways of growing food. A system which had jogged along, just about managing to feed a fixed or only slowly growing population, was not able suddenly to start producing more. More people to be fed meant that more money could be made from good farming. So naturally landlords wanted to get more out of their estates. The people of the country needed the food, and the landlords wanted to try and give it to them.

The old open field system was undoubted-ly slow and wasteful. Look at the fourteen hundred and ninety acres of Barton's West Field. Each one of these would have its narrow path around it, wasted space on which weeds could grow, or vermin live. After each harvest the cattle would be allowed to come charging on to the fields, as they had done for centuries, to graze until they were slaughtered before winter set in. For the hay from the communal meadow land was only enough for winter feed for horses, and a few beasts for breeding. The rest had to be killed and sold in the autumn.

But in some parts of England and in some other countries there were new ideas about all this. Root crops, turnips and swedes, were being grown for winter feed, both for humans and cattle. But customary pasturage rights prevented the open fields from being used for root crops. New crop rotations were being talked about which, by using roots and clover, cut out the wasteful fallow year altogether, and made the land immed-iately much more productive. But in the common fields the animals – including the weedy scraggy beasts of the poorest farmers – relied on the fallow field for pasture. How-ever many new and profitable ideas for farming a landowner might have, if his land was scattered in strips all over a series of open fields, he had no chance of putting these ideas into practice.

Enclosures

And so, like many other parishes, Barton was "enclosed". What this meant was that a special Act was presented to Parliament, asking for permission to enclose the common fields. Parliament agreed, and appointed three lawyers to go into the whole question. It was the job of these Com-missioners, as they were called, to find out, first of all, whether the owners of three-quarters of the land (*not* three-quarters of all the landowners) wanted to enclose. Then they had to find out who owned all the various strips of land, and what claims each person had to common and grazing rights. Then they had to draw a new map, dividing up the fields and commons between all those who had land or claims on the old open fields. They had to allow for roads on the new plan, often they made these roads with wide grass verges which could be let for grazing or haymaking, the money from the rent going to help with the cost of keeping the road in good repair. When they had sorted out these and many other questions, they held meetings of all landowners, and listened to any appeals against their findings.

If there were no appeals, or if the appeals did not succeed, they finally signed the papers and plans. These papers, known as the Enclosure Award, were kept as the record of the land ownership for that particular area. Each landowner should now have a piece or pieces of land equal in value to his old strips. He had the job of fencing and draining his land, and he could then go ahead and farm it as he pleased. Most modern farming and stock breeding dates from the days following the enclosing of the common fields.

From the point of view of growing more and better food, there is no doubt that the move was an excellent one. But how did it affect the villages?

In Barton, there were 126 landowners listed, who, the Commissioners agreed, were entitled to a share of the enclosed land. The Award lists them all by name, with the amount of land they were given in the final share-out. Three of them got more than 600 acres each – these three between them had about two-thirds of all the land. Another seven got more than 100 acres each. These ten big landowners had 81 per cent of all the land. The other 19 per cent was divided between 116 owners, of whom 37 had less than 2 acres. All these owners, big and small, had to fence and drain their land, and then arrange their own way of farming it.

The New Farming

For the big farmers this was the chance to use new methods, and to draw ahead of the old slow ways of their village. All over England

12. A prize ram.

13 Pedigree cattle.

14. "Turnip" Townshend.

15. Thomas Coke of Norfolk: in the background is his house, Holkham Hall.

landlords and farmers were doing this. The names of some of the most enterprising have gone down in history – like that of Viscount Townshend, who was one of the first to realise the possibilities of root crops. He used a four-year rotation, growing turnips and clover and never leaving the land fallow. The turnips he used for winter feed for his cattle, keeping them alive and healthy. He was so proud of the results he achieved by this means, that he got the nickname of "Turnip Townshend" – it is, after all, not a bad thing to be remembered for. Another famous landowner, Thomas Coke of Holkham, in Norfolk, used these methods, and divided his land into model farms which became famous all over England. People made journeys to see the results of his planning – fine crops, strong healthy animals, neat strong houses for the farm workers and stables for the horses. By doing all this he increased the rental value of his estates from £2,200 a year, to £20,000 a year, and his tenants still made bigger profits than ever before.

In the breeding of animals, too, the enclosed farms shot ahead. No longer were all the animals in a village herded together, catching each others' diseases, scrabbling for what food was going. Now it was possible to choose out the best beasts for breeding, give them better food, keep them apart from the herd. The name of Robert Bakewell of Leicestershire is especially remembered here, particularly for his New Leicestershire sheep. One sign of the improvement in animal breeding is the fact that in 1710 the average weight of sheep sold at the London meat market at Smithfield was 38 lb., and by 1795 it was 80 lb.

All this improvement in agricultural methods was very exciting. Magazines were started, giving news of what was being done in different parts of the country, and describing the new tools and new crops which were being used. In 1793 the government set up the Board of Agriculture, to help and encourage the new farming. The secretary of the Board was called Arthur Young. Young was one of the keenest writers about the new farming methods, and he travelled all over England, seeing what was being done, and writing about it. It is from his writings and from the reports that he asked for, that we get much of our picture of the enclosures and improvements of the end of the eighteenth and beginning of the nineteenth centuries.

Young was enthusiastically in favour of enclosures. And yet, as he travelled around, he began to notice that all was not well. As we have seen, for the big landowners and farmers, enclosures were a great advantage. But what about the poorer people – the 37 men and women in Barton, for instance, with less than two acres? And what of the other people in the village, the cottagers, even the squatters? Gradually, as he looked around, Arthur Young came to the conclusion that, as he said, "By nineteen out of every twenty enclosure acts the poor were greatly injured".

How did this happen? First of all, there was the actual legal expense of the enclosure act, which had to be shared by the landowners. Then there were other expenses – draining and fencing the land where the new roads were to be built, fencing off the land which was given to the vicar in place of his tithes when the fields were split up, fencing in other odds and ends which did not belong to any one owner. In Barton, the costs of the act and these jobs came to £13, 18s. Each landowner had to pay a share of this. Then he had to drain and fence his own land. You can imagine that a man who had managed to jog along and make a poor living from a couple of strips in the open field would not be likely to have the ready cash for all this. So that a great many of the small landowners sold their allotments straight away. And money does not last as long as land. Even if the small man did not yield to the temptation to spend all his money at once in the nearest town, it would still only last him and his family for a short time. Then he would be a labourer, and depend on what he could earn by working for someone else, either in the village, or if there was no work there, he would have to move on to the nearest town and look for work.

The cottager without any land would probably be worse off still. If he could bring proof that his right went back for many years, he might get a small allotment when the common was enclosed, but many hundreds of cottagers and squatters would have no rights at all, even to the land their cottages stood on. Their scruffy donkeys and half-starved geese would have to go, and with them their chance of a livelihood in the village. There are many versions of a rhyme about the cottagers, who were often accused by the landlords of being thieves and gypsies:

> They clap in gaol the man or woman
>   Who steals the goose from off the common,
> But let the greater thief go loose
>   Who steals the common from the goose.

So the small landowner and the cottager were either forced to leave the village, or had to stay on as labourers, depending on someone else to give them work. And when we remember that the population was increasing, we can see that it must have seemed as though the enclosure movement was driving people off the land into the unhealthy and overcrowded towns. It may well have been that in some areas the enclosed farms provided more work for labourers than the old strips, but there were many more looking for work.

The feeling of injustice, the belief that they had been robbed by the rich enclosing landlords, remained very strong amongst the poor people of England, and their children.

The Village

The Nineteenth Century saw the slow decay of the village. New farming methods were only one of the many factors which helped this. The development of factory industry in the towns meant that the jobs like spinning and weaving by which many farm workers had made a bit of extra money were no longer possible. As transport became easier, people were able to move around looking for work or houses. The narrowness of village life, overshadowed as it was by the vicar and the squire, drove the more adventurous of the young countrymen away. The fact that girls could get work in the towns, as servants or in the factories, whereas there were very few jobs for girls in the villages, meant that the daughters of farm labourers left the village when they could, and then, of course, usually married away from home. Above all, the very low wages given to farm workers and the impossibility

16. Cabinet making. The work was hard and the conditions often crowded, but the craftsmen worked at home or in workshops attached to their houses, and so were near their families, instead of working in factories away from home.

in most places of a labourer ever working his way up into a more independent and better paid job, made farm-work something which the country as a whole despised. Although so much of the life of the country depended on the farm worker, he continued to be ill-treated and underpaid and looked down on, badly housed, his children badly educated. The old community of the village, in which each person had a position and a job, slowly disappeared, and by the beginning of the twentieth century England became a land of overcrowded towns and cities, with a countryside of dying villages around them.

The Game Laws

In the late eighteenth and early nineteenth centuries the game laws also got stricter. These were the laws which made it possible for a landowner to protect the wild game on his estate, from rabbits and pigeons to pheasant, grouse and deer. They were protected to provide sport for the landowners, and as the people of the countryside became poorer, so the laws to prevent them from getting a bird or a rabbit for the pot became more harsh.

These laws were not put into operation to help the farmers. In fact, most of the farmers did not like them at all. The tame, or partly tame birds which were raised for shooting ate the crops, and farmers were not allowed to shoot them. The only people who were allowed by law to shoot game were the very rich and their sons – less than one in ten thousand of the people of England. But they controlled Parliament, and they managed to get a whole series of Acts passed to tighten up the punishments for poaching. These got steadily more harsh from 1770 onwards. Poachers took to working in gangs, and there were pitched battles with gamekeepers. In 1816, when the end of the Napoleonic wars made life very difficult for the poor in the countryside, a law was passed which was said by Samuel Romilly, an M.P. who opposed it in the House of Commons, to have no parallel in the laws of any country in

17.   The iron forge, a painting by Joseph Wright of Derby.

the world. Under this Act any person who was found at night with a net for poaching in any forest or park could be punished by transportation for seven years. This applied even to unarmed men – mere possession of a net was enough. This was the high point of the campaign. Romilly and others were able to introduce later Acts which made the punishments rather less strict, but even so, poachers were still transported to convict settlements if they were found with guns or bludgeons. The justices who administered the laws were landowners, and they were all

too ready to convict poachers. A song from Liverpool at this time warns the "rambling lads" to

> Watch out for the gamekeepers,
>   Keep your dog at your command,
> Or you'll find yourself transported
>   To far Van Dieman's land.

The song goes on to describe the journey, until the convicts, the poachers among them, are landed in Van Dieman's Land (now

Tasmania) – and offered as labour to the farmers:

> They lined us up like cattle
>   And they sold us out of hand
> And yoked us to the plough, me boys,
>   To plough Van Dieman's Land.

The horrors of transportation hung over any criminal in the early years of the nineteenth century. It was a cruel and atrocious punishment. Now it was added to the penalties of being poor in the countryside.

The Poor Law

What help was, then, available to out-of-work labourers, or to widows, orphans and the sick or disabled?

The English Poor Law in the eighteenth century was chiefly based on a set of regulations made in the reign of Elizabeth I. By these laws each parish was responsible for its own poor. It had to raise a poor rate from all the property owners and out of this either find work for the unemployed, or pay them enough to live on until they found work. It had also to keep orphan children and others who had no one to support them, and to provide either hospitals or workhouses or money for the sick. This system worked for two hundred years – it was suited to a fairly small population, in which every person in each village was known. It had one great disadvantage for the poor people, however, which got worse during the eighteenth century. This was that in order to get relief, the poor person had to be "settled" in a parish. He could only get relief from his own parish.

The Acts of Settlement

There were various ways in which a person could be settled. He could work for a certain length of time in one place. If he had been born in a village or owned property there, he was considered to be settled there. Women got "settled" in their husband's parish when they married. But the point was that in times of bad harvests, when work was hard to get, a labourer could not just go and work in another village, where things were better. Villages did not want to allow new labourers to "settle", because they would then have to look after them if they were ill or out of work. Each parish was anxious to get rid of its own poor, so overseers of the poor sometimes smuggled people into neighbouring parishes. The effect of all this was to make movement of poor people much more difficult. They could not follow work, nor could a man move into another village when he married, to get, say, a better house or job, because the other village would not want a new family who might soon, with their children, come to depend on the poor rates.

As unemployment in the villages got worse, there was less work for the women and children to do at home, at the very same time it became more difficult and dangerous for the men to provide wild game for food, and it remained the most difficult thing in the world for a poor or unemployed family to go around the country looking for work.

Only in places where there was a real shortage of workers did the authorities ignore the settlement Acts. In the manufacturing districts it was easier to move in and find work than in the farming villages.

The Speenhamland System

In the 1790's, food prices rose because of the war. But the farm labourers' wages did not go up. There were too many men looking for work, so that the farmers were able to pay the lowest wages. Many people, in the House of Commons and in the country, thought that the government, or the local Justices of the Peace, ought to fix a living wage for farm workers, and punish those farmers who would not pay it. A group of Justices met at Speenhamland in Berkshire in 1795, to consider suggestions on this question. They discussed the whole matter of the labourers' wages, and came to a very important decision. They did not decide to fix a wage which the farmers had to pay. But they did agree that wages were too low. So they decided that

18.   The poacher, a drawing of a countryman trapping a hare in a noose. The smock the man is wearing is the working dress of an agricultural labourer at the beginning of the nineteenth century.

in their districts, they would fix a wage, according to the price of bread, to which every labourer would be entitled. It would include an allowance for his wife and each of his children. If the labourer was unemployed, he was to be allowed this amount of money from the parish poor rates. If he was working, but not earning enough, he was to get the difference from the poor rates. This should mean that every labourer got enough to live on, however dear bread was, and however many children he had.

This method of paying poor relief became known as the *Speenhamland System*. On the face of it, it looks a fairly sensible way of doing things. In the North of England it was used as a sort of unemployment pay in times of bad trade, and it seems to have worked. But in the South and Midlands, in the farming districts, its effects were disastrous. First of all, if the farmers knew that the parish would make up their men's wages, they did not bother to pay a living wage. So a great many labourers, even when working full-time, were still getting poor relief. And since they got it anyway, there was no particular reason why they should work too hard or look for better jobs. To make sure there was no "slacking", the parish usually made the unemployed do degrading work, like breaking stones, for their unemployment "pay".

The effects on the family were very bad. There was no reason for a man to wait to marry and have a family until he was earning a good wage. He probably never would be. So people tended to marry younger and younger, and have their children earlier. This may well have been the main reason why the population in these depressed and poverty-stricken counties went up faster than in other parts of the country.

The Effects of Speenhamland

So, the labourers suffered. Their wages were kept down; their chance of improving their position by hard work was lost. The small farmers also objected. They paid poor rates, but many of them did not employ day labourers. They either did the work with their own family, or had a living-in farm hand. So they objected to paying poor rates which went to make up the wages of the rich farmers' workers. The effect in the country-side was to divide the rich farmers from the poorer farmers, and to divide off the poor people altogether into a new depressed class, living on charity, discouraged from using their own abilities to the full to find work, or to do the work they had.

To see this system at work we cannot do better than to look at one actual case. In 1830, a member of Parliament visited Bedford Gaol. He saw and spoke to many of the prisoners. Among them were two brothers named Lilley. They had been caught together poaching, and had fired on and wounded the keeper who had disturbed them . . .

They were two remarkably fine young men, and very respectably connected. The elder, twenty-eight years of age, married, with two small children. When I enquired how he could lend himself to such a wretched course of life, the poor fellow replied: "Sir, I had a pregnant wife with one infant at her knee and another at her breast; I was anxious to obtain work, I offered myself in all directions, but without success; if I went to a distance, I was told to go back to my parish, and when I did so, I was allowed – what? Why, for myself, my babes, and my wife in a condition requiring more than common support and unable to labour, I was allowed 7/– a week for all; for which I was expected to work on the roads from light to dark, and pay three guineas a year for the hovel which sheltered us".

The other brother, unmarried, received 6d a day.

These two brothers, found guilty of wounding the gamekeeper, were hanged that spring.

Chapter 3

The Industrial Revolution

The population of England was growing. There were more mouths to feed and more backs to clothe. At the same time, England's trade was expanding. As the eighteenth century went on, British industry was becoming more highly organised. Even before they started to use water-power or steam power to drive their spinning machines, some manufacturers began to gather their workers together into factories where they could watch them at work.

The Beginning of Factories

To begin with there were very few of these factories. On the whole, working people did not like the idea. They did not like the idea of "public" work. Work was something you did at home. You were paid by the results – it was nobody else's business how you worked. So to begin with the factories tended to be in workhouses or orphanages. But they were efficient. The merchant could plan his sales better if he could watch the work progressing. So some of the bigger merchants began to finish the cloth in factories. The weavers would do the weaving in their own homes, then deliver the cloth to the merchant. He would have the final processes – brushing, mending, fulling – done in his own workshop. Then he knew that all the cloth would look alike when he had got it ready for sale. He would know when it would be ready. Even those who did not have any of the work done in a factory, began to organize the work more. Instead of going to the local markets and buying cloth from the weavers, they would take orders, then put out the yarn to the weavers, and pay them for their work

when it was finished. If there were not enough weavers to do the work, the merchant might buy some looms and either let them out to people to use in their own homes, or rent a shed or house and have the weavers work there for him. So that, although in 1760 there were not very many people working in what we should recognize as being a factory, there were very many who worked for a master, on *his* materials, sometimes with *his* tools.

Kay's Flying Shuttle

The pressure was all the time to increase the production of cloth. Even in the early part of the eighteenth century it took 12 spinners to keep one weaver supplied with yarn. But in 1733 John Kay invented a "flying shuttle". The shuttle is the piece of wood which carries the weft of the cloth through the threads of the warp, which are threaded on the loom. It is like the needle taking the cross threads in darning. Until Kay's time, the shuttle had to be thrown across between the threads, and on a broad piece of cloth it needed two men – one to catch and one to throw. Even on a narrow width the weaver had to throw the shuttle from one hand to the other, but with Kay's invention he had simply to tap it from side to side with two sticks – which was both quicker and more accurate. This meant that weaving was greatly speeded up, and the weaver needed even more spinners to keep him at work. It was at this time, in the middle years of the eighteenth century, that the wives and children of farm labourers, even in parts of the country quite far away from

27

19. Hargreaves' Spinning Jenny: one worker could spin on a whole number of spindles.

the main wool and cotton weaving centres, were able to earn money by preparing and spinning yarn for the weavers. Merchants from the West Riding would ride up into the Yorkshire dales to put out wool for spinning, and to collect it, and the farming families in the West of England relied on the spinning of women and children to make a living wage. It was at about the time when enclosures were becoming widespread in the countryside, that the labourers and cottagers lost this way of earning extra money.

Machine Spinning

In 1764 a weaver, James Hargreaves, invented a machine which would spin several threads at once, instead of just one at a time. He called it jenny, a corruption of the word gin, or engine. The spinning Jenny greatly speeded the production of yarn, but two more inventions brought about a far greater change. In 1769, Richard Arkwright, a barber by profession, invented a water frame, which used the power from a waterwheel to turn a slightly different kind of spinning machine. This was known as Arkwright's water frame. In 1775, Samuel Crompton, a weaver, combined the two, and made his *Mule*. This used the principle of Hargreaves' jenny, with water power. It could turn hundreds of spindles at a time, and produce cotton yarn at a great rate. These inventions made two very important changes in the whole system of manufacturing cloth. In the first place, it became possible to produce fine and regular thread in very great quantities. In the second place, because of their size, and cost, and the fact that they needed water power to run, they had to be used in a factory.

So it is really with the introduction of Arkwright's frame and Crompton's mule that factories become an *essential* part of the textile industry. As we have seen, many merchants had already seen their advantages, but now they had really come to stay. It is important always to remember that changes take time, and in the days we are speaking of, when so many of the inventions were totally new, it took longer for people to see their value than it would take to-day. Even so, by the end of the eighteenth century, the *dominant* method of spinning, in both wool and cotton textiles, was machine spinning. This meant that the farmers' wives in the outlying districts had lost a means of making extra money at home. Even in the districts nearer to the weaving centres, very much less hand spinning was done. To make up for the loss of money in the home in these areas, the women and children increasingly went to work in the factories.

The Factory Workers

For a while, the great increase in the yarn that was available meant much more work for the weavers. In Yorkshire and Lancashire particularly, people flocked into the weaving areas. It did not take long to learn the trade of a weaver, and with the good supply of yarn and the excellent trade which resulted partly from the contracts for soldiers' uniforms during the Napoleonic Wars, there was a golden age of weaving. Indeed, the manufacturers, who wanted cheap labour for their cotton spinning mills, found that at first they could not entice the weavers' children in.

So the people who worked the earliest cotton spinning mills were what were called "pauper apprentices". While trade and industry in the north were expanding, and work was getting more plentiful, the agricultural villages in the south and midlands were stagnating. The local Poor Law authorities there and in London were finding it more and more difficult to put orphan children, or the children of the very poor, in

20. Inside an early cotton mill. The frames on each side moved backwards and forwards by power, and the girl worker joins the threads, while the boy under the frame cleared the waste material.

any sort of work. So that when they heard that manufacturers in the north were finding it hard to get workers for mills, they saw their opportunity. Hundreds of these little "Parish apprentices" were sent into Lancashire and Yorkshire. It is almost impossible to imagine the conditions in which these first little mill workers lived and worked. No one bothered very much about them. The water mills, placed by the best streams, were far enough away from other buildings to prevent any interference by outsiders with the children.

Child Workers

Once inside the mills the children from the age of six onwards were usually put to work as piecers – that is, they had the job of joining the threads. The very little ones had to crawl under the machines to keep them clear of waste, and others were doffers – they had to replace the big bobbins when they became full of yarn. John Fielden, a manufacturer from Todmorden, who himself had started work in a cotton mill at ten years of age, once tried to work out how far one of the children in his mill walked in a day. He found that in twelve hours, which was the usual working day, the distance covered would be twenty miles. There were no chairs or stools in these early mills, and children were beaten if they sat on the floor. So for twelve, thirteen, fourteen or sometimes sixteen hours a day, these small children worked standing up in the hot damp fluffy atmosphere of the cotton mills. They were often not allowed proper breaks for meals, but had to eat their bread while they were cleaning down the machines. It is hardly surprising that they were seldom hungry, or that they had to be given medicines to make them sick when they swallowed too much of the cotton fluff which filled the air. At many of the mills shifts were worked by day and night, and it was said that the beds in the apprentice houses were never cold. When one lot of children crawled out of bed, the others who had been working crawled in.

Boys and girls slept together, several in a bed, between horse blankets.

Factory Laws

The general public took surprisingly little interest in the lives of these little paupers. It was, in the end, one of the manufacturers who got the first law passed to protect them. The *Health and Morals of Apprentices Act*, of 1802, was introduced by Sir Robert Peel the elder, father of the man who was later to be Prime Minister of England. Peel was the owner of a very big cotton factory. The local magistrates had twice complained of the treatment of the apprentices at Peel's works.

However, the Act which resulted from his interest said that the children were not to work more than twelve hours a day, not counting meal times, and that these hours must be taken between 6 in the morning and 9 at night – that is, there was to be no more night work. The children were to be given lessons in reading, writing and arithmetic, and an hour's religious instruction every Sunday. They were to have a suit of clothes once a year, and girls and boys were to sleep in separate rooms, and not more than two in a bed. You would hardly think that anyone could quarrel with these rules – unless they felt that they did not go far enough. But, as with every other Act that was introduced later to protect the factory children, employers from all over the country cried out in complaint. They declared that it would ruin the cotton trade – that unless they were allowed to work some of the children at least at night, they would go bankrupt, and that to take an hour or two from the working day to educate the children "would amount to a surrender of all the profits of the establishment . . .". They need not have worried. The government had made very little provision for enforcing this Act.

The Free Labouring Children

But another change was taking place. This was connected with the discovery of steam power. This meant the factories did not have

21.   Early steam mills in Manchester.

to be by the side of fast-running streams, and the employers found that in the towns it was more profitable to use "free labour". At first, as we have seen, the weavers did not allow their children to go into the factories. But in the early nineteenth century there were too many weavers especially as the machines did more and more work. Weavers' wages fell and many families had to send their children to work in the factories.

We learn about the conditions under which these children worked mainly from a series of government reports. There were people, Robert Owen of New Lanark in Scotland, John Fielden of Todmorden in Lancashire, Richard Oastler of Fixby Hall, near Huddersfield in Yorkshire, who, together with Michael Sadler and Lord Ashley in Parliament, devoted their lives to trying to improve the conditions of these little factory workers. They saw to it that committees were appointed, and that these committees got to know the facts about the way the mills worked. From the pages of

these reports and from the debates in Parliament we can build up a picture of life in the early cotton, wool and worsted mills.

The Health and Morals of Apprentices Act was passed in 1802. It was sixteen years before another Act concerned with the factory children was introduced, and it still concerned only cotton mills. The debate around this Act is interesting for the efforts by employers and economists to prove, not only that children were necessary to the industry, but that the cotton trade was doing them a great service by employing them. Lord Lauderdale produced doctors who claimed that working for twelve or more hours in a mill was good for children. People were impressed by these arguments, and the bill was not passed. A year later the debate was opened again. This time doctors were called who declared that the effect on the children's health was indeed disastrous. Perhaps even more impressive was the evidence given by some of the men whose job it was to keep the children at work. One explained to the committee that his master

31

22. Child workers in a cotton factory, an illustration from a novel written to help the campaign for better working conditions in the factories.

made him beat the children to keep them at work:

"What master was that?"

"Mr. Luke Taylor; I have seen him with a horse whip under his coat waiting at the top of the place, and when the children have come up, he has lashed them all into the mill as if they were too late: and the children had half a mile to come and be at the mill by five o'clock."

But the Act which was finally introduced had little effect. There were no inspectors appointed, and six years later only two convictions had ever been made under it.

Until 1832, the year of the Great Reform Bill, the few acts which were introduced into Parliament were of little help to the factory children. They applied only to cotton mills, but there were by now woollen, worsted, flax, and silk mills in which conditions were every bit as bad as in the cotton mills. There was no way by which the government could enforce the laws – a factory child could hardly complain to the magistrate if his employer asked him to work more than his legal day. In any case, even if some outsider – a clergyman or a schoolmaster for instance – did report a case of a factory which did not obey the law, it was often to find that the magistrates in the factory districts were all mill-owners themselves, and that they were not prepared to punish their friends.

Factory Reform Movement

Two kinds of people were mainly responsible for the gradual reform of the factories. One was the good employer. Amongst the many thousands of masters, large and small, a few stand out. John Fielden we have already mentioned. He entered parliament solely to fight for better conditions for factory workers, young and old. Another outstanding employer was John Wood, worsted manufacturer of Bradford. He made a fortune from the trade, but he spent a very large part of it on trying to improve the conditions of the children. It was Wood who introduced the factory movement's greatest leader to the cause. This was Richard Oastler, a land steward from Huddersfield. Oastler encouraged the factory workers themselves to form committees, called Short Time Committees. They organised petitions, meetings and demonstrations all over the factory districts. They ran their own newspapers, and gained the support of existing papers in Lancashire and Yorkshire. They provided evidence for the various committees of enquiry that were set up. And in the end, as we shall see in later chapters, they broke through the opposition, and forced a change in the law.

The Industrial Revolution

The great change in the way people lived and worked which took place in the towns during the second half of the eighteenth and the first half of the nineteenth centuries, is usually called "The Industrial Revolution". A

Revolution means overturning one kind of power, and replacing it by another. It is usually a word that is used about governments, but you can see why it has been used about the changes in people's lives at this period. It is quite a useful idea, as long as you remember that it did not happen, as a political revolution might do, by one set of people sitting down and planning a kind of war on another set. It all happened with very little apparent planning or purpose. And although something of the sort soon began to happen all over the world, it happened first in England.

As we saw in the textile industry, factories were organised with hand labour and with water power before the invention of steam engines that could work them. So steam did not start off the industrial revolution. Still, it did bring about some of the most startling changes. When steam was available, factories could be built anywhere, and the great smoky towns which we associate with modern industry grew up. By the middle of the nineteenth century, more people lived in towns in England than in the countryside, for the first time in our history. And this was largely the result of the steam engine.

Two men stand out in the history of steam. One was James Watt, the man who perfected the industrial steam engine, the other was Matthew Boulton, his partner, who made possible the development and manufacture of Watt's inventions.

James Watt

Steam as a source of power had been known since the time of the ancient Greeks. They had developed steam engines and steam turbines as a sort of toy. The principles had been used by later inventors and by the eighteenth century there were already a number of engines used in England. These were mainly pumping engines – the early ones being built on the model of one invented by Thomas Savery, called "The Miners' Friend, or an engine to raise water by fire"; the later ones on a rather more efficient model designed by

23. Richard Oastler, leader of the movement for shorter working hours in factories and for the abolition of child labour.

Thomas Newcomen. In 1769, when Watt started working on it, Newcomen's engine was used in hundreds of collieries all over England, to pump out water. Both these early engines had two great disadvantages. They had to rely on very poor workmanship in the making of their parts, with the result that accidents and explosions were common, and they needed a very great deal of heat to work, which meant that they were only really suitable for coal mines, where there was a lot of cheap fuel ready to hand. If you look at the diagram of Newcomen's engine on page 34, you will see why this last point was so. The cylinder in which the piston worked had to be cooled down by cold water at each stroke. This meant that it had to be completely re-heated before the next lot of steam was let in. Thus an enormous amount

33

24. Diagram showing the working of Newcomen's engine – a cumbersome machine which could only be used for pumping, and was only worth installing in mines where there was plenty of cheap fuel.

The ENGINE for Raising Water by Fire

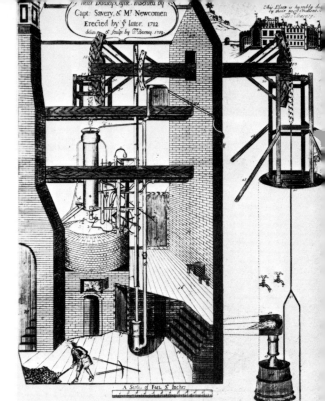

25a. Newcomen's atmospheric engine erected by him near Dudley Castle in 1712.

25b Drawing of Watt's 10 h.p. rotative steam engine 1787, from John Farey's *Treatise on the Steam Engine 1827*.

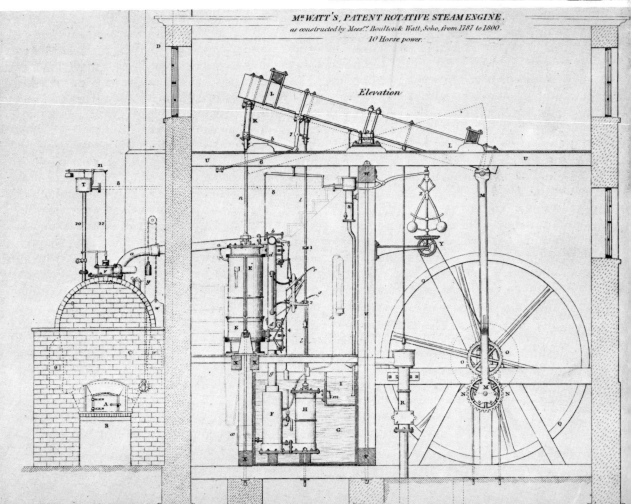

of heat had to be used just in re-heating the cylinder, before it even came to making the steam. Watt saw this waste of heat, and overcame it by using a separate condenser. In his engine p. 35, the cylinder containing the piston remained hot all the time, but the steam was condensed in a condenser. This engine could be used to work a much more efficient pump, operated by a great deal less fuel. It is interesting to note, too, that originally Watt wanted to use a furnace which saved fuel by consuming its own smoke, but as this would have been more expensive to build, the idea was never taken up. If it had been, some of the worst of the dirt and smoke of the early towns might have been avoided.

James Watt was a Scotsman, from Greenock. His father was a builder and merchant in a small way of business. Young James became a scientific instrument maker, but he had no desire to work the usual seven years' apprenticeship before he started on his trade. He had a mind which was able to grasp every aspect of mechanics and engineering with great speed, and he knew he would be bored by the long apprenticeship that custom demanded. There were no technical colleges or schools which could teach him, and he finally did one year's training in a London workshop before coming back to Scotland and setting up a small repairing and manufacturing shop in the University of Glasgow. Here he had a certain amount of regular custom, and, perhaps even more important to him, the chance to talk about his interests with some of the ablest men of the time, mathematicians and doctors and students. It was while he was repairing the University's model of a Newcomen steam engine that he was able to overcome the main problem and perfect his own engine. The money to make the models was given and lent to him mainly by one of the professors, who saw the very great possibility of his work.

But a project like a totally new kind of steam engine was enormously expensive. Every piece of the engine had to be made individually, at a time when iron and steel making was still very primitive. To make a working engine would cost thousands of pounds, and there were many times when Watt quite despaired of ever being able to build one. He had to earn his living at the same time, and although he would have liked to make money from his invention, he had very little hope of doing so until he met Matthew Boulton.

Matthew Boulton

Matthew Boulton was an entirely different sort of man from Watt. Where Watt was nervous, sickly, and always turning his mind inwards on some problem which he carried in his head or on his drawing board, Boulton was a natural business man and showman. He delighted in projects for making goods and for making money. He was always prepared to risk his money on an idea. He organised and managed a huge works employing 1,000 men at Soho, Birmingham. He was the ideal partner for Watt, his courage and daring allowed him to risk many thousands of pounds that he had made in other enterprises, until finally the partnership began to make some money. They had very many problems to solve, both mechanical and financial before this happened. The great break-through came when Watt invented a way of adapting his steam engine for rotary drives – so that it could be used to turn machines and not only for pumping. It was soon in use in the new cotton mills, and Watt was able to enjoy a comfortable old age on his profits. Boulton was not so happy; for him retirement was separation from all that made his life interesting, and we are told that as an old man he used still to "totter down the hill to see what was going forward at Soho".

Boulton and Watt had introduced a new and important industry to England – the manufacture of heavy machinery. Their problems with workers were just the opposite of the cotton masters. Here were no factories to be worked by little girls. They needed a constant supply of skilled mechan-

26. Boulton and Watt's works at Soho, Staffordshire.

ics and engineers, and these were very difficult indeed to get, or to keep. There were laws to prevent skilled workmen from leaving the country, but they nevertheless went to most European countries, tempted by handsome salaries. They were lured away by rival firms in England, sometimes taking important inventions with them. Watt had not much sense of how important a good engineman was – perhaps because to him the work seemed simpler. He was always trying to sack men who made mistakes. "If possible", he wrote to Boulton on one occasion, "have the whole brood of these engine-men displaced, if any others can be procured; for nothing but slovenliness, if not malice, is to be expected of them . . ." Fortunately Boulton knew better.

Iron

The great advances in machinery which the inventions and work of Watt and Boulton brought about were only possible because at the same time great advances were being made in the manufacture of iron and steel. England had always used a great deal of iron, but at the beginning of the eighteenth century two-thirds of the high quality iron

for manufacturing was imported from abroad – mostly from Scandinavia and America. It was used to make many important things. In one great iron works near Newcastle, which Arthur Young visited on his tour of the north in 1768, "They manufacture anchors as high as seventy hundredweight, carriages of cannon, hoes, spades, axes, hooks, chains etc. etc." Soon there would be added to this list boilers and other parts for steam engines.

The great difficulty about the extraction of iron from ore in England was that, until the early years of the eighteenth century, the furnaces for actually getting out the raw iron had to be fired by charcoal. It was not possible to use coal for this, and so the iron works had to be sited near good supplies of wood. In many parts of the country, wood was grown especially to provide fuel for the iron furnaces, and the trade of charcoal burning was carried out on many hillsides. The wood had to be burnt for a long time in very slow fires, covered with earth, before it became charcoal suitable for furnaces. There simply was not enough natural forest in England for this trade, and so it was cheaper to import foreign iron ready to be worked.

27.   The iron works at Coalbrookdale.

The next stage, in which the iron was melted down and worked or cast, could be done with certain types of coal, so the iron-works tended to be established near the coal fields – in Newcastle, Rotherham and South Wales. As well as wood and coal, the iron works needed a good supply of water to drive the great hammers, and of all the English rivers, the Severn was the best for this purpose. It was therefore, above all, in the valley of the Severn that the iron works flourished.

The Darbys of Coalbrookdale

The secret of using coal instead of charcoal for furnaces was discovered by Abraham Darby, an iron-master of Coalbrookdale in Shropshire. At first the method was kept secret by the firm, and used only for cast iron. But in about 1750, the second Abraham Darby, son of the inventor, used it to make higher quality iron, which could be worked as well as cast. The Darbys were Quakers, and were not interested primarily in making profits from their inventions. They did not take out a patent for their method of using coal in blast furnaces, and they refused orders for cannons and other weapons of war. In spite of this, their works increased greatly, and they were kept busy making all kinds of goods for peaceful use. It was at Coalbrookdale that the first iron rails were made in 1767. Until that time rails made of hard wood had been used in many mines for carrying trucks, drawn by ponies or children. In 1779 the company made the first cast-iron bridge across the River Severn. In the quiet valley the great iron works grew and spread out. In 1776, Arthur Young visited them:

> Coalbrookdale itself, he wrote, is a very romantic spot, it is a winding glen between two immense hills which break into various forms, and all thickly covered with wood, forming the most beautiful sheets of hanging wood. Indeed, too beautiful to be much in unison with that variety of horrors art had spread at the bottom; the noise from the forges, mills, etc. with all their vast machinery, the flames bursting from the furnaces with the burning

of the coal and the smoak of the lime kilns, are altogether sublime, and would unite well with craggy and bare rocks ...

The Darbys were good employers, but many of the iron-masters had a very bad name. The town which grew up around the works at Merthyr Tydfil was said, even as late as 1848, to be as filthy as Bombay, in its total lack of drainage or rubbish disposal, and in the overcrowding of its houses. In between there were varieties of good and bad employers. The ironmasters were much bigger men than most of the cotton masters. There were not so many of them, and their factories and works were much larger. Some of them coined their own money in their works, and paid the workers with it, and as they owned the shops and houses around, they could force the men to use it. Since the ironmasters were also usually the magistrates in their own districts, they had the law on their side. The few strikes or protests which did occur at the beginning of the nineteenth century were more like outbreaks of civil war, in which the employers had on their side all the forces of the law, and the workers were driven to use methods of terrorism rather than of peaceful negotiation. It is hardly surprising that in the rest of the country, the iron towns were regarded rather like the frontier towns in the American West – places in which you might get rich quick if you worked hard, but in which the life was tough and brutal.

The improvements in the steam engine which better methods of manufacturing iron and steel made possible, also brought great advantages back to the iron industry. Steam hammers and steam-blown furnaces increased the efficiency of the works. By the end of the eighteenth century, instead of importing two thirds of the iron we needed we had begun to export iron. By the end of the 1820's we were exporting four times as much bar-iron as we were importing from abroad. The English iron and steel industry had become firmly established.

Other Factors in Industrial Advance

Iron, steam, and the moving of the textile industries into factories – these are three of the most outstanding things in the Industrial Revolution. But there were other changes and inventions which had a great deal of effect. For one thing, it was no good inventing machines if there were no materials strong enough to make them, or workmen and tools which could work with sufficient accuracy to follow the designer's plans. An example of this can be seen in the development of the steam engine. In the days of the Newcomen pumping engine, the cylinders were still often made of wood, bound with metal hoops. The designers had to expect mistakes of half an inch in a cylinder of 28 inches diameter. Airtight seals were nearly impossible if work could not be done more accurately than that. So that when Watt produced his first models, one of the great designers of the time said "neither the tools nor the workmen existed that could manufacture so complex a machine with sufficient precision".

It was the work done in the iron industry which produced better metal and more accurate boring machines, and so made Watt's engines possible. Even so, it was said that as late as 1830, a fitter who could work to one-sixteenth of an inch was a good workman. So it is important to remember that all the developments which took place in the nineteenth century, for instance in the use of railways, or the development of electricity and gas for power and lighting, depended on the fact that improvements were being made all the time in tools, machines such as lathes and milling machines, and in the combination of metals. Aluminium, for instance, only became widely used in industry after 1886. It would be impossible to imagine the modern aircraft industry without it, yet it is the inventor of the flying machine whom we all remember, and not the man who first produced aluminium in an electric furnace. There is not space here to go into the story of these developments. For our purposes, it

28. "Late for the mail", in spite of the uneven roads, horse-drawn vehicles could go at a good speed when necessary, in this case, to put a passenger on the mail coach.

is just necessary to remember always that the industrial revolution was brought about by the work of hundreds of mechanics, scientists and engineers, as well as a few great inventors.

Roads

All the advances in trade, in the use of new kinds of power, made it more necessary to be able to move goods and fuel easily about the country. But English roads in the mid-eighteenth century were quite dreadful. Travellers constantly complained that carriages got stuck in the mud, or even overturned on the bumpy tracks. If two vehicles had to pass each other, one sometimes had to go back for miles. The pack-horse tracks which crossed and re-crossed the country were only suitable for carrying small loads by pack-horses in single file. Heavy loads of coal were usually taken by coastal ships rather than by road. In 1760, when the period covered by this book opens, there were a few good roads being built by the turnpike system. This was done by groups of trustees being appointed by the government, who raised money from amongst the landowners in a given district. They then built a road, and got the money to keep it up by having toll gates at which every-

one who used the road had to pay, according to the size of his vehicle or load. This method of road building is used today in some countries to make motorways, and it has the advantage of getting the money from the people who actually use the road. It was not very popular with the people in the English countryside in the eighteenth and nineteenth centuries, however. The local farmers and villagers objected to paying tolls. They had been quite happy with the old bumpy tracks, and thought the new turnpike roads had been built for travellers and traders from outside at the expense of the local people. There were riots and demonstrations against these roads, in which local people attacked and destroyed the toll gates.

John Metcalfe

There are three outstanding names amongst the eighteenth-century road builders. Like the developing industries the new roads called for special abilities, and there were no schools for road-building engineers. Perhaps the most remarkable road engineer was John Metcalfe, a Yorkshireman, known as blind Jack of Knaresborough. The son of poor parents, he went completely blind after an attack of smallpox when he was six. In

40

29. A pack-donkey carrying raw wool.

30. A toll gate on a turnpike road, in 1806. If this is an example of a well-maintained road, the others must have been pretty terrible.

spite of his blindness, he became a first-rate rider, and found his way all over the wild and trackless moors of Yorkshire. In fact he earned his living for a long time as a guide and as a carrier. By 1765, when he applied for the job of repairing part of a local highway, he was so well-known locally that he was given the job, although he did not have any particular experience. He made such a success of it that he decided to give up his whole time to road-building. How was a blind man able to plan and build some of the best roads that England had ever had? The answer probably lies in Metcalfe's combination of imagination and great attention to detail. He was a huge man, of enormous energy, and, with his long stick feeling the way, he used to pace every step of the route to be covered, feeling the differences in the soil and rocks. He attended to every detail of the plans, from the first routing of the road to the rations for the men working on it. And all these plans and details he was able to carry in his head. He worked on until he was over seventy, building the great trading roads connecting up the main Yorkshire towns, and the tolls of Lancashire and Cheshire. In 1793, he retired, bought a small farm, and wrote his life story – or rather dictated it.

He went on farming until he died at the age of 93.

Thomas Telford

Thomas Telford was the son of a shepherd. Like Metcalfe he came to road building without previous experience, having been a stonemason by trade. He built hundreds of miles of roads in the West and Midlands, including forty-two bridges, and also constructed the Ellesmere canal, one of the engineering wonders of the time.

J. L. Macadam

The third name is more familiar to us than either Metcalfe or Telford. We still call the smooth surface of our roads *Macadamised*, after J. L. Macadam. He first used small bits of granite to surface roads, packing together into a sort of natural smooth concrete. Before his time, road surfaces had been built up of large smooth stones or flints. His new system was used all over the world. Apart from the surfacing, he also came to know more about road-building than any one else in the country, and planned and supervised the building of roads for thirty-four different boards of turnpike commissioners.

When we think of the development of roads, then, we remember particularly

41

31a.   A canal crosses the river – the Rolle canal and aqueduct near Torrington, Devon.

31b.   The canal and barges going through the Great Hill called Harecastle, Staffordshire.

31c.   A horse-drawn barge passes a windmill on the canal near Liverpool.

Metcalfe, Telford and Macadam. When we turn to the building of canals, we come to a man who was in some ways even more remarkable.

James Brindley

In 1759, James Brindley was asked by the Duke of Bridgewater to build him a canal between Worsley and Manchester. The Duke was a big coal owner, and he was finding that to get his coal to Manchester from Worsley by cart or pack horse was costing him nine or ten shillings a ton, for a journey of only seven miles. He therefore asked Brindley, who worked for him as an engineer, to design and build a canal. France had already begun to build a series of inland canals, but in England, apart from a bit of digging out to help some of the shallower rivers, nothing of the sort had been done before. Brindley was quite uneducated – he never learned either to read or to write, but he attacked the problem. Road-building was a complicated business, with embankments and bridges to be planned. But an artificial water-way presented even bigger problems. Brindley used two rules. One was always to build a new bed for his canals, never using the soft beds of existing rivers; and the other was always to keep the line of the canal level, not to use locks to raise or lower the water. So his first canal began with an underground gallery, and reached Manchester finally by crossing the River Irwell on an aqueduct forty feet high. By this means it flowed level all the way. When it was finished, it was regarded as the eighth wonder of the world. After that, Brindley was kept very busy. The first canal was such a success, and lowered the cost of transport so much, that the Duke planned a bigger canal, from Manchester to Liverpool. The result of this was to halve the cost of transport between the two cities. For the last years of his life, Brindley worked without ceasing. He seldom made even simple plans of his great projects, but carried all the details in his head. When a very difficult problem arose, he would go to bed for several days, working out the details in the quiet of his room. Like Metcalfe he had the imagination and the memory to be able to deal with every detail of a complicated scheme.

Brindley died in 1772, before his greatest canal, the 93-mile Grand Trunk Canal from the Trent to the Mersey, was finished. But he had started a fever. In less than thirty years since the first canal had been started, England was covered with waterways. Without them it would not have been possible to move around the great loads of coal needed for the steam-driven factories. It would have been far more difficult to move the increasing loads of manufactured goods, particularly breakables like pottery, which the industrial revolution made possible.

An enormous amount of money was spent on the building of canals. On the big and much-used canals people got a good return for their money, for they became very profitable. Many of the owners and shareholders must have felt very secure in having such a constant source of profit available to them. But the day of the canals was short. As early as 1784, William Murdock, the engineman who worked for Boulton and Watt, built, for his own interest, a model of a steam traction engine, which ran at eight miles an hour. No one was very excited about this – but it was a foretaste of something that was to put many of the canals out of business before long.

Railways

Murdock's steam car, and other models which had been made in France at about the same time, were for running on roads. It was Richard Trevithick, who first thought of using a steam traction engine on rails. There were miles of wooden, metal-plated, and iron rails in mines and works in various parts of England. At the iron works in Coalbrookdale there were twenty miles of rails, along which horses drew loaded waggons. Trevithick built a steam locomotive for use there in 1803. It drew ten tons of ore and 70 passengers at five miles an hour. Although they

32.   The Lickey Inclined Plane, a stretch of the Birmingham and Gloucester Railway, opened in 1840.

33.   *The President*, an early steamship, built in 1839.

34. Grand Junction Railway works, 1849. Building rolling stock for the world's railways became one of Britain's major industries.

were not very efficient, and tended to break down rather often, these steam engines showed the possibility of a new means of transport. The man whom we remember above all for his early steam locomotives was George Stephenson.

George Stephenson

Stephenson carried on where Trevithick had left off. He made improvements in design which increased the possible speed of steam locomotives. In 1821 a plan for a public railway line was drawn up, to run between Stockton and Darlington. It was to be worked "with men and horses or otherwise". Stephenson gave a demonstration of his steam engine, and it was adopted. The line – the first public railway in England – was opened in 1825. In 1830, in spite of opposition from canal owners and landowners and farmers, a Liverpool to Manchester railway was opened. This time the directors had

organised a competition with a prize for the best locomotive to run on the line. Stephenson's *Rocket* was not only the best, it was the only one which fulfilled all the conditions for the prize. At the trial it pulled 30 passengers at 30 miles an hour.

The railway had arrived. From 1830 onwards lines spread all over the country. By 1848 there were 5,000 miles of railways in Britain. Steam locomotives on land and steam ships at sea speeded up transport at home and abroad, and made it possible for manufacturers and trade to go on increasing throughout the whole of the nineteenth century. In less than a hundred years there had been a revolution in transport, from packhorses and wooden sailing ships to vessels of steam and iron. And even while the railway was coming into its own, as the greatest wonder of the steam age, scientists in England, France and America were making new discoveries about the uses of electricity. As early as 1822 Faraday discovered the fundamental principles of the electric motor, and in 1831 of the dynamo. Although it was fifty years before these principles began to be applied to large scale industry, they were already pointing the way ahead for those who could imagine their possibilities.

35. Stevenson's *Rocket* wins the competition for the new Liverpool–Manchester line in 1830.

Chapter 4

Eighteenth-Century Politics

We have looked at some aspects of the lives of the people of England during the later part of the eighteenth century. Now let us look at the way in which they were governed.

The King in Parliament

If we think of government to-day, we think of Parliament – the House of Lords and the House of Commons, and the Queen or King. This was the same in the eighteenth century. The country was governed by *the King in Parliament* and laws had to pass both houses and then be signed by the King, as they still do to-day. In many parts of the world – in fact in nearly all countries in 1760, kings or princes ruled without any elected parliament to control them. They sometimes had a group of nobles to advise them, rather like the House of Lords, but an elected House of Commons existed in few places except England. For this reason there was a rather odd situation. In England itself there was considerable discontent with the system of government, for reasons which we shall look at in a moment, but to most of the rest of the world, England seemed to have the best kind of government in the world.

The House of Lords

The King of England in 1760 was George III, the third monarch of the house of Hanover. In the House of Lords sat the hereditary peers and the bishops. All the peers were Lords, Dukes and Earls because of the family they had been born into. The king could make a man a peer, but if he did, it was a title which then went on through the man's

family for ever. These peers sat in the House of Lords purely by right of their title, not their property or anything else. Although it was possible for a woman to have a title – to be a peeress because her father had been a peer – peeresses were not allowed into the House of Lords. So the Upper House was made up of all the peers, including the King's sons, who were all Royal Dukes, and in addition the bishops – the heads of the Church of England.

The House of Commons

The House of Commons consisted of 432 Borough members representing the towns and 122 county members, representing the countryside. Oxford and Cambridge Universities each had two members, making a total of 558.

Election of Members of Parliament

In the countryside – or rather in all parts of England which did not count as a borough, the members were elected by the freeholders. Any man over 21 who owned property which was worth 40/– a year in rent, was allowed to vote for a county member. Voting was open – that is each voter had to sign his name in a book – and any one could look at this book. The result was that the county seats were mostly controlled by the very big landowners.

In England very few small farmers were freeholders at this time. They might own some property freehold – perhaps their house, or part of their land – but they usually rented land as well from a big landowner. Or a small freeholder might be a tradesman who owned his own shop or workshop, but

47

36. Elections in the eighteenth century often degenerated into drunken brawls between people who anyway had no vote. This is an imaginary picture of an eighteenth-century scene in Covent Garden, London.

he would depend for his custom on the rich families around. So that the person who *really* decided the election was the biggest property owner around. It was quite accepted that the tenant voted with his landlord, the shopkeeper with his biggest customer. And the poll books were open for any one to check up and make sure that his tenants had voted properly. What this usually meant was that there was no point in any one standing for parliament who was not supported by one of the big landowners, so that in most country seats there was only ever one candidate – the local landowner's friend. In 1761 there were elections in only three of the county seats. All the others sent back their members without opposition.

In the towns things were rather different. For one thing there was not one single qualification for voting, as there was in the countryside. For another thing, some of the towns which had been quite big places when they had first been given a member of Parlia-

ment had dwindled into tiny villages, or even, in at least one case, into uninhabited fields, with no-one living in them. But they still had the right to send one or more (usually two) members to Parliament, as they had had a hundred years or more earlier. So that although Birmingham, a thriving manufacturing town, sent no member, but was counted as part of the county of Warwickshire, Old Sarum, a grassy hill in Wiltshire, sent its two members as if it was a flourishing city.

In about twelve of the old boroughs the system of voting allowed every man over twenty-one who was head of a household to vote. In Preston, he did not even have to live in the borough, only to have spent the night before polling day there. In a big borough, this could mean that there was something like a genuine election. In a smaller borough it could mean that gangs of people could be hired by the candidates and brought in to vote – and the one who could hire the most voters would win the election. In some boroughs freeholders could vote, and here the same kind of influences were likely to be brought as in the countryside. But in some boroughs the right to vote went with certain houses only, so that whoever owned these houses could choose the candidate; in still others the system was that only a freeman of the borough could vote – and often that only a freeman of the borough could be a candidate. Since the freemen were usually a small group who had the power to decide who else could be a freeman, they could often use their powers to make a candidate pay to become a freeman. Sometimes they would ask for a straight money payment, sometimes for some gift to the town, a hall or some other public building. In general, with very few exceptions, votes were for sale. If the voter was lucky enough to be fairly independent, he could sell his vote to the highest bidder. In some areas he would get actual money, in most others a good dinner or two and plenty to drink in return for his vote. If he was not lucky enough to be able to use his vote as he pleased, he would vote for his landlord, or his best customer, but since it was the general custom to treat the voters handsomely on election day, he would probably get something in the way of free food and drink, and probably a ride to the polling station.

Borough Elections

There were many different kinds of voting arrangements in the boroughs, but they can be divided into three main groups. The first small group of "open" boroughs had enough voters to have a "real" election. Even if votes were bought and sold, there might be a real contest as to who could buy the most voters. All sorts of tricks were used – "bottling" was a favourite. Supporters of one side would get voters of the other side drunk and then lock them away somewhere until polling was over. As polling often went on for two or three days, this could be a difficult and costly proceeding. Many battles were fought and heads broken as supporters of one side fought to rescue "bottled" voters from their kidnappers, while the defenders tried to keep their victims either imprisoned or too intoxicated to be able to vote.

The second group of boroughs were the "pocket" boroughs. These were smaller boroughs which were in effect owned by one man or one family – that is, they were "in his pocket". Since he owned the voting rights, he could nominate the two members who were to represent the borough. Some big landowners owned several pocket boroughs, so that they might have the power to nominate as many as a dozen members to the House of Commons, as well as sitting in the House of Lords themselves.

37. Old Sarum, a modern aerial photograph of the "accursed hill".

The third group were the "rotten" boroughs. These were small boroughs which were not actually in the possession of any one owner, and which often put themselves up for sale quite shamelessly to the highest bidder. Of course, a rotten borough did not necessarily send back a "rotten" member. Some of the very ablest politicians sat for rotten boroughs, from William Pitt to the reformer, Horne Tooke. But nobody elected them.

One result of this old system of sending members to Parliament was that in order to get there you had to be either extremely rich, or the friend or follower of someone extremely rich. In order even to qualify to be a candidate, you had to own land worth at least £600 a year in rents for a county member, or £300 a year for a borough member. Members of Parliament were not paid, so they had to be rich enough not to have to earn their own living. The cost of elections was sometimes quite fantastic. In 1790, Lord Penrhyn spent £30,000 trying to get his man returned in Liverpool – without success on that occasion. As you can imagine, some of the voters, who might be quite poor people, were very glad to be able to make something of their right once in seven years. William Cobbett, who was one of the people trying to get the whole system altered, reported that at Honiton in Devonshire:

> After . . . I addressed . . . the people of the place, telling them how wicked and detestable it was to take bribes, most of the corrupt villains laughed in my face; but some of the women actually cried out against me as I went along the streets, as a man who had come to rob them of their *blessing* . . .

So the corrupt old House of Commons was not elected democratically. It certainly did not represent the common people of England, or even the main body of property owners in England. But this does not mean that it served no purpose. It was there, its members watched the way wars were fought, taxes raised and public money spent. And this did at least mean that the King and his ministers had some check on their actions. To people in countries where the kings had no such body to watch them and criticise them, the English seemed particularly well off.

Criticism of the System of Government

In England itself, criticism of the House of Commons came from many different directions. The world and the country were changing, and some of these changes were going to affect the old system of government.

We will look at two events which had great effects on English political history during the years after 1760. One was a great and world-shaking event – the War of American Independence, one was a short-lived scandal, mainly confined to London – the affair of John Wilkes and *The North Briton*. But although they were very different in size and importance, they were connected, and both influenced the way politics developed in the dramatic years of the late eighteenth and early nineteenth centuries. The Wilkes affair came earlier, so let us look at it first.

The Political Power of George III

If you look back at the short account we have had of the political system at this time, you will see that power and money went very closely together. If a man wanted to have political power, he had to have enough money to buy Parliamentary seats. But the richest man in the country, or certainly the one with access to the most money, was the King, and it is not surprising that, as well as the power which he had as king, he should also want to use his money to get himself more support in the House of Commons and in the government.

The King's efforts were unpopular with those politicians who did not enjoy his favour, and also with the much greater number of people who paid taxes. People like the merchants of London, who made their money by trade and not by owning land, saw that the more power the King and the few very big landowners got, the more they would try and raise money by taxing tradesmen and merchants to pay for their wars and for their corrupt politics. In London and nearby were the greatest numbers of seats whose members were elected by freeholders – the big borough of Westminster, in particular, and the county of Middlesex, whose freeholders were mostly independent merchants and tradesmen. So that when opposition to the increasing construction power of the king began to develop, it did so mainly among the London merchants and tradesmen.

John Wilkes and "The North Briton"

In April 1763, the leading article of a small weekly journal called *The North Briton* contained an attack on George III's speech from the throne at the opening of Parliament. It was not a violent attack, but it was very critical of the policies the King had advocated.

The North Briton was edited by John Wilkes. Wilkes was Member of Parliament for Aylesbury (he had paid £7,000 for the seat) and was in many ways a thoroughly disreputable character. He was a member of the notorious "Hell-Fire Club", a society which was said to practise black magic, and which shocked many respectable people. He was a writer of satirical verse, much of it indecent, a gambler, a dueller, a man of enormous vanity – in spite of the fact that he also had a quite hideous squint. Not, somehow, the sort of man you might expect to find as the leader of an important reforming movement. But he had the most important thing. He was a man of great personal courage and daring. His vanity and his great sense of humour sustained him when he was standing alone against the might of the King and Government, and his courage and resilience led him to go on fighting when most men would have retired defeated.

The King chose to see in Wilkes' editorial an outright attack on himself. He therefore declared that the issue of *The North Briton*,

38. John Wilkes, editor of *The North Briton,* who became a popular hero by challenging the powers of the King and the Government.

Number 45, was illegal, and his ministers issued a "general warrant" for the arrest of everyone concerned with publishing it. This "general warrant" did not specify particular names, but simply anyone who was concerned with the offending paper. In all, forty-eight people were arrested before Wilkes himself was also taken. Wilkes immediately declared that he could not be arrested, since M.P.'s are protected by Parliamentary privilege from arrest whilst they are still members. His case, and that of the other people arrested, was brought into court, where the judge declared that Wilkes was right, and that he could not be arrested legally, and furthermore that the issue of a general warrant was not allowed by English law.

This decision of the court was a great defeat for the Government. All the people who were worried by the King's policy of increasing his power were, of course, delighted, particularly the merchants and people of London. Their delight was even greater when all the arrested printers and booksellers brought actions against the government for wrongful arrest, and received handsome compensation.

But the triumph of Wilkes was short-lived. The House of Commons expelled him from membership, and he was declared an outlaw while he was out of the country. Anyone else would have recognised defeat. But Wilkes had seen his chance in the enthusiasm of the London people, and at the next election, in 1768, he defied his outlawry and came back to London. He presented himself as parliamentary candidate for Middlesex, and was elected by a large majority. Rather unwillingly the Government once more arrested him.

"Wilkes and Liberty"

Whilst Wilkes was in prison, waiting to be tried, his popularity in London reached fever pitch. The number "45" was painted on houses and buildings throughout the capital and the surrounding areas. Demonstrations in support of Wilkes were held outside the prison, and at one of these, the temper of the London people was changed by the action of the authorities. Soldiers were used to clear the crowds and in the process killed six demonstrators. Now it was not merely a matter of Wilkes' personal popularity, but blood had been shed in his support. The authorities were frightened of more serious demonstrating. When Wilkes was finally brought to trial, the judge declared his outlawry to be "bad law", and cancelled it, sentencing him instead to a term of imprisonment and a fine for issuing "Number 45". This was a triumph, for the imprisonment was of a most informal kind. Wilkes was able to have his friends about him, and to prepare the next stage of his attack.

The story of Wilkes and his followers is a story full of bravado, humour, and the continued bold storming of all the bastions of authority. For the next six years, as M.P., Alderman of the City of London and as Lord Mayor of London, Wilkes continued to be the hero of the freeholders and the common people of London. He encouraged the people to meet, to demonstrate, even on occasions, to strike, in support of what they believed were their rights, and undoubtedly held back to the King and those who were advising him to try and increase his personal power. Wilkes himself even introduced an unsuccessful Bill into the House of Commons to lessen some of the worst of the corrupt practices. The whole episode was part of a process by which people were awakened to the possibility of direct action by the ordinary people to change and influence governments.

The Yorkshire Reformers

In the seventeen-eighties a less spectacular, but nevertheless very influential movement amongst the smaller landowners and freeholders, starting in Yorkshire and spreading to many other counties, helped to increase the general discontent with the worst of the old practices. Amongst the politicians themselves there were attempts by the able and honest to remove the worst abuses, although all attempts to get the House of Commons to reform itself failed. By the 1780's, however, there was a great deal of serious thought amongst all sections of the population about the best way to achieve a reform of Parliament. It was events in France which eventually strengthened the hands of those who were opposed to any change, and enabled them to hold back the processes of reform for nearly half a century.

The American Colonies

The main functions of the Government were, as we have said, the raising of revenue, and the prosecution of wars. As our period opens, England was fighting the last years of a Seven Years' War with France. The Treaty of Paris which ended the War in 1763, left

England undisputably in control of North America and most of India. It strengthened her position in the West Indies, and established her as a country with a large and profitable empire. But it had been, as George III said, "a bloody and expensive war". Trade had been interrupted, armies had had to be raised and fed. While the war was going on, smuggling and tax evasion had increased. So that one of the first functions of a peace-time government was to increase taxation and improve the methods of collecting it.

There were thirteen colonies in North America. They had been set up at different times, and each colony was in separate touch with England, and taxes and customs duties were paid directly to England. When the new English Prime Minister, George Grenville, began to look into ways of increasing revenue from taxation and other duties after the war, he found that the North American colonies between them contributed only £2,000 a year in customs, and that the cost of collecting that £2,000 was more than £6,000. In the years that followed, the British government tried to prevent smuggling in the American colonies and to increase the customs duties they could collect. They also tried to raise money by direct taxes, to pay for soldiers whom they sent out to help the American colonists against the Indians. As the American colonists reacted to these demands, several things became clear.

First of all, the thirteen colonies which had existed separately for years, began to see that they had a great deal in common. They felt, indeed, that they had more in common with each other than with England, and gradually, out of the group of separate colonies, a new country emerged. Then they also saw that they were being asked to send money in taxes to a government in which they had no representatives. At the end of 1773, ten years after the ending of the Seven Years' War, the famous Boston Tea Party took place. As a protest against the duty they were asked to pay on tea, a group of American colonists, disguised as Red

39. American colonists, wearing Red Indian dress, hurl tea from the tea-ships into the harbour at Boston.

Indians, boarded three tea-ships in Boston harbour, and hurled the tea chests into the sea. The tea duty was not enormous, but the Americans had demonstrated that they would no longer pay duties which they had no say in imposing. The following year representatives of all the colonies met to discuss ways of avoiding what they considered to be unfair taxes. In 1776 a Congress of the American colonies met at Philadelphia on July 4th, and adopted the Declaration of Independence. The United States of America had been born, a new nation which stood not only for the right of the people of America to have their own government, but for a kind of government which would be free of the old forms of corruption which existed in England. The new men in America had learnt from European experience, including

40.   The American Declaration of Independence, July 4, 1776.

the experience of Wilkes and the London radicals, and the new state was to be an inspiring experiment in democracy.

The American War of Independence

After the Declaration of Independence, the Americans fought against Britain with great effect. They got a great deal of help from the French. The French government was glad of a chance to avenge its defeat in the Seven Years' War, and yet, by helping America and sending its soldiers and sailors to help the colonists, the old reactionary government of France was signing its own death warrant. Undoubtedly one of the factors that led to the French Revolution of 1789 was the experience which Frenchmen gained of democracy in the American War.

Effects of the American war

In 1783 the War was ended by the signing of the Treaty of Versailles. By this treaty, England recognised the independence of the American colonies – henceforth to be known as the United States of America. Britain also lost some colonies to the French and Spanish.

The experience of the American War was a great blow to the old system in England. Obviously it was not efficient, even at raising money and fighting wars. The King's personal prestige had suffered, both from the defiance of Wilkes and the demonstrations of his followers, and in more serious ways, from the failure of his government to deal with the American situation. In 1780, the English House of Commons had passed a famous resolution that "the power of the Crown has increased, is increasing, and ought to be diminished". For a few more years the King tried to exercise the old kind of personal influence, but in 1788 he had the first of a series of spells of madness, which lasted with shorter and shorter intervals for the rest of his life. In 1811 he became totally mad, and his son was made Regent in his place. Although the kings and queens who followed him in the nineteenth century had more influence in many ways than a modern monarch has in a democratic country, after

The map shows the area covered by the American colonies at the time of the revolution. The thirteen colonies were New Hampshire, Massachussetts, New York, Connecticut, Rhode Island, Pennsylvania, New Jersey, Delaware, Maryland, Virginia, North Carolina, South Carolina, and Georgia.

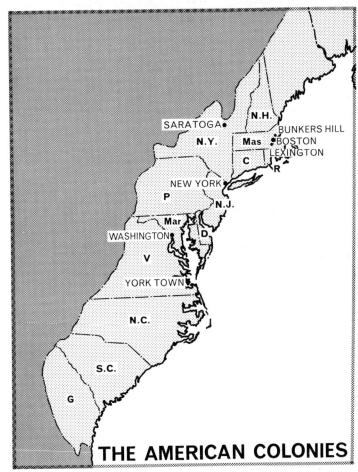

THE AMERICAN COLONIES

1788 the direct power of the crown in day to day politics continued to decline. We shall see in later chapters how the powers and nature of the two houses of Parliament also changed.

Political Divisions in England

There were two main political groups in England in the eighteenth century, the Whigs and the Tories. It is not necessary to try and see what each group stood for – indeed it would be very difficult to do so. Mostly the parties were the personal supporters of the great political men of the day. It is not really until we come to the French Revolution and the wars which followed it, that we begin to see any clear differences between them. The Tories were in power at the time of the Revolution, they had the task of putting down the reform movement in England and of fighting the war overseas. The opposition in Parliament was a small group of Whigs who stood for peace abroad and reform at home.

Pitt and Fox

There were two outstanding men in politics during the last twenty years of the eighteenth century, the Tory leader, William Pitt, and the Whig, Charles James Fox. Like most of the political leaders of George III's reign, both these men were members of great political families. Pitt's father was the Earl of Chatham, a great Whig statesman of the earlier years of the eighteenth century, Fox's was Lord Holland, also a Whig. Fox was ten years older than Pitt, and came into politics thirteen years earlier. Fox became an M.P.

41. William Pitt (centre) in a French cartoon.

when he was nineteen, in 1768, and Pitt when he was twenty-two, in 1781.

Fox had had only a few months' experience as a member of the Government when Pitt became Prime Minister in 1783. For the next twenty years Pitt led the government, and Fox led the opposition. But unlike the earlier Whig and Tory party differences, the two men really did stand for different things. Pitt would have liked to see a reform of Parliament in the 1780's. He would also have liked to see the Catholics given more freedom to take part in the government of Britain and particularly in Ireland. But once the French Revolution had broken out, he became the chief opponent of any sort of reform in England. He introduced the series of acts during the 1790's which put down the popular societies and outlawed the move-

ment for the reform of Parliament for thirty years. He also persuaded the Irish parliament to vote itself out of existence in 1800, and to join with England in the Act of Union without, in the end, giving the Catholics their political freedom.

Fox welcomed the French Revolution, and tried his best to keep England at peace with France. He never gave up his belief in the need for the reform of Parliament, and for the people of England to play a much greater part in choosing the government of the country. He and a small band of supporters fought the various repressive acts which Pitt introduced into Parliament. He was not a popular leader like Cobbett or Hunt (see Chapter 7): he was an aristocrat, and believed that if the people had the chance to vote they would vote for men like

42. Charles James Fox.

himself to lead them. He believed passionately that England must have a free press and the freedom of public meetings and open discussion of all political questions.

Pitt and Fox died in the same year, 1806. The Tories continued to be the Government until the end of the Napoleonic wars in 1815, and for some years afterwards. They continued, as we shall see, to try and hold back any movement towards the reform of Parliament, and to keep up Pitt's policy of the repression of the press and the restriction on public meetings and the expression of opinion. But Fox's ideas, also, remained alive in members of his party, and it was his friend, Charles Grey, as leader of the first Whig Government of the nineteenth century who finally introduced the Reform Bill of 1832 (see Chapter 8).

The Radicals
There were always some Members of Parliament who did not follow either political faction but who voted independently. Also there were, of course, a great many people outside the House of Commons, particularly amongst those who had no vote, who did not think like either of the two main groups.

The most important group of people outside the Whig and Tory groupings were the *Radicals*. This word comes from a word meaning *root* – the idea being that a radical is a man who wants to get to the very root of a problem in order to solve it. He is prepared to make big changes in order to achieve the right solution to a problem. We shall be coming across the radicals in politics all through the next hundred years. The important thing to remember is that there were radicals in both parties and in neither. Most working men who were interested in politics were radical, for without a radical change it was impossible to imagine working men ever taking part in politics.

Chapter 5

Empire Trade and Shipping

During George III's reign, Britain came to be the world's greatest sea power. There was a period between the Seven Years' War and the Napoleonic War when it looked as though Britain might lose her sea strength. Her battleships were allowed to rot, and her commanders were punished for the political mistakes of the Government. Things were particularly bad during the struggle with the American colonies. It was failure in her sea-power more than any other single factor which led to the defeat of Britain in the American War of Independence. But things were improved after this lesson, and by the time of the final struggle with France at the turn of the century it was her sea power which decided the war in Britain's favour. Britain was left triumphant in the struggle for trade routes and trading posts which were the key to the enormous profits from commerce in the East and the Americas.

India

The British Empire in the eighteenth century consisted mainly of trading posts and military and naval stations. There were some actual settlements – that is, lands in which people from Britain had settled and begun to work at farming or mining, nearly all in North America and the West Indies. In India and West Africa the Empire was made up of trading posts, and of military and naval posts to guard them. The main business of the Empire was trade.

In India trade in spices, silks and other fine textiles was carried on by a company, the East India Company. During the Seven Years' War the British and French East India Companies had fought for control of the Indian trade, backed up by their respective governments, and Britain had come out the winner. But in the course of the battle to get the exclusive rights to trade in different areas, the East India Company had found itself having to take over large parts of India and govern it. It would have been easier if they could have found Indian rulers who would have given them a trading monopoly, and enforced it. But the Indian princes were not prepared or not able to do this, so that gradually the important areas were taken over by the Company; British troops were stationed in them to keep order and to protect the interests of the Company. In 1757 Robert Clive won control of the rich province of Bengal at the battle of Plassey. By 1763 Britain had driven out France from most of India, and she continued to take over more and more of the government of the continent.

North America

By 1763 Britain was also in control of Canada and the rest of North America. This was nothing like such a profitable area as India. Furs from Canada and a certain amount of cotton and tobacco from further south made up the main trade with England. There was a far greater volume of trade after the American colonies had split away from the Empire.

The West Indies

Britain's greatest source of wealth, apart from India, was the sugar islands of the West Indies. Although there were other sources of

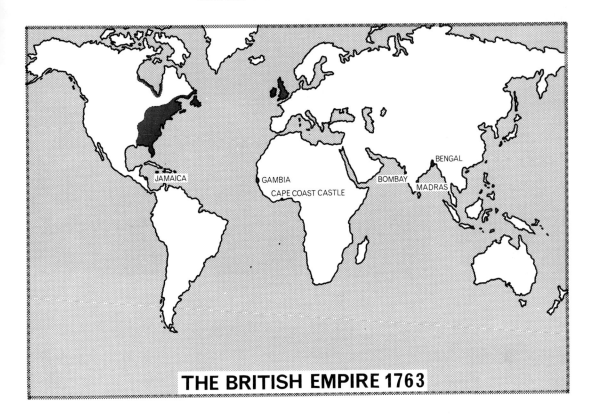

THE BRITISH EMPIRE 1763

sugar in the world – the East Indies for example, by far the greater part of Europe's sugar came from the West Indies. It played a part in what was known as the *triangular trade*, a trade which made the fortunes of many of the richest families in England.

The Triangular Trade

Britain produced and exported many kinds of manufactured goods. These included cotton and woollen cloth, shoes, knives, guns, pottery and metal ware of all kinds. Ships loaded with British-made goods sailed to the West coast of Africa, and here they exchanged their goods for slaves. One trader to Africa carried aboard, in 1787:

Cotton and linen goods, silk handkerchiefs, coarse blue and red woollen cloths, scarlet cloth, coarse and fine hats, worsted caps, guns, powder, shot, sabres, lead bars, iron bars, pewter basins, copper kettles and pans, iron pots, earthen and glass ware, hair and gilt leather trunks, beads of various kinds, silver and gold rings and ornaments, paper, coarse

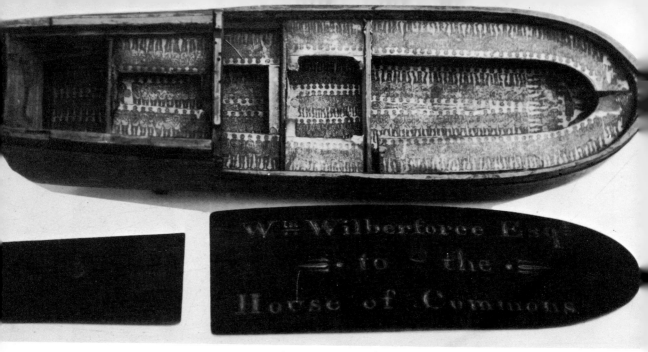

43. This model shows how closely the slaves were packed.

44. Young African slaves being stowed aboard the slave-ship.

and fine checks, linen ruffled shirts and caps, British and foreign spirits and tobacco.

All these goods were eagerly welcomed in Africa, and could be exchanged directly for slaves. One trader for example, received a "fine negro" from a prince, in exchange for thirteen beads of coral, half a string of amber, twenty-eight silver bells and three pairs of bracelets for his women. As the trader could sell the negro for sixty pounds or more in the sugar islands, he had obviously made a very good bargain.

The slaves were mostly bought from African dealers in exchange for money or goods. They were then loaded aboard the special slave ships, packed as closely as possible, and taken by the "middle passage" across the Atlantic to the West Indies. Here they were sold, and the ships loaded with sugar, molasses and rum. The third side of the triangle was complete when the ships returned to Bristol or Liverpool with their cargoes.

This three-cornered trade in goods, slaves and sugar made the fortunes of many English traders. Money flowed into the ports and into the city of London in greater amounts than ever before in England's history. In 1770, Alderman William Beckford, former Lord Mayor of London, died, leaving a million pounds. He was a member of a famous West Indian trading family, and has the distinction of having been the first English millionaire. Like many other merchants, he had built a huge house on his estate in the country, which he furnished in the most lavish style. He also had interests in banking, for with the growth of the fortunes of the merchants came the development of London as a world banking centre.

Objections to the slave trade

There were people in England who had the strongest objections to the slave trade. But as long as it was the source of such great wealth, the struggle against it was a hopeless one. Landowners hoped for a daughter of a West India merchant to marry into their family and bring her money to help improve their country estates and farms. Industrialists and merchants were glad to be able to borrow money from the new banks or from the sugar merchants themselves to develop new ideas and new forms of trade. Only a few humanitarians complained of the price in human suffering that was paid by the poor Africans. The opposition was very much strengthened by the publication in 1776 of *The Wealth of Nations* by Adam Smith. This book had an enormous influence on the growth of English industry. Its contribution to the argument about slavery was to say, not as the Quakers and others said, that slavery was bad or wicked, but that it did not pay:

> It appears from the experience of all ages and nations that the work done by freemen comes cheaper in the end than that performed by slaves.

So slavery was under a two-pronged attack. It was wicked and it was expensive. Led by William Wilberforce, Member of Parliament for Hull, and one of the best speakers in the House of Commons, a small group worked in Parliament to get the government to pass a law abolishing the Slave Trade. Thomas Clarkson toured the country outside, collecting information and evidence about the trade. Clarkson was able to show that not only the Africans suffered by the trade. English seamen died far more often – at least ten times as often – on the slavers than on other merchant ships. Disease and the need for speed in delivering the live cargoes were the main causes of this.

Wilberforce introduced motions in Parliament against the slave trade in 1789, 1791, 1795 and 1804. He met with firm opposition from the West Indian interest, for the riches of some of the merchants had been used to buy rotten boroughs, and the trade was well represented in the House of Commons. But the arguments of the anti-slavers gradually won support and shortly before his death in 1806 Charles James Fox introduced a measure that "all manner of dealing and trading" in slaves was to be "utterly abolished, prohibited and declared to be unlawful" for any British subject. It became law in 1807. The U.S.A. made slave-trading illegal in 1809, France in 1815, Spain and Portugal in 1820.

Abolition of Slavery

The ending of the slave trade was a great victory for the "abolitionists" as its opponents were called. But slavery itself continued to exist in the West Indies and in North and South America for many years after the ending of the trade. Wilberforce lived to see its ending in all parts of the British Empire, in 1833.

In the Southern States of the United States of America, tobacco and cotton growing were carried on by slave labour for another thirty years. Slavery was to be one of the major questions in the civil war in which 620,000 Americans died between 1861 and 1865. It was not until after the end of the war that slavery was finally abolished in North America, in 1865.

Trade and Industry

We saw in Chapter 3 that the great changes which we call the Industrial Revolution took place in Britain before the rest of the world, and made Britain the world's leading industrial power. This industrial development could not have happened without the money which was already coming into the country through her trade with the rest of the world. Britain was a small country, not particularly well supplied with raw materials. Why then was she such a great trading nation?

One reason for her success was the skill of British sailors and shipbuilders, which made the British merchant fleet able to take the lead in getting to the Far East and the sources of rare spices and other goods which were increasingly in demand in Europe. Then the British Government was far more

45.   The Bank of England in 1816. Centre of Britain's trading empire, the Bank of England dominated the City of London in the late eighteenth and early nineteenth centuries.

sympathetic to trade and industry than most European governments – even though the merchants and manufacturers thought it was usually too favourable to farmers and landowners.

Even in the middle of the eighteenth century Britain's home manufactured goods were limited. Woollen cloth or wool made up over half of her home production. The countries of the Far East, and many countries nearer home in Southern Europe and the Mediterranean did not want a great deal of woollen cloth. So much of the trade which British merchants carried on was in re-exported goods – that is things brought from outside Europe in British ships, and either worked on in Britain and then exported to Europe, or even exported straight away. Other European countries took three-quarters of all exports from British ports in the middle of the eighteenth century, but only half of the exported goods which were actually made in Britain. By the end of the eighteenth century the trade in re-exported goods to other parts of Europe was even greater. So Britain was able to buy timber, pitch and hemp for ship-building, and bar-iron for all kinds of iron work until her own iron industry caught up with her needs around the turn of the century. She was also able to pay for grain from other European countries by selling them goods obtained from tropical and Eastern countries.

Here, as with the development of industrial change, it was the skill of the traders and the lack of restriction by the government which made Britain rich, and not any rich resources within the country itself. As a result Britain was already the greatest industrial and trading nation at the beginning of the nineteenth century.

Chapter 6

The British People during the French Revolution and the French Wars

No country exists by itself, and we can never study the history of one country completely separately. It has very often been true that events in other countries have had as much influence on the way English people thought as what was actually happening at home. One of the most outstanding examples of this was the events of the French Revolution at the end of the eighteenth century.

France in the Eighteenth Century

During the century or so before the French Revolution, England had fought five wars against France. Our period opened with the ending of one of these, the Seven Years' War. France, mostly out of hostility to Britain, had helped the Americans to break away from British rule in the 1770's. France was, in fact, *the* enemy as far as Britain was concerned. This great nation, on the other side of the channel, was a rival for trade and for colonial expansion. She was also, for the common people of England, the great example of despotism. She had an absolute monarchy, her Parliament had not met for nearly two hundred years. She had large military and police forces. At her head was the King, and a nobility which enjoyed far greater privileges than the English – a nobility which had no interest in trade, or in new ideas or new inventions. These French nobles oppressed not only the peasants, who made up the majority of the population of France, but also the lawyers, writers, teachers and business men who made up the middle classes.

Constant wars had made France poor. Taxes were getting heavier, and the people who paid the taxes had no say in governing the country. What was more, the nobles, who had all the power and most of the wealth in the country did not have to pay taxes themselves. In 1788 there was a bad food harvest, followed by a very bitter winter. The peasants, small farmers who grew most of the food in the country, worked by such old-fashioned methods, that very few of them had any spare supplies. In the country-side there were famine conditions, and the poor and hungry people began to come into the towns, particularly Paris, in search of work and food.

The Government did nothing. Discontent of all kinds increased. People in the middle and lower classes began to demand action. Some Frenchmen had fought with the army in America; there they had seen an inefficient authority overthrown by determined military action, and replaced by an elected Assembly which represented the whole people.

The French Revolution

In 1789, the French Revolution broke out. Two important events occurred in that year. The first was that the King, Louis XVI, summoned the *States General*, the French Parliament, that had not met since 1614. He hoped that this council – made up of representatives of the Church, the Nobility and the Commons, would help him to solve the problems of famine and money shortage with which he was faced. But the middle class members of the States General were not prepared simply to be advisers to a King whom they did not trust. They decided

46. The beginning of the French Revolution: the King calls a meeting of the States General.

to become a Parliament of the English kind, and changed their name to the *Constituent Assembly*. While they were in session the second dramatic event occurred. Dominating the Eastern side of Paris was the Royal fortress of the Bastille. It was a state prison, and was believed to hold stores of arms. On July 14th, 1789, the workers of the region attacked it, broke in, in spite of gunfire from the soldiers inside, killed the governor and proceeded to take the whole great building apart, stone by stone.

The Bastille was a symbol of the power of the old system in France. With its overthrow ended the absolute power of the French kings and the French nobility. The Revolution went through very many stages before France had internal peace again, and since we are concerned with the history of England, we have not the time to trace the whole story. But the effect of the Revolution was great on England in a number of ways.

Effects in England

First was the effect of the downfall of an old and apparently powerful despotism. Follow-
ing the British defeat in America, it looked as though the ordinary people were breaking through into the Governments of the world at last; reformers in every country were encouraged, while the old Governments became alarmed, and began to see threats to their existence in any talk of change or reform. This was particularly true in England, where Parliamentary reform had been very much in the air before the Revolution, and had been supported by a great number of people of differing political views.

The second way in which the French Revolution altered the history of Europe, was in the series of wars which followed it. Although one of the causes of the downfall of the old system had been its wasteful spending on foreign wars, the new system soon developed its own warlike policies. The Napoleonic wars engulfed Europe from 1792 to 1815. Napoleon Bonaparte, a young soldier in the Revolutionary army, rose to be first General of the Republican Army, and finally Emperor of France. As the wars progressed his power became greater, until

47. The storming of the Bastille.

finally the Revolution, which had begun as the establishment of a democratic system of government, ended in his personal dictatorship.

War was partly forced on to the French Republic by the hostility of the old governments of Europe, many of whom welcomed escaping French nobles, and wanted to put them back in power. But the Republic itself developed ambitions to make the whole of Europe into Republics, and as one by one the old Governments fell before the vigorous and efficient armies of the new France, it looked as though the whole face of Europe would be changed.

When the first news of the setting up the Constituent Assembly in France reached England, nearly everyone, from the Government downwards, was pleased. The Fall of the Bastille may have given some people second thoughts, but to the reformers, and to many writers and thinkers who hated the cruelty and injustice of the old system, the destruction of the ancient prison was a symbol of a new life. Charles James Fox, the Whig leader, called it "much the greatest event that ever happened in the history of the world"; in the potteries, Josiah Wedgwood, the pottery manufacturer, welcomed "the wonderful revolution", which he thought was the beginning of a new age. William Blake, the poet and painter, Robert Burns, the Scottish poet, and many others sent enthusiastic greetings to the new government in France, and the poet William Wordsworth, then aged nineteen, went across to France, and wrote enthusiastic verses about:

France, standing on the top of golden hours,
And human nature seeming born again . . .

The fact that the Revolution had taken place in France, which had seemed so strong, and so impossible to change, gave English reformers new heart. The movement for the reform of Parliament gained new strength.

British Parliamentary Reformers

Three groups of people now began to work for changes in the British system of electing members to Parliament. In 1792 the Society of the Friends of the People was started by a group of young Whigs, many of them aristocrats and Members of Parliament themselves, who wanted more chance for the common people to have a say in elections. Another society, the Society for Constitutional Information, which already existed, began to meet regularly in 1791, and gave a great welcome to events in France. This group was led by John Horne Tooke, a radical lawyer, who actually sat for a short time as Member of Parliament for Old Sarum. Societies like this one started up in most of the great towns and cities in England, and worked for reform at home, and support for the new French Government. The members began to call each other "citizen", in the style of the French Revolutionaries, instead of "sir" and "mister". They were mostly tradesmen, small industrialists and people of this sort.

The third group were the Corresponding Societies. The London Corresponding Society was founded in 1792 by Thomas Hardy, a London shoemaker. Its members were working men, who paid a subscription of 1d a week, and it, too, soon linked up with similar societies in other towns. As well as calling for votes for all men, the Corresponding Societies wanted other reforms, including :

> taxes diminished, the necessaries of life more within reach of the poor, youth better educated, prisons less crowded, old age better provided for . . .

48.   William Wordsworth.

So, in the early 1790's, the people who wanted change and reform in England were more organised than ever before, largely as the result of events in France. But also there was a strong reaction amongst those who had always been opposed to change. After all, the French Revolution had begun as a move towards reform, and was now becoming a violent and aggressive force, sweeping across Europe.

War with France

The Whig party in the House of Commons was split by the question of France. One group, led by Charles James Fox, continued to believe in reform and to oppose war with France. But the majority of the Parliamentary Whigs disliked the revolution, and thought that it showed how dangerous reforming ideas were. They wanted to see France defeated, and joined with the Tories in forming successive governments to fight France and to keep down the reformers at

49. Tom Paine, whose book *The Rights of Man* was the basis of the Reform Movement in England in the late eighteenth and early nineteenth centuries.

them, since Marie Antoinette, wife of the King of France, was an Austrian princess. News of plans for the invasion of France by Austria and Germany reached Paris. The royal family, having tried and failed to escape from Paris, was imprisoned, and in September 1792 the monarchy was abolished and France declared a Republic.

In 1792, Tom Paine, the author of the *Rights of Man* a book which supported the Revolution, left England, where he was threatened with prosecution for his writings, and arrived in France. He was made a citizen of the Republic, and became a member of the French Parliament. In 1793 he opposed the proposal to execute the King, urging that it was enough for the republic to do away with the idea of monarchy, without actually killing the King. But the King was beheaded, and Paine himself was imprisoned for two months. The Revolution was taking a strange course. Many aristocrats had been beheaded before the royal family. Now it was the revolutionaries themselves who were being imprisoned and beheaded, as one group replaced another. Until the autumn of 1794 the government was in the hands of men who, although they may have been harsh and bloodthirsty in many of their actions, were still trying to build a republic based on the revolutionary slogan of "Liberty, Equality and Fraternity". But after the downfall of Robespierre in July 1794, the government fell, first to a group of five 'directors', and then to the personal dictatorship of Napoleon Bonaparte. After Napoleon had made himself Emperor of France, it was very difficult for the reformers in Britain to get very much inspiration from France.

The Scottish Reformers

In England, Scotland and Ireland the reformers became the object of Government attack once England was at war with France. Spies were used to find out what went on at meetings of reforming societies, and as the result of the reports of these men many

home. From the beginning of 1793 England was at war with France, a war which lasted, with only a short break in 1802–1803, for twenty-two years.

These twenty-two years were important and eventful ones for the whole of Europe. Events moved very rapidly in France itself. The Revolution had begun with the two aims of overthrowing the old power of the nobility, and of setting up a more democratic form of government which would improve the condition of the people. To begin with, it seemed possible that a fairly moderate programme of reform would achieve these aims. But it soon became clear that the old nobility were not going to submit tamely to being turned out of their positions of privilege. It was also clear that the King of France was not prepared to become a constitutional monarch, even to the same degree that the English kings were. The French nobles who had fled from Paris organised resistance to the new government in Austria and Prussia. Austria in particular was sympathetic to arrests were made. The first to be arrested were the Scottish reformers. In 1793, when Paine had been arguing against the beheading of the King of France, a young Scottish lawyer, Thomas Muir, had also come to Paris, representing the supporters of the French revolution in Scotland, to urge the Government not to cut off the King's head. When he returned to Scotland, he was arrested, along with several others, and brought to trial on a charge of treason, found guilty, and sentenced to fourteen years' transportation to Botany Bay.

Most of the leading Scottish reformers, and some delegates from London to a Scottish meeting were arrested and sentenced soon after Muir. Their sentences were all very severe, but the most extraordinary was the sentence of death passed on a man called Robert Watt. Watt was accused of organising an armed conspiracy. At his trial, he showed that he had organised the conspiracy on instructions from the Government. He had been told to spy on the reformers, to supply them with arms, given to him for that purpose by the Government, and to encourage them to engage in a conspiracy, so that he could betray them. The Attorney-General, for the Government, agreed that this had indeed been the case, but claimed that they had had to dismiss Watt for unreliability. We shall probably never now know the full truth about this strange story – only that the wretched Watt was indeed hanged, drawn and quartered as a traitor.

English Trials

The Scottish sentences and the strange affair of Robert Watt caused a great stir in England. There were protests and meetings in all the great towns, and the Government decided to act against those Englishmen whom it suspected of sympathy with France. The Government now moved against the reformers in London. Three of the leading figures were arrested – John Horne Tooke, of the Constitutional Society, Thomas Hardy, the secretary of the London Corresponding

50. John Thelwall.

Society, and John Thelwall, journalist and friend of the poet Wordsworth. All three came up for trial at the Old Bailey on charges of High Treason, the trials beginning only ten days after the horrible death of Robert Watt.

The London trial caused a great sensation. Hardy, the shoemaker, faced his accusers with courage and dignity. Tooke persisted in treating the whole trial with the greatest flippancy, and pretended to be bored with all the proceedings. Thelwall was more dramatic. He had prepared a long speech to the jury, and wanted to deliver it himself – "I'll be hanged if I don't" he told his defending counsel, Thomas Erskine. "You'll be hanged if you do" was the reply. Erskine's defence of the three men was brilliant, and the prisoners themselves obviously impressed the jury. When the verdict on Hardy was expected, the streets outside the court were crowded with people. The jury were out for three hours, while the court waited in "an awful silence and suspense". When called upon to deliver the verdict, the foreman of the jury was so strung up that he only

69

51. Richard Parker, "admiral" of the mutinying fleet at the Nore, presents the demands of the sailors to Admiral Buckner.

and the war. Taxes were high, and many of them were on food. In October 1795, King George III drove in his state carriage to open Parliament. A crowd of perhaps 200,000 Londoners crowded the streets, booing and shouting – "down with Pitt!", "give us Peace and Bread!" "no War!", "down with George!", "no King!", "no Pitt!". The window of the Royal coach was pierced and the royal head narrowly missed, probably by a pebble, although George III not unreasonably thought he had been shot at.

The Government acted in two ways. They opened negotiations for peace with France (which in the end came to nothing) and they brought in laws against the popular societies. An Act was passed forbidding all meetings of more than fifty people, and making any speeches attacking the King, the Constitution or the Government illegal. Fox and his group opposed these measures in the House of Commons, for they still believed that peace and Reform would do more to solve England's problems than repression.

Two more important things happened before England was quiet again.

Mutinies in the Navy

In 1797 there were serious mutinies in the Navy. The crews of the fleets at the Spithead and the Nore mutinied, took over the ships and put their officers ashore. They wanted better pay and conditions – we have already seen (Chapter 1) some of the things they were protesting against. The naval mutinies were strongly influenced by events in France. It is not surprising that cruelty, the press gang, bad food and small and irregular pay should have caused mutinies. But the fact that they took place at this moment was certainly due to the increased discussion of the "Rights of Man", and to the influence of the French Revolution. At one point the mutineers passed a resolution that they would hand over the fleet to the French "as the only Government that understands the Rights of Man".

managed to whisper "not guilty" before he fainted. But the crowd outside soon got the news, and it was spread all over England. It did not prevent many local reformers from being arrested and imprisoned by local magistrates' courts, but the death penalty and the heavy punishment of transportation were not used against them.

In the two years after the trials of Hardy, Tooke and Thelwall, England was in a ferment. 1795 was a year almost of famine in Europe. In France and in England there were bread riots – that is demonstrations, mainly in the market towns and cities, in which huge crowds gathered to protest against the high price of bread. Often they broke open shops and stores and forced the merchants to sell bread at low prices. Sometimes they were just great demonstrations of hungry people, blaming their hunger on the Government

The mutineers were in the end defeated. Many improvements were made in sailors' conditions, and some of the worst officers were not returned to service. But the leaders of the mutiny were rounded up and those who did not manage to escape to France were severely punished. Richard Parker, "Admiral" of the Floating Republic of the Nore, was hanged at the yard-arm of H.M.S. *Sandwich*, off Sheerness. Every ship of the fleet sent a boatload of men to witness the execution, and to see for themselves what became of mutineers.

More Acts were introduced as the result of the mutinies. One of these made it punishable by death to "administer an illegal oath" – that is to persuade people to swear an oath of allegiance to an organisation. Another introduced the death penalty for "attempts to seduce the armed forces from their allegiance".

Before the mutinies in the Navy had been finally put down, the British Government was faced with a much larger rebellion – this time among the people of Ireland.

Ireland

In 1790 Ireland had her own Parliament, and made most of her own laws. She was still under the rule of the King of England, and had to provide troops for the British forces, but an Irish Parliament met in Dublin, and carried on much of the business of government.

We have seen that the British Parliament at this time was elected by only a very small minority of the population. The Irish Government was elected on more or less the same system, but the result was even less representative of the people of Ireland than the Parliament at Westminster was representative of the people of the rest of the British Isles. The main reason for this was the religious question.

There were three main religious groups in Ireland. Most of the ruling families were members of the Church of Ireland. This was an established Church, like the Church of England, with its Bishops, higher clergy and parish clergymen. This was the Church which collected the tithes in the villages, and membership of which was needed to hold any important office in the State or the Government. But unlike England, where the majority of the people who went to Church supported the Church of England, the very great majority of the Irish people were not only not members of the established Church, but were actively opposed to it. Some belonged to non-conformist Protestant sects who made up the second religious group. These people tended to be concentrated mainly in the Northern Counties of Ireland. But the vast majority of the people of Ireland were then, as they are now, members of the Roman Catholic Church. Under English law (and Ireland, although she had her own Parliament, was controlled by the same laws in these matters as England) anyone who was not a member of the Established Church had to put up with certain "disabilities." They could not study at the Universities, for example, or hold most important public appointments. The Catholics suffered from the most severe prohibitions – they could not become Members of Parliament let alone members of the Government – in fact until 1793 they could not vote even if they had the necessary property – and so they found themselves under the rule of men who were not only outside their Church, but actively hostile to it. This was, of course, the position of Catholics in the rest of the British Isles, but since they were in a minority in most parts of the Kingdom they knew that a change in the law would probably not make a great deal of difference to their political position. The Irish, on the other hand, knew that if Catholics were admitted to political power the majority of their representatives in Parliament would be Catholics. So that their discontent with the law as it stood was of quite a different order from the discontent of the minority groups in England.

As the result of the exclusion of the Catholics from political life, the Irish Parliament was even more corrupt than the British. A few big, Protestant landowners controlled all the elections, and the laws which they made were made only in the interests of this small, powerful and wealthy minority.

The United Irishmen

This was the background to the Irish view of the French Revolution. Like reformers in nearly every country, the Radicals in Ireland – who were mostly Protestants, many of them non-conformists – welcomed the Revolution. An organisation was formed in the North of Ireland, called the United Irishmen. They hoped that the Revolutionary Government in France would help them actively with arms and troops to end the English connection altogether and establish an independent Republic of Ireland. But there was also support for France among the Catholic peasantry in Southern Ireland, in spite of the fact that officially the Catholic Church in Ireland was very opposed to the French Revolution.

The British Government were rightly worried by the situation. In the midst of a war they were faced with widespread disaffection at home. Some of them recognised that the Irish had grievances but they believed, as with the navy, that first the rebellion had to be crushed, and then the grievances might be considered.

The full and bloody story of the crushing of the United Irishmen, first by the arrest of the leaders in the north, and then by the suppression of risings among the country people in Wexford, Antrim and Down, cannot be told in detail here. But it was clear enough to the British authorities that the real cause of the rising was not sympathy with France, but centuries of misrule in Ireland itself. The rebellion was suppressed, but what was England to do about the basic situation?

The Act of Union 1801

The government feared that if it gave political rights to Catholics, Ireland would declare itself independent of Protestant England. But if Ireland were to be brought back into the British Parliament, like Scotland and Wales, then the Catholics could be given their freedom, because they would then only be a small minority of the whole population of Great Britain.

In the end, it was not very difficult to persuade the Irish Parliament to vote itself out of existence. Since the seats in Parliament were in the control of so few people, they could be bought – and it was in fact mainly by straightforward bribery that the rulers of Ireland were brought to agree to the Act of Union of 1801 by which Ireland became joined to England for the purposes of Government.

The Catholics who might have been expected to oppose the Union were led to believe that a Union would mean that they would gain their political freedom. The man who led them to hope for this was the Secretary for Ireland, a young Protestant nobleman, Robert Stewart, Lord Castlereagh. He had already become hated in the country for his part in the very cruel punishments which had been given to those who took part in the risings. In 1801 he became associated with the betrayal which the Catholics felt when it was learnt, after the Union had been accomplished and the Irish Parliament had gone out of existence, that the Catholics were not to be given political rights. Pitt, the English Prime Minister, had been unable to persuade the King to accept the idea of Catholic emancipation. He resigned from office for a time on this question, but he made no further attempts to carry the question and to keep faith with the Irish, when he returned to power. The crowds in Dublin chanted:

A high gallows and a windy day
For Billy Pitt and Castlereagh

The English Government, as we shall see,

had laid up for itself a store of future trouble by settling the Irish question in this particular way. There was one more rebellion while the war was still on, in 1803, but it was on a small scale and was easily suppressed. But it was to be well over a hundred years before there was real peace in Ireland.

Effects of the Napoleonic Wars

The wars in Europe lasted for more than twenty years. All through the nineteenth century the people of the countries which had been at war looked back to those years as the "Great War" which had made so many changes. France produced, in Napoleon Bonaparte, one of the greatest military geniuses of all time, and England produced, in Horatio Nelson, one of the world's greatest naval commanders. In the end, the brilliance of the British sea strength and the combined land forces of the other European powers prevailed, and Napoleon was defeated. But, before he was defeated, he had ruled over nearly the whole of Western Europe.

In the countries which the French armies conquered many important changes took place. Europe had been for centuries divided into tiny kingdoms and principalities, some independent, some coming under the rule of the greatest single government, the Austro-Hungarian Empire. The countries which we now know as Italy and Germany were divided up into a whole number of small states. Most of Italy was ruled by Austria or by kings who were supported by Austria. Now the kings and princes had been overthrown, and the Emperor of Austria defeated. Under Napoleon Northern Italy was treated as if it was one country. Roads were built, laws were brought in for the whole area, one Government ruled it all. Although the French were finally driven out, and Italy was given back to her Austrian overlords, the Italians did not forget. Napoleon had reminded them that Italy was a country with its own history and language. In the next hundred years modern Italy grew

up and broke away from Austria, largely as the result of the Napoleonic period.

Nationalism – that is the coming together of all people who spoke the same language, like the Italians and the Germans, into a single country, was one of the results of the European wars. Another was the growth of republicanism. Although a king of France was put back on the throne after Napoleon's defeat, he did not stay long. Before the middle of the nineteenth century, France was again a Republic. Kings and Emperors throughout Europe were never as safe on their thrones again after the experiences of the American and French Revolutions.

Effects of the Wars in England

Inside England the war had many different effects. There is no doubt that after 1800, when Napoleon was dictator of France, sympathy for the French died down in England. As usually happens in war time,

52. Lord Castlereagh. The strange unbalanced statesman, who earned the hatred of the common people in Ireland and in London, and whose funeral, after his suicide in 1822, was booed and jeered at in the London streets.

people began to hate the enemy. Threats of a French invasion, and stories of French atrocities strengthened these patriotic feelings. In the farming areas of the South of England many people were doing well out of the war. More land was ploughed up to grow grain than had ever been used before. Grain prices were high and on the whole farmers large and small lived well.

In the manufacturing districts, however, things were different. War had interfered with trade, and the demand for goods of all kinds, especially textiles, varied very much from month to month. At the beginning of the war the need for soldiers' and sailors' uniforms had given a great deal of work to the textile districts. In order to get the work done, new ideas and methods had often been introduced. For example, in the stocking-weaving areas around Nottingham, the manufacturers had discovered that they could make stockings quickly and cheaply by cutting them up out of large pieces of material instead of knitting each stocking separately on a properly shaped frame. These "made-up" stockings were not much good – they were not properly finished off, and they soon came to pieces, but they were cheaper to make than the properly finished article. In the woollen districts of Yorkshire the manufacturers introduced machines for finishing woollen cloth – a job which had always been done by skilled craftsmen.

When the trade began to fall off, the manufacturers did not stop using the newer, cheaper methods of producing goods, but kept them going, and sacked the older skilled men. The Acts passed by Pitt in the 1790's had made all Trade Unions illegal, so the men had no way to protest against this. In any case, it is always difficult to make an effective protest when there is a great deal of unemployment. And so it was in this situation that there occurred outbreaks of machine breaking.

The Luddites

The first to act were the stocking knitters of

Nottingham. They attacked the "wide" frames on which the shoddy stockings were woven. Any workshop in which these frames were used was likely to be attacked in the night by bands of men, who soon reduced the wide frames to rubble. These men called themselves Luddites, after the leader of the movement who was nicknamed Ned Ludd. This was not a real person, but a name which was used in many parts of the country at different times. A Luddite membership card from Yorkshire which was sent to the Home Secretary by a magistrate has written on it:

No General but Ludd
Means the Poor any Good . . .

and a poem called *General Ludd's Triumph* circulating in Nottinghamshire at the time begins:

Chant no more your old rhymes about bold
　　　　　　　　　　　　　Robin Hood,
His feats I but little admire
I will sing the achievements of General Ludd,
Now the Hero of Nottinghamshire . . .

In Nottinghamshire the Luddites at first had some success. The manufacturers went back to the narrow frames and properly finished work, for which the payment was higher. The troops in the district found it very difficult to arrest any of the machine breakers, who obviously were protected by the people of the weaving villages. Although the penalty for machine-breaking was already fourteen years' transportation, the Government decided to make it harsher still. A law was introduced and passed in Parliament to make machine-breaking punishable by death.

In spite of the increased punishment, Luddism spread throughout the manufacturing districts. In the weaving and cloth-finishing villages of the West Riding of Yorkshire, masked men gathered at night and

53. A hand-operated stocking frame for knitting single stockings (right).

smashed the heavy iron shearing-frames. These frames were made by a famous Yorkshire machine-maker, Enoch Taylor. The great hammers which were used to smash the machines were made at the same iron-works, so the Luddite cry was "Enoch made 'em, Enoch shall break 'em". In Lancashire steam-looms were attacked, usually by gangs of up to sixty men, for the steam-looms were housed in large factories, and not, like the stocking-frames or shearing-frames in small workshops. During the last years of the Napoleonic wars there were more British troops engaged in patrolling the manufacturing districts of England to protect property against the attacks of the Luddites than there were engaged in the Peninsula campaign.

This was the state of England, then, during, the last years of the war. Farmers were prosperous, and the Southern counties were calm. But throughout the Northern counties things were very unsettled. Trade had suffered from the war. Pitt's acts had made it impossible for people to form Trade Unions or to protest in ordinary peaceful ways, so that discontent showed itself mainly in outbreaks of machine-breaking and violence. The writer, Sir Walter Scott, in a letter to a friend, said "The country is mined below our feet". This sense that things were unsafe, that you never knew where violence was going to burst out next, was very widespread. Once the war was ended, many problems at home had to be tackled.

The End of the Wars

In April 1814 Napoleon abdicated as Emperor of France. He was banished by the allied powers, Prussia, Russia, Austria and Britain, to the island of Elba. The leaders of the victorious allied powers met to discuss peace terms, and the re-settlement of Europe after the long years of Napoleonic rule. But it was difficult for countries who had in fact spent a large part of the war years in squabbling amongst themselves to begin to agree on anything important. Before they had made much progress Napoleon escaped from Elba and landed again in France. An army of Frenchmen flocked around him, and for 100 days he was again emperor of France.

The armies of the allies were put under the English commander, the Duke of Wellington. He commanded a force of 100,000 men, of whom half were British. He was supported by the Prussian commander, Blücher, with a rather larger force. Against them Napoleon had only 120,000 men. The armies joined in battle at Waterloo in Belgium, where the French were at last decisively defeated.

After more than twenty years of war, in which French armies had overthrown kings and wiped out national boundaries, the map of Europe had to be drawn again. It is not part of the subject of this book to go into these European settlements, but since they were to affect the British people indirectly, it is worth looking at the general principles on which they were made.

54. Lord Byron, the poet, spoke in the House of Lords against the death penalty for machine-breaking. He also wrote a "Song for the Luddites".

England was represented at the post-war conferences by the one-time Secretary for Ireland, Lord Castlereagh, who had become Foreign Secretary in 1812. As was to be expected, he had little sympathy or understanding of the ideas of nationalism and democracy which had grown up in Europe during the years following the French Revolution. He supported the other European statesmen when they put a Bourbon king back on the throne of France and handed back the other states of Europe to their old, despotic rulers. But he did insist that France must not be punished with too great severity, and prevented the more extreme among the European leaders who would have liked to try to reduce France to a minor power.

* The final settlements taken usually tried to restore the old ruling families who had been driven out by the Napoleonic armies, and to guarantee that they would remain secure on their thrones. As the result, the next fifty years were to see a series of revolutions within the main European countries, in which the principles of nationalism and republicanism were to drive out many of the old ruling families and to draw new frontiers on the map of Europe.

55. The Charge of the Life Guards at the Battle of Waterloo.

Chapter 7

After the Wars

In 1815 England was at last at peace, after more than twenty years of war. The French prisoners who had been kept in London's Fleet Prison, or held in the convict ships off Portsmouth, were set free, some of them after ten years or more in prison. English prisoners returned home, and the soldiers from the overseas armies went back to their towns and villages and their peace-time jobs.

But after the first cheering had died down, it became clear that the peace was going to be, if anything, worse than the war. The next fifteen years were to be some of the blackest in the whole of England's history.

The Royal Family

The English Royal Family was as unpopular and as undeserving of popularity in these years as it ever has been. George III, still King in name, was blind, deaf and insane. His sons, of whom seven were still living in 1815, were for the most part regarded with considerable mistrust. The eldest son, the Prince Regent, who was soon to become King George IV, was despised and disliked by most of his subjects. While his father was ruling and the government was predominantly Tory, the Prince was an ardent radical. When he became Regent, however, instead of showing favour to his former friends, as they might have expected, he became a strong Tory like his father. He thus managed to earn the enmity of both political groups, as well as getting the reputation for insincerity and changeableness.

For the Whigs and radicals, it was probably a good thing when the Prince became a Tory. Wellington, the Tory leader, said of the Royal Princes that they were "the damndest millstones that were ever hanged round the neck of any government . . ."

Princess Charlotte and Queen Caroline

George's wife was Caroline of Brunswick. He had married her in 1795, and as soon as their only child was born they lived apart. Caroline's behaviour was almost as much open to criticism as her husband's, and their private lives and constant quarrels provided an endless source of gossip. One wit wrote of Caroline during the last great scandal:

> Gracious Queen we thee implore,
>   Go away and sin no more
> Or if that effort prove too great,
>   Go away at any rate!

Their only daughter was Princess Charlotte. She was a plain, good-natured girl, who lived quietly and simply. She became extremely popular with the people of London, who looked forward to the time when she should become Queen, and end the rule of the unpopular princes. In 1817, however, the Princess, who had married a German prince, died. Soon after this, the Prince Regent declared that he was going to divorce Caroline, his wife. A long and scandalous investigation into Caroline's private life followed, which produced no definite result. In 1820, the old king, George III died, and Caroline, who had been living in Italy, returned to become Queen of England. Her husband, however, refused to allow her to take part in the coronation ceremony. Some of the Parliamentary radicals took the Queen's side, and the people of London joined in the quarrel with enthusiasm. For all her peculiarities, it was still possible to see her as the victim of cruelty by the unpopular George IV. In the weeks before the coronation, Parliament was asked to pass a Bill taking away Caroline's titles, but there was such support for her among the people of London, that the Bill was withdrawn. This was celebrated by the London crowds as a great victory, which was also, of course, a defeat for the King. At the coronation ceremony, however, Geoge persisted with his refusal to recognise his wife, and would not have her in Westminster Abbey. While the solemn ceremony was taking place, the Queen was hammering at the locked door of the Abbey, cheered on by enthusiastic crowds. The monarchy had never been the object of so much public ridicule.

Caroline died very soon after her husband's coronation, but the King's reputation and dignity never really recovered from the scandal which accompanied his ascent to the throne. When he died in 1830, *The Times* newspaper wrote:

> There never was an individual less regretted by his fellow-creatures than this deceased King. What eye has wept for him? What heart has heaved one sob of unmercenary sorrow?... If George IV ever had a friend – a devoted friend in any rank of life – we protest that the name of him or her has never reached us...

William IV

Next on the throne was George's brother, William. He was far more popular. Although not nearly as intelligent as his elder brother, he had more idea of how to get on with the people around him. He was king for only seven years, but these were years, as you will see in Chapter 8 in which some of the most violent political activity of the century took place. Those who thought William a particularly stupid man, probably did not consider what might have happened during the Reform Bill crisis if his brother

57. Queen Caroline. George IV's treatment of his wife turned her into a popular figure. Radical politicians of all kinds used her case to attack the King.

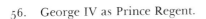

56. George IV as Prince Regent.

58.   Samuel Whitbread.

had still been king. But most people seem to have felt about him rather as *The Times* did, which wrote on his death in 1837:

> His late Majesty, though at times a jovial and, for a King, an honest man, was a weak, ignorant, commonplace sort of person... Notwithstanding his feebleness of purpose, his ignorance and his prejudices, William IV was to the last a popular sovereign, but his very popularity was acquired at the price of something like public contempt...

After William's death, his niece, Victoria, became Queen. We shall see in later chapters how the public attitude changed towards the monarchy during her reign. When she came to the throne as a young girl of eighteen, she was welcomed with relief by a country which had grown very tired of the sort of kings and princes who had ruled over it for half a century.

The Government

At the end of the war, the government in power was led by Lord Liverpool. He was a Tory, and his government was made up of Tories and some Whigs who had joined the government during the war. This was the sort of government which had been in power since 1794, and which was to remain in power for another fifteen years. Their main concern was to make a settlement in Europe, and to keep Britain peaceful and prosperous. They did this by supporting landowners and farmers with the Corn Laws, and by opposing any attempts to alter the system of government, either by admitting Catholics into political life, or by making any reforms in the election of members of parliament. Some of the younger men in the government were in favour of a certain amount of change, but they were in a minority.

The Opposition

The government was opposed within parliament by a section of the Whigs. As we have seen, the two parties were not divided by great differences, and during the war years many of the leading Whigs had co-operated with the Tories. But the section of the party which was made up of the former friends of Charles James Fox, spent most of the war years in opposition. The leader of this group was Lord Grey. He and his followers believed that a reform of Parliament must come about, and as the years went by and the country became more and more disturbed, they became convinced of the need for moderate reform. As well as the Whig reformers, there were a few independent radicals in the House of Commons, men like Sir Francis Burdett, Samuel Whitbread and Henry Hunt, who, at different times in the years between the war and the Reform Bill opposed the Government on a whole number of questions, and who were in favour of a more far-reaching reform of Parliament than Lord Grey and his followers.

Henry Brougham

But as well as the older, Fox-ite Whigs, and the small number of independent radicals, another important kind of politician was coming forward in these years. The most outstanding among them was a Scottish lawyer, Henry Brougham.

Brougham differed from the old Whig reformers – he was not an aristocrat himself, and he did not believe in the idea of the aristocracy as the "natural" leaders of the country. He wanted the middle classes to be given the vote, and to be included in the government of the country, for he believed strongly in the middle class virtues. These were the virtues of hard work, common sense, and a respect for property and for money. He was in favour of reforming many of the old laws of England, to make the law more reasonable and easier to understand. He was amongst the M.P.'s who worked for the freeing of slaves. In the quarrel between King George IV and Queen Caroline, Brougham became legal adviser to the Queen, and so made himself very popular with the people of London. It was perhaps his experience at this time which gave him a great interest in public opinion. He believed that there was a wide interest in political matters in the country, even amongst people who had no vote. This was the time in which newspapers were becoming more widely sold in the country, and Brougham and his friends made sure that their speeches were fully reported. We are used, nowadays to the idea that political leaders should speak to the people outside Parliament, as well as to the members inside, but in the early nineteenth century this was a new idea. It seemed strange to many of the old school of politicians that a political leader should defend or explain his views to the public at any time except perhaps during an election. George IV complained, in 1823, about " . . . the passion which seems to exist for speech-making out of time and out of proper place . . ." But Brougham and his friends saw that the middle classes were going to take a more and more important part in the life of the country in the future. If this was to happen, politics could no longer be carried on by a small group of people in London, who all knew each other and who met regularly at each other's houses. Britain was moving into an age when people all over the country – manufacturers in Lancashire and Nottingham, businessmen in Edinburgh and Newcastle – were going to take part in politics. Much more public discussion would be needed, politicians would have to travel and meet their followers, and newspapers would have to take the latest news into every part of the country.

The Utilitarians

As well as wanting more people to take part in political life, Brougham and those who thought like him wanted other changes. Most of these changes were in line with the ideas of the philosopher Jeremy Bentham, who put forward the principals of *Utilitarianism*. Bentham believed that ideas and institutions should be judged by whether they helped to increase human happiness and well-being. He was attracted by the slogan of "the greatest happiness of the greatest possible number". He looked at laws and institutions, and asked whether they contributed to the greatest possible happiness. If they did not, he thought they should be abolished, however ancient or holy they appeared to be.

Bentham's followers supported the reform of Parliament, the reform of prisons and punishment of crime generally, the simplification of many laws, the provision of education for the whole population, and many other changes, most of which were achieved as the century went on. This philosophy of reason and common sense appealed very much to the middle classes, who tried to carry on their businesses on these lines. Perhaps unfortunately, the ideas sometimes became very much over-simplified. Reason, common sense, utility can be dangerous if they are not mixed with imagination. It was easy for the idea of what was useful to become confused with what was profitable, and the middle classes were often accused of thinking that the only things

59. Jeremy Bentham, leader of the Utilitarians. He believed in looking again at laws and institutions, to see if they were really serving a useful purpose.

that mattered were things that could be bought and sold.

In the immediately post-war period, the middle classes were concerned very much with gaining various kinds of freedom. They wanted a reform of Parliament to admit them to a share in the election of a government. They wanted the removal of the many restrictions which applied to members of churches other than the Church of England – non-conformists could still not hold public office until after the Test and Corporation Acts were repealed in 1828. They wanted freedom of trade between countries, and freedom to carry on their firms at home without government interference.

The Poor

The majority of people in England in 1815 were poor. Historians have lately been discussing the question of whether the first effects of the Industrial Revolution were to make people more miserable, or whether to make them better off. Part of the argument is about rates of wages, and part of it is about the way people lived. We shall probably never be able to give a simple answer to this question. For one thing, we do not have reliable figures about wages. We may know that some workmen were paid more for their work after industrialisation had come to an industry, but we do not know whether they worked as regularly as before, or whether the work was more or less pleasant, easier or harder. We can make some guesses, and we can read what people thought at the time. There were some who thought that the factory system and the movement into towns were making people much more miserable, and others who thought people were happier and better off. The argument will probably go on for a long time. Certainly by the middle of the nineteenth century the money earnings and standard of living of the majority of people in the manufacturing districts had improved considerably over the earnings of their pre-industrial ancestors. In the years immediately after the Napoleonic wars, however, the war and the changes which industrialisation was bringing to the way of life of many of the people of England had created a state of great poverty and misery for many thousands.

The population rise which had been taking place since the middle of the eighteenth century, had resulted in more young men in the villages who were unable to find work, and who were not ever likely to find work in the country. There were no jobs for the soldiers who came home to their villages. The factories in the towns mainly wanted women and children as workers, and trades such as weaving and framework-knitting which did employ men had become over-full during the war, and could not take in the returning men. Trade fell off after a short post-war boom, and work became even scarcer.

Unemployment and distress were to be found in every part of England and in every trade. The people looked to the government to take some action which would improve things. But the only actions which the government took seemed to make things worse. The Corn Laws kept up the price of bread. Laws against Trade Union action and against all forms of political activity and against the expression of opinion in the press made it clear that the government was relying on the use of force to keep order, rather than trying to remedy things.

Two things happened. In some districts, especially in the agricultural areas, there were riots, rick-burning and the destruction of property. The labourers demanded better wages and lower bread prices.

In other areas, particularly in the big towns and in the manufacturing districts there was a great revival in the movement for Parliamentary reform.

The Reformers

> As to the *cause* of our present miseries, it is the enormous amount of the taxes which the government compels us to pay . . .

This was the voice of William Cobbett – the greatest of the Radical journalists. His weekly *Political Register* sold 60,000 copies a week in 1816, far more than any "respectable" newspaper. A cheap edition of it, nicknamed *Twopenny Trash* opened with an "Address to the Journeymen and Labourers", which was later printed as a separate pamphlet. Cobbett knew how to speak to the ordinary working men and labourers in language which they understood. Always clear and simple, very often funny, he wrote in a new way for a new audience, putting forward the view that the only way to improve things was to sweep away the old corrupt system of government, and replace it with one elected by the whole people. Reforming clubs grew up all over the country. To begin with they were organised by the tradesmen and manufacturers, who had no vote, and who thought the government favoured landowners and farmers at the expense of industry. Gradually, however, they began to include artisans and working men. Some of the older reformers were

60. Rick-burning was the only way the poor people in the country-side could make their protest felt. In this drawing, the labourer is explaining to the clergyman that the burning hay-rick behind him is the result of years of oppression. He had been first turned out of his farm to make way for a new fox covert for hunting, then turned out of his cottage for not paying tithes.

rather horrified by this development. In Sheffield one manufacturer, who had always attended reform dinners and meetings, complained now of a dinner at which "the dinner tickets were priced so low that the company, with few exceptions, were of the lowest rank . . ."

It was clear that not only the manufacturers and merchants were now in favour of reform, but a very wide section of the people. A movement was growing for a really sweeping reform of Parliament, by which everyone over twenty-one should have the vote.

The combination of great distress and a growing movement for reform frightened the government. They tried to crush the reform movement by every means at their disposal. One means which they used more freely than it has been used before or since in this country, was the planting of spies and *provocateurs* in the reform clubs. Spies had often been used, before, of course, to report the activities of groups who might be dangerous. But now the government encouraged its agents not only to report, but actually to suggest plans for risings and armed action. In case after case evidence was

61. William Cobbett, the Radical journalist, who wrote for journeymen and labourers, and brought the arguments for the reform of Parliament to the ordinary people.

given after the arrest of leading reformers that the violent episodes in which they were said to have taken part had been suggested, often actually started, by a confessed agent of the government. Most notorious of all these provocative agents was one known as "Oliver the Spy". He had toured the manufacturing districts, encouraging rebellion. When his record became known, many juries refused to convict men arrested on his evidence, but at least three were hanged as the result of his activities, and many more suffered arrest and imprisonment.

Government repression

There were three men in the government who were held to be most responsible for the extreme harshness and repression of this period. When the poet Shelley wrote about the state of England in 1819, he described the three men in the characters of Murder, Fraud and Hypocrisy.

I met murder on the way –

He had a mask-like Castlereagh . . .
Very smooth he looked, yet grim;
    Seven bloodhounds followed him:

All were fat; and well they might
    Be in admirable plight,
For one by one and two by two,
    He tossed them human hearts to chew
    Which from his wide cloak he drew.

Next came Fraud, and he had on.
    Like Lord Eldon, an ermine gown;
His big tears, for he wept well,
Turned to millstones as they fell;

And the little children, who
Round his feet played to and fro,
Thinking every tear a gem
Had their brains knocked out by them.

Clothed with the bible as with light
And the shadow of the night
Like Sidmouth next, Hypocrisy
On a crocodile came by.

Lord Castlereagh, the Foreign Secretary, had earned a reputation as a harsh, even vicious administrator when he was Secretary of State for Ireland early in his career. He was an unbalanced man, who cut his own throat in 1822 to avoid blackmail or an unpleasant scandal. His funeral procession was greeted with cheers and groans by the crowds in the streets of London.

Lord Eldon was Lord Chancellor in the Government. He was a professional lawyer who had been made a peer in 1799 after a very successful legal career. He had been the leading counsel for the prosecution in the trial of Thomas Hardy and the other London Reformers in 1794. He was in office when many measures were taken by the Government which the reformers held to be against the ancient laws of England. *Habeas Corpus* (that is the law which makes it impossible for people to be held in prison for more than a short time without being brought into court and tried) was suspended in 1817, and the Six Acts of 1819, which put severe limits on the right of people to hold meetings and on the right of newspapers to publish what they thought was important,

62. The Pentridge Rising. An imaginary and very blood-curdling picture of the leaders of the Pentridge Rising. The unsuccessful rising was instigated by Oliver, a government spy, in the pay of Lord Sidmouth.

were passed during Eldon's years of office.

Lord Sidmouth was the Home Secretary, the man directly responsible for the control of the spies and agents who provoked military and semi-military risings amongst the starving people in the manufacturing districts. In 1817, when the four leaders of the Pentridge rising were condemned to be hanged, Sidmouth was ill in bed, but he "derived more benefit from the termination of the Derby trials than from all that the medical men could give him . . ."

These, then, were the most prominent members of the government which tried to put into operation the "continental" system of control in England. The lack of success of their methods, and the fear which they aroused amongst people of nearly all classes were important reasons for the eventual introduction of Parliamentary Reform, and the growth of the Democratic system of government in England.

Peterloo

In spite of the government's efforts, enthusiasm for Reform grew. Middle and working class opinion was shown by the refusal of many juries to convict radicals and reformers and by the growing number of peaceful demonstrations. On 16th August, 1819, there occurred an event which was to have a lasting effect on the history of civil rights in England. On that day the reformers of Manchester and the surrounding districts had organised a great demonstration in favour of the reform of Parliament. Each of the weaving villages on the Pennines had arranged for its own con-

63. The massacre of Peterloo. Compare this picture with the picture on p. 77 of the Battle of Waterloo.

tingent to attend, banners had been made, women and children had made new dresses, caps and bonnets. The speaker was to be Henry Hunt.

Amongst those who set off for Manchester on the morning of 16th August was young Sam Bamford, leading radical in the small Pennine town of Middleton. In later years he wrote a famous autobiography – *Passages in the Life of a Radical*, in which he described the preparation in his town:

> By eight o'clock on the morning of Monday, the 16th August 1819, the whole town of Middleton might be said to be on the alert: some to go to the meeting, and others to see the procession, the like of which . . . had never before taken place in that neighbourhood.
>
> First were selected twelve of the most comely and decent-looking youths, who were placed in two rows of six each, with each a branch of laurel held presented in his hand, as a token of amity and peace; then followed the men of several districts in fives; then the band of music, an excellent one; then the colours: a blue one of silk, with inscriptions in golden letters, "Unity and Strength" "Liberty and Fraternity"; a green one of silk, with golden

letters "Parliaments Annual", "Suffrage Universal"; and betwixt them, on a staff, a handsome cap of crimson velvet with a tuft of laurel . . . next were placed the remainder of the men of the districts in fives. . .

So, in their best clothes, with flags flying and the band playing, the Middleton people set out to walk into Manchester. All along the route they were joined by contingents from other towns, including many girls and women and young children. Everyone was wearing their best. Bamford said "I noticed not even one who did not exhibit a white Sunday's shirt, a neck-cloth, and other apparel in the same clean, though homely condition . . . ."

From all directions processions such as this one converged on St Peter's Fields in Manchester. On a central rostrum, Henry Hunt and other speakers stood up, prepared to speak to one of the greatest crowds that had ever assembled in England. But scarcely had they begun the meeting, when, from the edge of the crowd, a group of mounted soldiers rode in towards the speakers. When their horses could not force a way through the densely packed people, the riders drew their swords and hacked about them to clear a path. As the crowd began to realise what was happening, and to fall back, the soldiers pursued them, hitting out with the flats and with the edges of their swords. Other mounted troops appeared, and soon the great field was full of people trying to escape, and heaps of people, alive and dead, who had fallen and been trampled. One man who escaped described some of the things he saw:

> ... When I got to the end of Watson street, I saw ten or twelve of the Yeomanry Cavalry, and two of the Hussars cutting at the people, who were wedged close together, when an officer of Hussars rode up to his own men, and knocking up their swords said, "Damn you, what do you mean by this work?" He then called out to the Yeomanry, "For shame, gentlemen, what are you about? the people cannot get away". They desisted for a time,

but no sooner had the officer rode to another part of the field than they fell to work again ...

Apart from a few brickbats, the cavalry met with no opposition, for the people had been especially asked to bring no weapons, not even walking-sticks, as proof of their peaceful intentions. When the field was clear, at least five hundred people had been wounded and eleven killed.

The original group of horsemen had set out to arrest the speakers, on charges of sedition – that is of plotting to overthrow the government. But the Yeomanry, who were a volunteer force, made up of the local gentry, had undoubtedly gone very far beyond this. The evidence of the witness just quoted, and the evidence of other witnesses at the inquests which followed, suggest that the regular soldiers, the Hussars, had been less bloodthirsty than the Yeomanry. But the wit who coined the name

64. Peterloo. A cartoonist of the time shows the yeomanry charging the unarmed crowds at the Manchester meeting, encouraged by the Prince Regent. Orator Hunt protests from the platform.

of *Peterloo* for the encounter, after the battle of Waterloo, was comparing the event quite literally to a battle, and with good reason.

The reaction to Peterloo was immediate. There has been a great deal of discussion as to whether Lord Sidmouth instructed the Lancashire magistrates in advance to attack the demonstration, and we may never know the full truth about this. But he reacted immediately by sending his congratulations to the magistrates and military on their "prompt, decisive, and efficient measures for the preservation of the public peace . . ." He was supported in this by the Prince Regent.

Protests, however, flooded in. The Lord-Lieutenant of neighbouring Yorkshire, Earl FitzWilliam, protested at the action of the Manchester authorities, and was removed from his office by the government. People of all classes throughout the country were shocked and horrified, and perhaps the government's support of the massacre did more to discredit it than any of its other activities. In London, William Hone and George Cruikshank sold thousands of copies of their satirical pamphlets attacking the government and the "victors" of Peterloo.

They proposed a "monument" and a medal to be worn by the warriors, on which the slogan of the anti-slavery movement appears – "Am I not a man and a brother?" with the answer "No! You are a poor weaver". The picture of the "free-born Englishman" after the passing of the Six Acts, shows him starving, gagged and in chains. In a bitter satire, The *Political House that Jack Built*, they described . . .

THE PEOPLE, all tattered and torn,
Who curse the day wherein they were born,
on account of Taxation too great to be born,
And pray for relief from night to morn,
Who in vain, petition in every form,
Who, peaceably Meeting to ask for Reform,
Were sabred by Yeomanry Cavalry, who
Were thanked by the man all shaven and shorn,
All covered with Orders – and all forlorn;
THE DANDY OF SIXTY, who bows with a
          grace,
And has *taste* in wigs, collars, cuirasses and
          lace;
Who, to tricksters and fools, leaves the State
          and its treasure,
And when Britain's in tears, sails about at his
          pleasure . . .

Chapter 8

Popular Movements and the Reform of Parliament 1819–1832

Trade Unions and Friendly Societies

The middle years of the 1820's were very good ones for English industry. Money was being put into building big cotton factories, and trade with other countries was booming. It was a good time for the working people to organise themselves into Trade Unions. In 1820 Trade Unions were illegal, but this did not prevent them from coming into existence. It only meant that they had to be given other names. So they were often called Friendly Societies – that is societies whose members joined together to save money for times of sickness or to pay for their burials. Anything which these societies did to raise wages or to improve working conditions had to be done secretly. In 1824, Francis Place, the well-known London Radical, managed to persuade a group of Radical Members of Parliament to try and repeal the Combination Acts, which made Trade Unions illegal. Place believed that the Unions would be better working in the open than working in secret. He even thought that they would begin to die out if they were not "underground". But he was wrong about that.

Joseph Hume's bill to repeal the Combination Acts was passed in 1824, and immediately there was an outbreak of strikes for better wages and better working conditions. Many employers blamed the Government for allowing Hume's bill to pass, so in 1825 another Trade Union Act was passed which put some limits on what Trade Unions were allowed to do. In particular this Act forbade any form of "molesting" by Trade Unionists. This meant that if there was a strike, the Union members had to be very careful how they tried to persuade non-Union workers not to take the places of strikers. In fact, it made the organisation of strikes very difficult, but it did leave the Unions as legal organisations. From 1825

65a.   Trade Union Card of the West of Scotland Female Weavers.

65b.   Trade Union Card of the Cordwainers.

65c.   Pictorial Heading to the List of Resolutions drawn up at a meeting of London Hat Finishers,
25 May 1820.

onwards the Trade Unions were able to work in the open, although they still had many years to go before they were able to set up the solid forms of national organisation which grew into the modern Trade Union movement.

The Reform of Parliament

The boom of the mid-twenties did not last. A period of bad trade followed, in which there was unemployment all over the country. Again people who were hungry or out of work, and people whose businesses were doing badly, looked at Parliament and thought they could improve things if only it could be reformed. The important question was – Could the House of Commons ever reform itself? Many people thought the idea was absurd. They thought that in the end, England would have to have a revolution, as France had had. The only possible hope of changing things without a revolution, would be to frighten the Members of the House so much, that they would reform themselves out of sheer terror.

Nearly every one in the country had some reason for thinking that reform was necessary. The great advances which had made England the leading industrial country in the world had been carried through, as we have seen, by men who had almost no say in the government of the country. They thought that the running of their businesses was being hampered by laws which favoured landowners and farmers, and that people who worked hard for their money were taxed heavily, while people who merely owned land got off very lightly. The working people, in town and country, thought no one would ever take notice of their miseries unless they had a vote to cast in the election of Members of Parliament. Together the middle and working classes made up the very great majority of the population.

In Parliament, even in the Government, there were people who were no longer satisfied with the old ways of governing. Some of them thought that if the Government acted to improve things, people would forget about reform. So some measures were introduced which would have been unthinkable in the days of Sidmouth and Castlereagh. The Combination Acts, as we have seen, were repealed in 1824, and in 1829 Catholic Emancipation was granted. This meant that at last Catholics were allowed to sit in Parliament. It was of very great importance in the history of Ireland where Roman Catholics were the great majority of the population. Robert Peel, who was Home Secretary, introduced measures to lessen some of the very harsh punishments for crime, and Huskisson, who was President of the Board of Trade, made some moves towards making trade more free.

But the Tories, who were the governing party, only succeeded in dividing their own followers by these reforms. One section, led by the Duke of Wellington, thought that even such limited concessions were dangerous, whilst for the more thorough-going reformers they did not go far enough. The Whigs, who were the opposition party, took the leadership on the question of Reform within the House of Commons.

In the General Election of 1826, two boroughs were so corrupt in their conduct of the election – particularly in the open bribing of electors – that a bill was passed in 1827, taking away their right to return members. A Bill was then introduced, which proposed to give these two spare seats to Manchester and Birmingham, neither of which two great towns had the right to send a member to Parliament. But so determined were the majority of Members of the House to have no reform of the old system, that even this reasonable proposal was defeated.

Bitter Winter of 1829–30

The winter of 1829 to 1830 was one of great distress in the countryside. The poor labourers were driven to desperation by their condition, and by the feeling that no one in

66.   The hulks in Portsmouth Harbour. These were rat-ridden old ships used as prisons for long-term convicts, or as temporary prisons for convicts awaiting transportation.

the country cared what happened to them or their families. During 1830 there were a series of outbreaks of violence all over the Southern and Eastern counties of England, which have come to be called "the Last Labourers' Revolt". Machines, such as threshing machines, which seemed to be putting men out of work, were smashed; ricks and barns belonging to unpopular employers were burnt, and again and again written appeals were sent to landlords and magistrates, asking for reasonable poor relief, the remission of tithes, lowering of rents and an increase of wages. Although thousands of people took part in these outbreaks, it was very difficult for the magistrates to get anyone to come forward and give evidence about the destruction of property. The rioters did not kill or seriously injure anyone. Sometimes they would disable a valuable horse belonging to an unpopular landowner, and on more than one occasion the local Overseer of

the Poor got a ducking in the village pond to punish him for his meanness or arrogance. But when Special Commissions of judges were sent into the countryside to try those rioters who had been arrested, they showed no mercy. Nine men were hanged, 457 transported, and several hundred imprisoned.

The labourers did not usually connect their miseries with the unreformed House of Commons. But others made the connection for them. Cobbett tells how, as he rode past the uninhabited green hill that was the "borough" of Old Sarum with two M.P.s, he met a labourer returning from work:

I asked him how he *got on*. He said, very badly. I asked him what was the cause of it. He said the *hard times*. "What *times*", said I; "was there ever a finer summer, a finer harvest . . . ?" "Ah", said he, "*they* make it bad for poor people for all that". "*They*?" said I "who is *they*?" He was silent. "Oh, no, no! my friend", said I, "it is not *they*; it is that Accursed Hill that has robbed you . . ."

The Birmingham Political Union

"That Accursed Hill" – Old Sarum – continued to symbolise the unfairness of the old system. But the plight of the labourers, and the general distress in the country made many people decide to take action to change things. In Birmingham, which had been refused a Member of Parliament in 1828, a group began to organise in 1829. Under the leadership of Thomas Attwood, a banker, who believed that every man in the country should have a vote, a group of business men met and formed a "Political Union of the Industrious Classes for the Protection of Public Rights". At a meeting held in January 1830, between twelve and fifteen thousand people heard Attwood and other speakers call for the immediate reform of Parliament. They unanimously passed a resolution agreeing to form "a general Political Union between the lower and middle classes of the people of this town", and agreed that:

> ... in the opinion of this meeting, the general distress which now afflicts this country, and which has been so severely felt at different periods during the last fifteen years, is entirely to be ascribed to the gross mismanagement of public affairs; and that such mismanagement can only be effectually and permanently remedied by an actual reform of the Commons House of Parliament.

Birmingham was only the beginning. All over the country Political Unions sprang up to press for reform. Sometimes these were only organisations of the middle classes. In some towns there were two unions, one for the middle and one for the working classes, but most of them were a union of the two – of what Attwood called "the industrious classes". They held meetings, and collected thousands upon thousands of signatures to petitions, which were sent up by the cartload to Parliament. Henry Hunt, the most radical of all the reform leaders, who had been the speaker in St. Peter's Fields in 1819, was elected Member of Parliament for Preston in 1829. In Parliament he found a few more radicals, men such as Joseph Hume, who

wanted Manhood Suffrage, that is the vote for every man in the country. The Whig party was in favour of some reform. Some of the Whigs, like Henry Brougham and Lord Durham, wanted a considerable widening of the franchise, others, like the leaders of the party, Lord John Russell and Lord Grey, wanted to go more slowly, and make less sweeping changes. The Tories would have liked to keep the question within the House of Commons and to have an agreement between the parties about the best sort of reform to make. But as 1830 went on it became clear that the King, George IV, had not much longer to live. At that time, the death of the monarch always meant a General Election, and the reformers began to get ready, and to organise their forces throughout the country. The King died on June 26th, and a month later his successor, William IV, prorogued Parliament.

The General Election of 1830

There followed eighteen months of excitement and turmoil. The reformers seized their chance to make use of the limited scope there was to win votes in favour of Parliamentary Reform. Henry Brougham, a candidate for Yorkshire, the biggest constituency in the country, asked the voters to return him on a programme of reform:

> We don't live now in the days of Barons – we live in the days of Leeds, of Bradford, of Halifax, of Huddersfield. We live in the days when men are industrious and desire to be free. I am for extending the rights of voting in the great towns of England. I go a great deal further. I am for extending the right of voting to that class of people who have no right now in any town of England – inhabitant householders – and I am for shortening the duration of Parliament.

Suddenly, in the middle of the election, a dramatic event occurred across the channel. In France, the restored Bourbon monarchy had been trying to go back to the old idea of a powerful king and a limited Parliament. In July, the King, Charles X, published a series of orders which were to limit the power of the elected parliament, and abolish the freedom of the press. Paris rose in protest, and after a short struggle, the king was forced to flee with his closest ministers. His orders were cancelled, Parliament asserted itself, and a new king, Louis Philippe, the former Duke of Orleans, was put on the throne. When the news arrived in England it caused great excitement. In three days the people of France had overthrown a despotic regime – the people of England were ready to draw a lesson from them.

In spite of the small number of people who had a vote, it soon became clear that the election was going to the reformers, Cobbett wrote:

> In Norfolk the old Tory, Woodhouse, has been shoved aside by a man who has pledged himself to Reform. In Cambridgeshire the Duke of Rutland's brother, or cousin, or something has been put out by a private gentleman, who made a solemn declaration he would vote for radical reform. In other counties no very great change as to the principle of the men, but everywhere reform has been sounded in the ears, and nowhere has there been found a man bold enough to say that he was not for some degree of reform in parliament . . .

Some of the members of the Government were in the House of Lords, and the others were mostly members for rotten boroughs. So they themselves were returned, but without very many of their former supporters. Before the new Parliament assembled, the situation was made even more tense by news of a revolution in Belgium. As the French had done, the Belgians gained their ends in a very short time, overthrowing the Dutch rule which had been forced on them after the Napoleonic War, and setting up an independent government.

Parliament reassembled in October 1830. The Prime Minister, the Duke of Wellington, made a most emphatic statement against reform. He declared that the present system was the best in the world. But the new Parliament contained a majority of members favouring Reform, and within a week of this statement, the Duke's government was voted down in the House of Commons, and the King sent for Lord Grey, the Whig leader, to form a government.

Immediately, all over the country, meetings were called and petitions organised, urging Lord Grey to carry out the reform of Parliament. All through the winter there were demonstrations. It was clear that the question could no longer be put off, and in March 1831, the long-awaited Whig Reform Bill was introduced.

The Reform Bill

Although the Bill did not propose to give the vote to all adults, it did go much further than most people really expected. Rotten boroughs were to be abolished, and many two-member boroughs were reduced to having one member only. The seats thus freed were to be given to new constituencies, made mainly from the towns of the industrial north and midlands.

In the boroughs the qualification for voting was the occupation of property worth at least £10 a year in rent. This would only include fairly well-off people, indeed in the one or two old "open" boroughs many voters would lose their votes. But it was estimated that the Bill would create 60,000 new electors in London, and 260,000 in the rest of England. In the counties the vote was to remain with the 40/– freeholders, with the addition of a small number of the wealthier tenants.

Many of the reformers were disappointed that the working people were not included in the proposed bill. What was more, there was no provision for a secret ballot to protect the new voters. As long as voting was not secret, people might be afraid of losing their job if they did not vote as their employers wanted. But they realised that there would be a struggle to get the Bill through at all, so most of them rallied round it, calling for "The Bill, the whole Bill, and nothing but the Bill". Many of them thought that if they could get this measure of reform passed, they would more easily get further concessions in the future.

They were right to expect a fight over the Bill. It passed the House of Commons by a single vote, and was then defeated in the committee stage. The members of the House of Lords declared that they would not pass it unless many changes were made, and Grey knew that the country would not agree to such changes. So he resigned.

The election which followed was the most exciting in the history of the country. Everywhere where voting was possible, people turned out, refusing to sell their votes and voting in favour of reform candidates. At Old Sarum, where there were no genuine voters, the ceremony of "electing" the two members was gone through under the elm tree on the top of the green mound. Soon afterwards, a body of some two hundred

Radicals, convinced that this was the last election which would ever be held there, marched to the spot, cut down the tree, and distributed pieces of it as souvenirs. Lord Grey again became Prime Minister with many more supporters in the House of Commons than he had before.

The Bill passed the new House of Commons by 136 votes. Grey now knew he had the support of the country, and he determined that if the House of Lords would not let the Bill through, he would ask the King to make enough new peers to swamp the Tory majority among the existing House of Lords. But it was well known that the King was not at all happy at this possibility, and in spite of the threat, the Lords again turned down the Bill. Now the country was at fever pitch. All the people who had believed that a revolution would be needed to get reform seemed to be proved right, and in some

67.   The French Revolution, July 1830. Events in France in the summer of 1830 gave new hope to the Reformers in England.

68.   Reform Bill Riots. Nottingham Castle ablaze during the agitation of 1831.

69.   An artist's impression of the town of Bristol, ablaze during the Reform Bill riots of 1831.

places the crowds were no longer satisfied with peaceful demonstrations. In London the Duke of Wellington's windows were smashed with stones, and the King's carriage was attacked. In the big provincial cities effigies of the Duke were burnt, in Nottingham the castle was attacked and burnt, in Derby the gaol was sacked, and in Bristol, riots which started as attacks on the carriages and property of well-known opponents of the Bill, turned into much more serious outbreaks of burning and demonstrating, and for several days the crowd was completely in control of the town.

At this point many even of the supporters of reform became alarmed. All through the country there was talk of arming and barricades. The Cap of Liberty, symbol of the revolutionaries in France, appeared in demonstrations. Respectable business men and tradesmen talked of starting a "run" on the banks – that is withdrawing all their money, so that trade was interfered with, and the Government would not be able to carry on. Moreover, the movement for reform was in some places getting altogether out of the hands of the moderate and respectable classes. This was particularly true in London, where there were two reform movements: the middle classes had the national Political Union, and the working classes the National Union of the Working Classes and Others.

Many of the members of the N.U.W.C. wanted very far-reaching reforms, including the complete abolition of the House of Lords, and the setting up of an English Republic. There were similar groups in some of the northern cities. The members of the House of Lords may well have remembered that it was the crowds in Paris and Brussels which had brought down the French and Belgian Governments, and have feared that the London people would go beyond the demands of the Whig Reform Bill.

So although the Duke of Wellington tried to form a Government, he found that many of his own party were not prepared to take the responsibility of continuing to oppose reform, and he was unable to form one. Finally, the Tory Lords gave way. To spare the King the embarrassment of having to create new peers, the Duke and many of his fellow Tory peers refrained from voting against the Bill, and it was finally passed.

Parliament had reformed itself – pushed and harried from outside as it was. There was very little violence, and the vote was kept firmly in the hands of people of property. For the working people it was only a slight step in the direction of their gaining any political rights, but it was a move, and it was certainly a grave defeat for the Duke of Wellington and his party of extreme Tories.

Chapter 9

The First Reformed Parliament

Results of the Reform Bill

The Reform Bill had made two important things clear about English politics. The first was that the Constitution could be changed. After 1832, it was no longer possible to argue that Parliament was not allowed by law to change itself. The second important thing about the 1832 Reform Bill, was that it recognised the change that had taken place in the kind of wealth that existed in England. For the past two hundred years, England had been changing from a country of great landowners, into one in which various forms of wealth existed – a country of bankers, merchants, shopkeepers, manufacturers, lawyers, teachers, writers. All these people helped to make up the wealth of the country, but until 1832 only the possession of freehold landed property entitled people to take part in the government of the country. In 1832 these other forms of wealth were at last recognised, and the people who made up the middle classes of society were allowed into the political system. The working people, those who owned no property at all, or very little, were still not admitted to political life, although many of them had taken a great part in the agitation throughout the country which brought about the Reform Bill. After 1832, one Englishman in every five had the vote. In Scotland, one man in every eight, and in Ireland one in every twenty.

Since the Whigs had been the party which had stood for reform, it is hardly surprising that they got in by a large majority at the first election under the new system. Indeed, it might have been expect-ed that the Tories who had opposed the Bill would never again be returned. But, as we have seen, there was a section of the Tory party which had already shown an interest in reform, even though they had opposed the Bill. Under the leadership of Sir Robert Peel they began to regroup as a new Conservative party. Three years after the Reform Bill, Peel issued the *Tamworth Manifesto*, a document which set out the ideas of the Conservatives in the new political situation. In this he accepted the new situation brought about by the Reform Bill, and expressed a willingness for moderate reforms of all kinds where there were real grievances. It was not many years before Peel was leading a Conservative Government.

Although the middle classes had been given the vote by the Reform Bill, this did not have an immediate effect on the sort of person who became a member of Parliament. Most of the members of the first Reformed Parliament were landowners or the sons of landowners. Only one of the old leaders of the radical movement was elected, William Cobbett. Henry Hunt lost his seat at Preston, and Michael Sadler, the factory reformer, lost at Leeds. The new voters were not in the main interested in voting in members of their own class, let alone anyone from a lower order. Even Richard Cobden, the owner of a calico printing works, and his friend and colleague, John Bright, who was a cotton manufacture, were regarded as "outsiders" when they were elected in the early 1840's. Although they were both men of very considerable ability, it was to be many years after their first entry into the

House of Commons before either of them got even a minor office in the Government. Government was still left in the hands of gentlemen, but these gentlemen were now aware that their votes came from the middle classes as well as from their own class.

Lord Melbourne

For the first two years after 1832, Lord Grey remained leader of the Whigs, and was Prime Minister. Then his place was taken by Lord Melbourne. William Lamb, Viscount Melbourne was, like Lord Grey, in the House of Lords when he became Prime Minister. He had been in the House of Commons for more than twenty years as a Whig member before he became a peer, and he had been chief Secretary for Ireland before he became Home Secretary in Lord Grey's Government. He was a strange man to be head of the Government in the Reformed Parliament, for he was by no means a reformer. He came of an aristocratic family and was a great believer in tradition. He was a man of very great charm – handsome, very well educated, sociable and easy-going. He was said to be lazy and careless of detail – a favourite saying of his was "Why not leave it alone?" He was also supposed to have told the Cabinet – "It doesn't matter what we say, as long as we all say the same thing . . ." His great achievement as Prime Minister was not as a reformer, but as the man who helped the young Queen Victoria to find her place as Queen of England.

Queen Victoria

William IV died in 1837, and was the last of the sons of George III to rule. Although Victoria was next in line to the throne, one more son of George III was still alive. This was Ernest Augustus, Duke of Cumberland – a fierce-looking figure, with one eye missing, from a war wound, and huge bushy whiskers. He was a very high Tory, and was extremely unpopular with most people in England, including many Tories. Victoria's Uncle, the King of the Belgians, writing to her at the time of her accession, told her that the

70.   Young Victoria.

Whigs and the Liberals in the country were her best friends, partly because "your immediate successor with the moustaches is enough to frighten them into the most violent attachment for you . . . " There is no doubt that most people in England welcomed Victoria to the throne, partly because she stood between Ernest Augustus and the English crown. Until she came to the throne, the Hanoverian Kings of England had also been Kings of Hanover, a small German Kingdom, but a woman was not allowed by law to inherit this throne. So Ernest Augustus became King Ernest I of Hanover, while Victoria became Queen of England.

Whatever his shortcomings in general as Prime Minister, Melbourne certainly made an excellent friend and adviser to the young Queen. Indeed, she became so attached to him, that at one point she refused to change her Whig ladies for Tory ladies when the Whigs were defeated and Peel formed a Tory government. This incident became known as "the bedchamber question", and it kept Lord Melbourne and the Whigs in office for two years longer than they would otherwise have stayed. But at the next election, they were defeated, and in 1841, Peel became Prime Minister of a Tory government.

The Whigs were in power more or less continuously from 1833 to 1841. What did they achieve in those years?

The Work of the Reformed Parliament

The three most important measures passed by the Reformed Parliament were a Factory Act of 1833, the Poor Law Amendment Act of 1834, and the Municipal Reform Act of 1835. All of these were measures which the new middle class voters would approve of, and all were to have very important effects on the life of the country. Let us look first at the 1834 Poor Law Amendment Act.

New Poor Law 1834

During the eighteenth century, foreign visitors to England had often been very impressed by the English Poor Law. Every parish was obliged to see that the poor in the district did not starve, that the sick, the widowed, the orphaned and the unemployed were given food and shelter. Conditions varied a great deal, and many poor people led miserable lives indeed. Nevertheless, parishes accepted their responsibility, poor rates were levied on property owners, and poor relief was paid. In days when there was no unemployment or sickness insurance, or any Old Age Pension, and when wages were too low for saving, nearly all working people needed Poor Relief at some time in their lives.

But at the end of the eighteenth century, population increased, many traditional sources of help for the poor disappeared, and, as we have seen, a new system was introduced by which relief was given according to the price of bread. This system, the Speenhamland system, had been in force since 1795. One of the first things which the Reformed Parliament did was to set up a commission to enquire into how it was working.

The Secretary of this Commission, whose report was issued in 1834, was Edwin Chadwick. He was a lawyer, a Utilitarian, friend and admirer of Jeremy Bentham. To his eyes the old poor law was untidy, wasteful and immoral. He and his fellow commissioners saw to it that the evidence they presented brought out the bad side of the old system. Nearly all their enquiring was done in the South of England, where the Speenhamland system had been most fully used, and where wages had been kept down by it. Even in the South, they looked at the worst places, where money was wasted, and people were not encouraged to work. The report declared that "in far the greatest number of workhouses" the able-bodied poor were kept in "sluggish sensual indolence". In general, it gave the impression that the poor were being supported in riotous and lazy leisure at the expense of the hard-working ratepayers. Although conditions in some of the workhouses and villages in parts of the South of England may have been as bad as the report showed, the fact is that it was a very unfair document. It made very little reference to the industrial districts in particular. Here the old poor law had not been used to make up low wages, but was used as a sort of unemployment pay, which enabled weavers and other workers to live in periods of bad trade.

The Bill which was introduced as the result of the Report of the Royal Commission, applied to the whole of England. It was based on the recommendations of the Report, and had three main provisions for the relief of poverty. *Firstly*, no relief was to be given to the able-bodied poor, except in a workhouse. New workhouses were to be built by groups of parishes. *Secondly*, any relief so given was to be such that the life of the person in the workhouse was to be "less eligible" (that is to say, more unpleasant) than the worst sort of life outside. And *thirdly*, men and women and boys and girls were to be separated on entering the workhouse, partly as a way of making workhouse life "less eligible" and partly to prevent them from having children, for the Commission-

ers and their advisers believed that one of the main causes of poverty was that the poor had too many children. The administration of the new Poor Law was to be in the hands of three Commissioners, who were to oversee things in the whole country.

Movement against the New Poor Law

The Bill passed into law with only fifty Members of Parliament voting against it. The main body of both the Whig and Tory parties supported it. Among those who opposed it were William Cobbett, his fellow member for Oldham, John Fielden, and Thomas Attwood, the banker who had led the Birmingham Political Union. Outside the House of Commons it was opposed by a great many people. Among them was John Walter, editor of *The Times*, the most influential newspaper in England. Lord Eldon, high Tory and former Lord Chancellor, declared that the Act was unconstitutional, while Richard Oastler, leader of the Factory Reform movement, and himself a Tory, saw in it the end of stable government in England. An ambitious young politician. Benjamin Disraeli, who was to be elected to the House

71.   The Unions: an artist's impression of the inside of a workhouse in the 1840's.

of Commons three years later, declared that the new law was "announcing to the world that in England poverty was a crime".

The Act was passed, and the new workhouses were built as soon as possible. In the South of England there was little resistance. Harvests were good in the two years following the Act, and there was also a boom in railway building, so that many labourers were able to find work. Certainly there was a dramatic reduction in the Poor Rates. In 1832 they had cost the country more than seven million pounds. By 1836 they had fallen to four and a half million.

The southern labourers accepted the Unions, as the new workhouses were called, without much protest. True, they changed the name to the "Bastilles", after the grim French prison, but they nursed their hatred silently. In the North, however, things were different. For one thing, there was already in Yorkshire and Lancashire, a movement, aiming at the reduction of working hours in the factories, consisting mainly of the working people. These people, weavers, combers, factory hands, were often in need of parish relief in times of bad trade, but they did not rely on it to make up their wages. They were hard-working and independent, and bitterly resented the attempt of the new Act to replace their relief by workhouse life. When the Commissioners tried to introduce the new system they were met with the strongest resistance. In Todmorden, where John Fielden had his works, they could not introduce it until after his death in 1848, and in Huddersfield and Bradford there were riots which held up the institution of the new workhouses until 1838. Branches of an Anti-Poor Law Association were set up in all the Northern industrial towns, and Richard Oastler, Feargus O'Connor and Joseph Rayner Stephens toured the North, speaking at huge demonstrations. The language used at some of these was violent in the extreme. Oastler believed that the Act was against the constitution, and that if necessary it must be resisted by force " . . . I tell you

Churchmen, I tell you Dissenters", he said at Rochdale, "before I would submit to such an Act, I would see the whole Kingdom in a blaze".

Nearly all the working people in the country, a formidable number of writers and journalists, and a band of fiery orators were in agreement in condemning the new Poor Law. But the Government, with the majority of the middle and upper classes behind them. won the day. The movement against the Act did not die out in the North, but it became engulfed in a much greater movement with wider aims, which began in 1837–8, and which we shall look at in the next chapter.

Movement for Factory Reform

Since the earliest days of the factories there had been a small number of people who were concerned about the hideous working conditions inside them. Employers like Robert Owen and Robert Peel the elder had done all they could, by example and by trying to get laws passed, to make things better, especially for the children. But the great majority of manufacturers did not want any regulation of hours or conditions of work. Their attitude was backed up by the politicians of the Utilitarian group, who believed that any interference even with the hours of work of children was an interference with freedom. So that by the time of the passing of the Reform Bill conditions in the factories were almost entirely unregulated. During the Reform agitation, a Committee of investigation into conditions of work in the factories was sitting under the chairmanship of Michael Sadler. Sadler was Member of Parliament for Leeds. He was a Tory, and one of the strongest supporters of the Factory Reform movement in the country. Although in 1832 he was a sick man, with only a short time left to live, he did not spare himself in the work of his Committee. They heard evidence from people who worked in the factories, from the parents of children who worked in them, from employers, clergymen and many others. Altogether, eighty-seven

72. Another view of a workhouse in the 1840's.

people gave evidence, and out of their answers to the Committee's questions, came the Report, published in August 1832.

This Report, officially called *The Report from the Select Committee on the Bill for the Regulation of Factories*, is one of the most famous documents of the nineteenth century. Many public libraries have copies in the reference departments, and it really is worth trying to get a look at one. Short excerpts that can be published in text-books can give little sense of the mounting horror that comes from reading more and more evidence of the working conditions in those mills. It is true that much of the evidence was marshalled by the Ten Hours movement in Yorkshire and Lancashire. They made sure that the worst conditions should be reported, and one may hope that there were many factories in which things were not as bad as some of these examples. Nevertheless, the evidence that was presented was enough to convince many doubters of the need for laws to control hours of work. Children in many mills worked fourteen to sixteen hours a day for weeks at a time. Their parents told of staying awake all night for fear of oversleeping and not waking the children for the mill. They told how the children fell asleep at night with their supper in their mouths, and woke too tired to eat before work. Late-comers to the mill might be fined a quarter of their day's pay or more – for being five minutes late. In families which owned no clock, children had been wakened and sent to work at two o'clock on a moonlit night to wait two hours outside the gate for the foreman to open up. One witness regularly saw the children who worked in the mill near where he lived running to work in the early morning, eating a piece of oat cake for their breakfast as they ran, and crying for fear of being late. Meal breaks during the long working day were short – a half hour for midday dinner and a quarter of an hour for breakfast and tea, during which the children often had to clean their machines. Sometimes they had to eat their meal while the machinery was running, and almost always it had to be eaten in the hot and fluffy atmosphere of a loom or spinning shed. And to enforce all these conditions, to keep the childen awake and at work, thrashing with straps and beating with rollers was the common thing. More than one overlooker said bluntly that the work could not be kept going without this continuous cruelty, for otherwise the children would fall asleep at their machines.

It is not surprising that added to the cruelty, long hours and small pay which the children received, was the fact that they had no education. Not only did they not go to school, but the little girls had no chance to learn cooking or sewing from their mothers. There were Sunday schools in many of the mill districts – often run by the mill owners, but there was little chance of even those children who went learning much there after a working week of the sort described in the Report.

Sadler had introduced a Factory Reform Bill into the last meeting of the Unreformed Parliament. It had asked for a ten-hour day for all workers under 18, with an eight-hour day on Saturday; no night work for people under 21, and no child under 9 to work in any factory. A book was to be kept in every factory in which the time of everyone working there was entered. Sadler was defeated at Leeds by the Whigs, and in the new Parliament the Bill was introduced again by Lord Ashley.

Lord Ashley (the Earl of Shaftesbury)

Before the Ten Hours Bill could be presented, the new Government sent commissioners into the factory districts to gather more information. Throughout Yorkshire and Lancashire they were met with demonstrations demanding the Bill. At Leeds hundreds of factory children gathered outside the commissioners' hotel, singing to a popular tune:

> We will have the Ten Hours Bill
> 　That we will, that we will;
> Or the land shall ne'er be still,
> 　Ne'er be still, ne'er be still;
> Parliament say what they will,
> 　WE WILL HAVE THE TEN HOURS BILL

Although the Commissioners were rather more cautious in their statements than Sadler had been, they nevertheless found the same evidence of cruelty, illness and overwork among the factory children. But their proposals for dealing with the situation were not as drastic as the Ten Hours Bill. In the end, it was their views which made up the Factory Act, passed in July 1833 by the Reformed Parliament. When Ashley's proposals were defeated, he withdrew his Bill, and the Act which was finally passed is known as Althorp's Factory Act, after the Leader of the House of Commons, who presented it. What did it contain, and how far did it differ from Ashley's?

Althorp's Factory Act, 1833

The first main difference is that Althorp took a much lower age as the ending of childhood. The main regulations apply to children under thirteen. No child under nine was to work at all, and those between nine and thirteen, only forty-eight hours a week. Young persons between thirteen and eighteen could work a sixty-nine hour week. Neither children or young persons could work at night. The really important thing about the Act was firstly that it applied to *all* textile industries (except that very little children were still allowed to work in the silk mills) and secondly that it provided for paid factory inspectors. In this it went further than the Ten Hours Bill, and it is above all this provision that makes it the first really effective Factory Act to be passed by Parliament. This does not, of course, mean that the inspectors got to work immediately, or that there was no avoidance of the law. But the important principle had been established, that it was the job of the Government not only to say what were the conditions of work in factories, but to see that its decisions were carried out by the employers.

Only ninety-three members of Parliament had voted for the Ten Hours Bill. The Ten Hour men were dismayed and depressed, and many working men became convinced that the Reformed Parliament was made up of their enemies. But the campaign for shorter hours continued, and was continued in Parliament by Lord Ashley, and by John Fielden, who had been elected M.P. for Oldham in 1833, in partnership with William Cobbett.

John Fielden

Fielden had worked in his father's mill as a child of ten. He tried in his own mills to make working conditions reasonable for all his workers, providing teachers for the children, and opportunities for rest and good food. But he became convinced that the example of individual good employers was not enough, and that the Government had to intervene to make all employers keep to at least some rules. He entered Parliament mainly to work for this cause. He was a quiet man, with a strong Lancashire accent, and often had difficulty in making his speeches heard and understood, but he was a man of very great ability as a business man and an organiser, as well as a writer. His pamphlet *The Curse of the Factory System*, published in 1836, is one of the best presentations of the factory workers' case. It was certainly right that he should be the man who, in 1847, finally introduced an effective Ten Hours' Act into the House of Commons, fourteen years after the failure of Ashley's first attempt.

Municipal Reform Bill

The third important law passed by the Reformed Parliament was the Municipal Reform Bill, passed in 1835. From this Bill comes most of our modern Local Government in the towns. Until this time, towns were ruled in many different ways, mostly

73. Letting children down a coalmine.

started when they had been much smaller. Now provision was made for Town Councils to be elected by the rate-payers in each town and city. There was not yet a lot for them to do, for things like town drainage and street lighting were not at first thought to be their responsibilities, but as the century developed, the local councils took over more and more responsibility, and were joined in 1888 by County Councils. Out of them grew our modern system of Local Government which deals with so many important matters from drainage to education.

The new voters, the middle classes, were pleased by the New Poor Law, and by the Municipal Reform Bill. They had therefore reason to be fairly satisfied with the Reformed Parliament. But the working people's dissatisfaction mounted. Another incident increased their sense that they had gained a

74. A demonstration of the Trade Unionists in Copenhagen Fields 21 April 1834, protesting against the deportation of the Tolpuddle Martyrs.

government that was more deliberately their enemy even than the old Unreformed House of Commons had been.

Tolpuddle Martyrs

It was at about the time of the publication of the Report of the Poor Law Commissioners in Spring, 1834, that a group of farm workers met in Tolpuddle, Dorset, to form a farm-workers' Trade Union branch. To join the Union, members were made to swear an oath of loyalty to their fellow-members.

After the Naval Mutinies in 1797 an Act had been passed making it illegal to "administer oaths". The leaders of the Tolpuddle labourers were arrested for organising this oath-taking ceremony. They had not yet properly formed their union branch, they had not called a strike, or even threatened to call a strike – in any case, Unions and strikes were both legal since 1824. But the six leaders arrested were sentenced to be transported for seven years.

Transportation at this time was the usual punishment for serious crimes. The convicted criminals were sent away, usually to Australia, in ships that were foul and overcrowded, and there hired out as convict labour to local farmers. It is almost impossible for us today to imagine the hardships involved, and it was rare indeed for anyone to return from such a sentence. For wives and families, the sentences might as well have been death, indeed so many men died in the convict ships on the way out, that for many it was in fact a death sentence.

The Protests Against the Sentence

There was great dismay when the sentences on the Tolpuddle labourers became known. Protests, petitions and demonstrations were organised throughout the country. In London, 27,000 Trade Unionists marched through the streets protesting. In the House of Commons a motion calling for a free pardon for the men was moved by Thomas

no Transportation, — no Nothing.

75. An anti-Trade Union cartoon of about 1830. Many middle class people were most indignant at the idea of the labouring people becoming concerned with politics.

Wakley, who spoke for two and a half hours in support of it. But only a small number of Members voted for a pardon – in this case eighty-four. After two years of petitions the Home Secretary did at last yield, and a free pardon was granted in 1836. But before then, the working people had again been given the impression that the Government was against them in every way. The same Government which had introduced the New Poor Law and taken away the relief which was given in support of low wages had also punished those labourers who had tried to get together to raise their wages. And the Tolpuddle labourers had only wanted to raise their wages from 7/– to 9/– a week. A Committee of London Radicals and Trade Unionists organised the protests in London against the sentences on the Tolpuddle Labourers, and helped to raise money for their wives and families. The secretary of this Committee, called the Victim Committee, was Henry Hetherington, the publisher of the *Poor*

Man's Guardian newspaper. His assistant was William Lovett, a Cornish carpenter, now living in London. We shall meet Lovett again, for he was to become one of the most influential radicals of the century, although he was not yet well-known. But already we can see a grouping of people – a very few radicals in Parliament, Fielden and Wakley prominent among them; some of the leaders of the Free Press movement, who were not only opposing the stamp duties, but who were writing in support of factory reform and in opposition to the New Poor Law; and throughout the country, but especially in the North, the two movements, the Ten Hours movement and the Anti-Poor Law Association. All these groups, together with some remaining Political Unions from the days of the Reform Bill agitation, and some former members of Trade Unions and Co-operative Societies came together in 1837–38 to form the Chartist Movement.

Chapter 10

The Working People Organise – Trade Unions, Unstamped Press and Chartism

We have seen how the changes which were taking place in England were affecting people's lives. The old way of life in the country districts was breaking down, and many people were leaving the villages. In the towns there were new jobs to be done, and new factories in which people had to work. The factory owners were a new sort of master, and as the towns grew in size other new men appeared. Shopkeepers and merchants became more rich and powerful. With the passing of the Reform Bill these new masters began to take their part in the government of the country, but the ordinary people were still left out, and seemed to have no power to make their views felt at all.

Early Trade Unions

In the twenty-five years or so following the end of the Napoleonic wars, the people of England tried in various ways to gain some control of the way they lived. We have already seen that one of these ways was by forming Trades Unions. The members of the unions hoped that, by joining together, they could have some way of keeping their wages up, and of controlling the number of hours they worked. They also wanted to see that trades were properly taught, and to have a say in the number of apprentices who were allowed to come into any industry. But the early unions were working under very great difficulties. They were very short of money, as their members earned so little, and there were all sorts of laws which could be used against them. So that, although there was never a time throughout the whole of the nineteenth century in which there were no

Trade Unions, and although they did have some successes from time to time, it is not until the second half of the century that they really began to have so much effect that we can say that they made a real difference to the wages that most people earned.

Robert Owen and Co-operation

Another way in which people tried to control their own working conditions was by *co-operation*. In the early days of the factories, it was sometimes suggested that the new machines were not being used to benefit the whole country. Many people thought that there were better ways of producing goods. One of the chief believers in a different way of doing things was Robert Owen, who put forward the idea of co-operation in industry. He thought that if people worked for themselves, and had a share in the profits on the goods they made, they would work better. It should, he thought, be possible to organise and plan production, to give good working conditions and well-produced goods. He himself managed a cotton mill in Scotland, at New Lanark, for many years, and showed that by giving decent houses to the workers, by providing schools for their children instead of putting them to work in the factory, not only were people happier, but the materials produced were better and profits higher. This was, however, not an experiment in co-operation or profit-sharing, only in enlightened management.

Several attempts were made to set up really co-operative workshops in various trades, and some of them succeeded for a

76.	Robert Owen's school for the children of the factory workers in New Lanark. Visitors can be seen watching the children's dancing lessons. Maps and pictures on the wall are used for teaching.

77.	Part of Robert Owen's community at New Lanark. The two buildings at the front on the left are a school and a public kitchen. The other buildings are cotton factories. In the foreground, right, is the town band.

time. But, the successes tended to be in the older hand trades like shoemaking and printing. In the new factory industries private industry and the profit motive held the field. It was not until the 1840's that any sort of co-operation began to succeed widely, and then it was not in the industries which produced the goods, but in the shops which sold them.

Trade Unionism and Co-operation, then, did not have very much effect on the lives of workers in these early years of the century. But in one field new ideas spread very rapidly. This was in the growth of a cheap press.

The Radical Press

In the eighteenth century printing and paper were dear, and books and papers were rarely seen in any but fairly well-off homes. But towards the end of the century more and more cheap pamphlets and newspapers appeared, and in the big cities, particularly in London, these were often read by the artisans and other workmen. It was mainly for this reason that the Government, when it passed the Six Acts of 1819, included one which put a heavy tax on newspapers, on advertisements in newspapers and on paper. In the years after the wars even a very small newspaper cost sixpence, which meant that very few households could afford to buy one. Of course, people did see papers – sometimes they clubbed together to buy them, and in the big cities they could be read in public houses or coffee shops. Even under these conditions a number of very radical weekly papers were published. Cobbett's *Political Register* was probably the most widely read. It was written for working men, and dealt with matters which were likely to interest them, written in a style which they could read and understand, but the tax did restrict newspapers for the poorer people.

Henry Hetherington and the "Poor Man's Guardian"

In 1831, the radical publisher, Henry Hetherington, made a frontal attack on the stamp duties. He published the first issue of a penny weekly newspaper, the *Poor Man's Guardian*. At the head of the paper was the motto "Knowledge is Power", and under the title ran the heading "Published contrary to 'Law' to try the power of 'Might' against 'Right'". In the first number, Hetherington clearly stated exactly which laws he was breaking, and he and his supporters set out as publishers of illegal papers.

For the next five years there was a flood of "unstamped" papers. Paying no taxes, they could be sold at 1d a copy, so that all but the very poorest working people could buy them. They were written for the factory workers as well as for the artisans, and they carried all over the country the messages of the Owenite co-operators, the factory reformers, the committees which worked to gain a pardon for the Tolpuddle labourers. and all the causes which were supported by radical reformers. Papers were published in London, Manchester, Bristol, and the West Riding of Yorkshire, and sellers were to be found in towns and villages all over the country. Some of the sellers were regular booksellers who kept the "unstamped" under the counters, some were wandering pedlers, some sold nothing but unstamped papers. Tens of thousands of copies were sold every week.

Of course, the authorities took action. In all as many as 750 people were prosecuted for selling and publishing these illegal papers. But, they were people who believed in what they were doing, and who were prepared to go to prison. There were many tales told about efforts to avoid the law. In one place the pedlers "sold" a straw, and gave away a free copy of the paper with it. In another, a penny was dropped into a grating, and the paper was pushed out, so that the seller could not be seen.

Finally in 1836, the Government was forced to alter the law. There had been so many prosecutions, and still the sales continued. The publishers of legal journals were

complaining that they could not sell newspapers for 6d when the "unstamped" were
available for 1d.

The 1836 Newspaper Act reduced the
stamp duty to 1d per issue, instead of 4½d,
although, it kept the duty on advertisements.
But it also increased the penalties not only
for publishing an unstamped paper, but
for being in possession of even a single copy.
The effect of this Act was to bring down the
price of newspapers from 6d or more to
about 3½d, and also to make it much more
risky to produce illegal papers.

By the late 1830's, the unstamped papers
brought together people all over the
country who were thinking in the same way.
In London the co-operators and Trade
Unionists and the publishers of illegal journals began to turn increasingly towards
another reform of Parliament. In the industrial north the factory workers and those
who were organising opposition to the new
Poor Law also began to see that they needed
to be able to influence Parliament directly.
The various movements of opposition to the
Whig Government began to draw together.

Feargus O'Connor and the Northern Star

1837 saw the founding in Leeds of the *Northern Star* newspaper. The *Star* was started by a
group of opponents of the New Poor Law,
led by Feargus O'Connor, who became the
owner of the paper. Feargus knew the importance of newspapers – he had seen the
way in which the unstamped papers had
helped to spread ideas. He also knew from
his own experience that the main newspapers of the day would not give space to
report the activities of the factory reformers
or of the opponents of the Poor Law, let
alone the Trade Unions and Co-operative
Societies. So he founded the *Star* to do just
this. It came out weekly, and cost 4½d. It
was written, like its unstamped predecessors,
almost entirely for working men to read.

Soon after the establishment of the *Northern Star* a meeting was held in London, at
which leaders of the London radical working

78. William Lovett as an old man. A self-taught
Cornish carpenter, he became secretary of the
first Chartist Convention, and later became well-
known as a teacher and educationalist.

men, including William Lovett, the cabinet
maker who had helped with the committee
for the Tolpuddle labourers, and Henry
Hetherington, who had been the publisher
of the *Poor Man's Guardian*, and Bronterre
O'Brien who had been its editor, met with
a few of the most radical Members of Parliament. At this meeting a programme was
drawn up for a reform of Parliament, which
was to go far beyond the 1832 Bill. It was
drawn up in the form of another Bill for
Parliament, and was given the name of the
People's Charter. This programme soon won
the support of the editors of the *Northern
Star*, and of the reformers in the north, and
within a month or two of its publication, it
became the programme for the biggest
movement of working people ever to have
taken place in England or in any other
country.

79. Feargus O'Connor, the red-headed Irish-man who was loved and admired by hundreds of thousands of English Chartists.

The People's Charter

The People's Charter consisted of a six-point programme for the reform of Parliament.
Point one was Universal Suffrage.

This meant the vote for all men over the age of twenty-one.
Point two was Vote by Ballot.

The vote had to be secret if people were not to be frightened into voting for the richest or most powerful candidate, and not the one they really believed in.
Point three was the payment of Members of Parliament.

If working men, or anyone who had to give up his job in order to be a member, were to stand for Parliament, there had to be some system of payment of members. Otherwise only rich men could ever stand.
Point four was the abolition of property qualifications for Members of Parliament.

At this time a man had to own property worth £600 a year before he was allowed to stand as a candidate.
Point five was equal electoral districts.

The Chartists wanted the same number of electors in each district, so that each Member of Parliament represented the same number of people.
Point six was annual elections.

The idea here was that if there was an election every year instead of every seven years, the Members of Parliament would have to take more notice of what the voters wanted.

A programme like this looks entirely reasonable to us today. In fact, apart from the last point, we now have all these things as part of our electoral system. We do not have annual parliaments, which would mean a General Election every year, but the length of parliaments has been reduced from seven to five years since Chartist times. But in 1838 the people in power thought that the Charter would mean the end of all that they thought was important. They thought the people who owned no property would pass laws – if they had the vote – to abolish all property, and that they would probably do away with the Queen, the Church and the House of Lords as well. So the proposals of the Chartists met with little support among the middle and upper classes.

The movement which gathered around the People's Charter and became known as the Chartist Movement was made up almost entirely of working people. There were some men of education, especially some doctors and teachers who had worked in the indust-rial districts, who helped, and there was a group of very able journalists who ran the Chartists' newspapers. But the manufactur-ing and land-owning classes were hostile from the beginning.

A "movement" means a great many people going in the same direction. The Chartist movement came to include many groups – the factory reformers, the oppon-ents of the New Poor Law, many of the writers, editors and sellers of the "un-stamped", people who wanted more education, those who wanted wages regulated – in fact almost every kind of reformer who believed that if all men had the vote, their own particular reforms would have a better chance of being carried.

The Chartist Petition

How did the Chartists set about getting their way? They did not have a vote, so they had very little hope of getting members elected to Parliament who would support the People's Charter. Instead they used a method which had become the traditional way for people who had no vote to make their opinions known. This was the petition. The Charter was drawn up in the form of a request to the Queen and the Government, and then signatures were collected all over the country in support of the "request". Meetings were held in all the big centres – cities and manufacturing districts, at which the leaders of the movement spoke, and the people who came to hear them, often tens of thousands at a single great open-air meeting, signed the petition and agreed to persuade their friends and neighbours to sign.

The National Convention

The petition was only one form of action. Another idea which the Chartists had was that of a National Convention. If they had no vote to send men to Parliament, why not set up their own parliament, and send representatives of those who had no vote? So the *National Convention of the Industrious Classes* was conceived. At meetings all over the country delegates were elected. Each area elected a delegate or delegates, according to the size of the local movement, who came up to London to sit in the Convention. The local Chartists paid the fares for their delegates, and paid them a small wage to live on while they were in London. This Parliament of working men met to consider what they would do next if their petition was rejected by the Government.

The Chartist Leaders

During the fifteen years or so that the Chartist movement remained active, its leaders were household names amongst the working people of Britain. There is only space here to mention one or two of the best known. Undoubtedly the most popular leader was Feargus O'Connor. He was an Irishman, and had the right sort of personality to be a mass leader. Big, handsome, red-headed, he was at his best when he was speaking to huge crowds. In those days before radio and television, people would walk miles to hear a famous speaker. Feargus had a fine voice, an Irish brogue, and the ability to make crowds laugh as well as cheer. He was the owner of the Chartist newspaper the *Northern Star*, but he did not edit it himself; he wrote a weekly letter which appeared on the front page, and the rest of the paper was written by the staff of journalists who ran it. In this way it represented not only the views of O'Connor himself, but those of a number of other leading Chartists.

One of the best-known writers amongst the Chartists was Bronterre O'Brien. Like Feargus, he was an Irishman, and had been trained as a barrister. He had worked with Henry Hetherington, and had edited the *Poor Man's Guardian* for several years, as well as other unstamped journals. He was particularly good at writing political articles in a clear and simple way. He was nick-named "the schoolmaster of Chartism".

William Lovett, was a joiner by trade. He had come to London from Cornwall, and had become interested in radical politics. He was a first-rate organiser – efficient and painstaking in every job he undertook. He was secretary to the first Chartist Convention in 1839. Unlike O'Connor, he was not a very good speaker. He did not have O'Connor's humour, or his quick understanding of ordinary people. Nor was he a competent journalist like O'Brien. His abilities were as an organiser, and as a man who always followed through and finished anything he agreed to do. He did not agree with

O'Connor and those who thought like him. The difference between them was that Lovett believed that in the end, the only way the working people would improve their condition was by education. He thought they should have the vote, and he thought that the government had a duty to educate all children, but he also believed that people could make a start in this for themselves, and that it was the duty of every man to learn all he could and to educate his children. O'Connor and those who thought like him thought that the first thing was for people to have political rights – that is, a chance to have a say in government, and enough to eat and good houses to live in. Then they could begin to think about education.

The difference of views between Lovett and O'Connor represented a real division in the Chartist movement. Although at times the whole movement worked together, there were always arguments which were about "physical force" and "moral force". The argument went more or less like this: the O'Connorites and those who believed in "physical force" said that any way in which the people could frighten the Government into granting the Charter was justified. If necessary let them arm and drill with arms, and threaten to march on London and force Parliament to agree. After all, armed uprisings had succeeded in forcing governments to act in other parts of Europe. They mostly believed that the Government would give in without a fight anyway, but they thought it was worth looking warlike. So all through the country there were groups of Chartists who were buying muskets and making and buying pikes. And after the working day was over, thousands of men turned out by torchlight on the hillsides of Lancashire and Yorkshire, and in the Welsh valleys, to practise drilling and marching.

Lovett and his followers, however, said that the Government would be more impressed if the working men showed themselves to be ready for the vote, not by marching and drilling and arming, but by mass meetings at

which their case was argued. They must show that they were reasonable and intelligent, and that they knew their rights and were determined to get them.

In fact, the division between the different views was not always very great. Many so-called "physical force" men – including O'Connor – did not really believe that their arms would ever be used. And many of the "moral force" people, including Lovett, were prepared to defy the law and to go to prison for their right to hold meetings and to publish what they liked. Men of both sides believed that it might be possible to have a general strike for the Charter. O'Brien was sure that if a strike were to be called, the other side would use force to try and break it, so he saw the strike as a "physical force" measure. But others held that a strike could go through quite peacefully. In 1842, at the time of the second National Petition, there was a strike in the manufacturing districts. It did in fact lead to several clashes with the soldiers, and both strikers and soldiers were killed, but the clashes were more in the nature of riots – there was never, in that year, any attempt at an armed uprising.

The most serious attempts at an armed rising in the Chartist period occurred in 1839, after the first National Petition had been rejected by the House of Commons.

The petition was presented, with over a million signatures, by Thomas Attwood, the Birmingham banker, who was now M.P. for Birmingham. He asked the House of Commons to consider the six points. He was seconded by John Fielden, the M.P. for Oldham. Altogether, forty-six M.P.s voted in favour of considering the Charter, and 235 voted against.

The Newport Rising

The Chartist Convention now had to consider what to do next. Some members wanted to call a General Strike, but it was decided that there was not enough support or enough money to do that. Although the Convention went on discussing the next steps, what

80.   An artist's imaginary picture of the Chartist attack on the Westgate Hotel, Newport, on the morning of 3rd November 1839.

really seems to have happened was that those Chartists who thought the time had come for more definite action left the Convention and went back to their localities. In several parts of the country, plans were laid for an armed uprising to force the Government to accept the Charter. The only one of the plans which was partly carried out was in South Wales. Here, on 3rd November 1839, a column of Welsh Chartists, led by John Frost, the leading Radical in the district, and former Chairman of the 1839 Convention, marched into the town of Newport on a dark, rainy night. The plan was for other columns to meet them, but for some reason the others did not arrive before Frost's column met a formation of armed soldiers. A brief exchange of fire took place, in which a number of the Chartists were killed. The rest scattered, some returning to their homes, others hiding in the woods, or making their way to Liverpool and other ports to escape from the country before they should be arrested for their part in the fighting.

It is clear that there were other plans for uprisings, in Wales and in Yorkshire, in Newcastle and some other districts. The failure of Frost's attack prevented the others from taking place. The Welsh rising was so small, and was so quickly put down, that it is difficult to see what the Chartists had hoped to achieve by it. There are several things to be said about this. In the first place, the successful revolutions in Europe in 1830 – for example those in Belgium and France – had been very small affairs in terms of the actual amount of force that was used. The Chartists may have thought that quite a small show of force would make the Government give way. They may also have expected more help from the soldiers. After all, most of the soldiers were working men, without votes themselves, and used to very brutal treatment. The Chartists probably hoped that they would refuse to fire. But the Government of England was very strong at this time. After the Reform Bill of 1832, it had the support of the middle classes, and the British Army was well-disciplined and obedient. The use of force by the Newport Chartists only gave the authorities the excuse to arrest and imprison Chartist leaders all over the country, and to weaken the movement still further.

On the morning after the Welsh rising, warrants were issued for the arrest of the five leaders of the march into Newport. Two of these – David Jones, known as David the Tinker, and John Rees, known as Jack the Fifer, because he played the flute for the marchers, escaped, and were never caught. The other three, John Frost, Zephenia Williams and William Jones, were all arrested within the next few weeks, and were put on trial for High Treason.

The verdict on the three men was guilty, and they were condemned to death.

When the sentence became known, Radicals and Chartists all over the country began to agitate on behalf of the three men. Finally, after three weeks spent in the condemned cell, when they were able to hear the noise of carpenters working to build the gallows on which they were to be hanged, a reprieve was granted. Instead of death, Frost, Williams and Jones were to be transported for life.

Transportation was a terrible punishment, but it was usual for many offences. In Monmouth three men had recently been transported for life for stealing a horse. So, in the company of criminals of all kinds, the Chartist leaders set out on their four months' journey to Van Dieman's Land in Southern Australia. Jones and Williams died in the colony, although both had ceased to be convicts long before they died. Williams, indeed, died a rich man, for he discovered coal and set up in business as a mine-owner. John Frost was in Australia for seventeen years, before he was finally pardoned and allowed to return home. He came back as strong a radical as he went out, and spent his last years in trying to get reforms in the convict system.

Imprisonment of Chartist Leaders

All over the country other leading Chartists were imprisoned. With Frost, Williams and Jones on their long journey to the penal colony went three Birmingham Chartist leaders sentenced for their part in riots which had shaken Birmingham. Theirs was not an armed march like the Newport one, but rather the violent reaction of a great crowd against the attempts by the police to prevent them from holding a public meeting. The other leaders who were imprisoned were mostly charged with sedition, unlawful drilling or "riotous assembly", and had fairly short sentences to serve, ranging from about six months to two or three years. But the local Chartists had to look after the families of the imprisoned men, and this, together with the campaigns for the release of Frost, Williams and Jones, kept them busy during most of the following year.

Chartism continued as a movement until about the middle of the 1850's. But it never, after that winter of 1839 to 1840, took on the aspect of a national revolutionary force. There were more meetings and demonstrations, and there were times when parts of the country organised in a military manner again.

The Second Chartist Petition

In 1842 a second national petition was drawn up. (It contained the same six points, and again hundreds of thousands of signatures were collected.) The petition, with three million signatures attached, was presented in May, by T. S. Duncombe, Member of Parliament for Finsbury. In the end, forty-nine M.P.'s voted with Duncombe, and 287 against.

As before, the Convention met to consider the next steps they should take. But the next

81a.   Chartists in Halifax attack soldiers who were escorting Chartists prisoners to a nearby railway station, after the plug riots in 1842.

81b.   Procession attending the Great National Petition of 3,317,702 to the House of Commons 1842.

move in fact came from Lancashire. In August, a strike in the cotton manufacturing districts of Lancashire set off a series of demonstrations known as the "Plug Riots". The strikers declared that they would not return to work until the Charter was the law of the land, and they set off, marching over the Pennines into Yorkshire. In each town and village they came to they stopped to persuade the local workpeople to join them in their strike, and in order to make sure that no work went on, they drew out the plugs from the boilers in the steam engines and let the water out of the mill dams. They were received with enthusiasm in the towns of the West Riding, and soon the movement and the strikes had spread throughout the textile districts and into the potteries and the Northern coalfields. But the strikers were without money or supplies. They had been forced into striking by a reduction in wages, and had no reserves to tide them over any length of time. The demonstrations were met in Yorkshire by armed cavalry, and several clashes took place in which both soldiers and strikers – and at least one magistrate – were wounded. Finally, the workers, returned to their work – many at lower wages.

The National Charter Association

By this time the Chartists had not only a number of local newspapers, as well as the *Northern Star*, but also a national organisation. It was known as the National Charter Association, and by collecting money and keeping a national committee in existence, it gave the movement something more like the form of a modern political party. As with a party, its meetings were attended by many thousands who were not actual members, but the Association was able to give some direction to these people as well as to its members, and it was also able to organise activities in between the big meetings.

Throughout the 1840's, the Chartists continued to meet in most parts of the country. They published newspapers and pamphlets, conducted educational classes for their members, and occasionally took part in elections. Since most of the Chartists had no vote, they could not hope to elect members to Parliament. But they found that they could use the machinery of elections in two ways. The first was what was called "exclusive dealing". Poor people could not vote, nor could they bribe voters. But most shopkeepers had votes, and the Chartists decided that they would only buy from shopkeepers who agreed to vote for radical candidates. So in some Chartist strongholds, radical innkeepers and shop owners found themselves getting all the custom of the working people. At least one West Riding grocer was able to retire on the profits he made during the 1847 election. Since there was no ballot, the people could read how voters cast their votes, and patronise those who voted for radical candidates.

The second thing the Chartists did was to appear on the hustings. At the time, elections were organised in the fashion which you may read about in Dickens' *Pickwick Papers*. When the day came for the candidates to be nominated to stand, they would all come together in the biggest public meeting place in the town – sometimes in the market square or some other open space. Here platforms called hustings were set up. Then, as each man was nominated by two electors, he had to make a speech asking people to elect him. After all the candidates had spoken, there was a vote by show of hands, and all the audience at the meeting held up their hands for the man of their choice. Then any candidate had the right to demand a poll – that is an election in which each elector had to write his name in a book. In order to cast a vote at a poll, each voter had to be on the electoral register, but at the hustings every one could put up his hands. So the Chartist candidates, who could usually find two electors to nominate them, would go to the hustings, and make a Chartist speech. Then they would very often win the vote on a show of hands, but when the Whig or Tory candidates demanded a poll, the Chartist would withdraw, as he knew he would not have the chance of getting elected on a vote by electors only. As you can imagine, the whole business added greatly to the excitement at election times, and gave the Chartists the chance to make speeches and put their case to huge audiences. In 1847 a really astonishing victory was gained. In this year, several of the Chartists actually went to the poll, though not really with any great hope of getting a big vote. However, in Nottingham, Feargus O'Connor, their leader, was elected, defeating a member of the Government. This was a great victory for the Chartists, and when a successful revolution occurred in France, early in 1848, they greeted it with huge meetings throughout the country, and the slogan "France has the Republic, England shall have the Charter!"

The Third Chartist Petition

The third Chartist petition was presented to Parliament in April 1848, and its acceptance was moved by O'Connor himself. But there were fewer signatures than in 1842, and even less support among the members of the House of Commons.

During the summer of 1848 there were meetings, and certainly quite a lot of drilling and arming especially in the textile districts. Many Chartist leaders were arrested, particularly those with a following in Yorkshire and Lancashire, and a group of London Chartists, who had been tricked by a Government spy into planning an armed uprising, were transported for life to Australia.

But even in 1848 the movement was dying out. The French Revolution and the others which followed in Europe helped to revive hope in England, but the numbers who turned out at demonstrations, and the number of readers of the *Northern Star* got steadily fewer. A movement of a fairly small size continued into the 1850's and the idea of political reform continued to be put forward by radical writers and speakers, many of whom had been Chartist leaders. In 1855 O'Connor died, and a crowd of over 50,000 followed his funeral. This was the last time the Chartists turned out in any great numbers, and after that the name ceased to be used.

Why was Chartism important, and did it achieve anything? By the time it ended, not one of the six points had become law. It was many years before any of them did. But the whole question had been brought out into the open. Although it took time for Parliament to accept the idea of everyone having a vote, from the time of the Chartists onwards, the main political parties took more notice of the working people, and tried to win their support. It was realised that the working people now took a real interest in politics, and were not just a crowd which could be hired to smash windows or cheer at election time.

And apart from the politics of Parliament itself, the Chartist movement gave people experience in other ways. Many former Chartists went on in the second half of the nineteenth century to build up Trade Unions, Co-operative Societies and other bodies. They also went into local government, where they were able to vote before they had the vote for Parliament. Chartists became aldermen, like R. M. Carter in Leeds and Thomas Livesey in Rochdale; Co-operative directors like Edward Hooson of Manchester, and leaders in almost all kinds of local organisations from reading rooms to council chambers.

Chapter 11

The Rich and the Poor

In 1845, Benjamin Disraeli published a novel called *Sybil*. Disraeli was at that time a young Tory Member of Parliament. He had spoken out against the New Poor Law of 1834, and was remembered for the speech he had made in 1839, when the Charter had been introduced into the House of Commons. In his speech he had said, among other things, that although he disapproved of the Charter, he sympathised with the Chartists. In *Sybil* he made the heroine a Chartist, and tried to show some of the reasons for the discontent which had helped to produce the Chartist movement. Near the beginning of the book comes a very famous passage. Egremont, the hero, meets two strangers, and begins to talk to them about the condition of England. At one point he says:

"... say what you like, our Queen reigns over the greatest nation that ever existed".

"Which nation?" asked the young stranger, "for she reigns over two".

The stranger paused; Egremont was silent, but looked enquiringly.

"Yes", resumed the younger stranger after a moment's interval, "Two nations; between whom there is no intercourse and no sympathy; who are as ignorant of each others' habits, thoughts and feelings as if they were dwellers in different zones, or inhabitants of different planets; who are formed by different breeding, are fed by a different food, are ordered by different manners and are not governed by the same laws".

"You speak of..." said Egremont hesitatingly,

"THE RICH AND THE POOR".

Many other writers and observers agreed with Disraeli that there were "two nations" in England in the first half of the nineteenth century. In the last two chapters we have looked at some of the people and some of the ideas of one of the nations – the poor people who lived in the cities and towns and who worked in the mines, the mills and on the fields. Now let us look at some of the people who made up the other nation, the rich.

As we have already seen, the rich, property-owning people in England fell into two main classes – those who owned land, and those who owned factories and other forms of manufacturing plant. Many of the land-owners were also bankers or rich merchants, and they made up the upper classes. The manufacturers and shopkeepers who had gained the vote in 1832 made up the middle classes. They were increasing rapidly in numbers during the nineteenth century. The first results of their vote, as we saw in chapter 9 were a series of measures which had the agreement of most wealthy people. However, it is worth noticing that some of the Members of Parliament who were against the New Poor Law, and who supported the reform of the factories were members of the Tory, or landowning party. Lord Ashley, Parliamentary leader of the factory movement is an outstanding example of this.

As time went on, it became clear that there were some things about which there was serious disagreement between the land-owners, and the industrialists. The most important was the question of *Free Trade*, and the battle between them took place over the *Corn Laws*.

The Corn Laws

During the wars with France it had not been possible for England to import corn from France and other European countries. English farmers had ploughed up every available scrap of land to grow corn and other grain crops, and these had sold for a very good price. When the war ended, the landowners were afraid that a lot of cheaper corn would be brought into England, which would bring down the price of corn at home. Since they were at that time entirely in control of Parliament, they were able, in 1815, to get laws passed to help them to keep up corn prices.

These laws were called the Corn Laws. They were quite straightforward: No foreign corn was to be imported into England, until grain at home reached a very high price. This meant that English farmers could keep up the price of grain, since no foreign grain was to be imported unless the harvest was so bad that there was a serious shortage. The result was dear bread.

The manufacturers were against the corn laws. In the first place, by keeping the price of bread high, they tended to keep wages up in the towns. In the second, the manufacturers wanted to get their goods around the world, to sell wherever there were people who wanted to buy. They thought that the government should not interfere with trade. By preventing foreign countries from selling us their wheat, the government was making it more difficult for those countries to buy our textiles and machinery. The "free traders" believed that if there was complete freedom, with no government interference, those countries would become richest who were most efficient at producing goods, and those industries would do best which produced at the lowest price the things that people wanted. And since they had no doubt that England had the most efficient industry and the most active and intelligent industrialists in the world, they were sure that the way to greatness for England lay in complete freedom of trade.

The landowners, however, had arguments on their side. If bread was to be cheap, they said, the only people who would gain would be the millowners and their associates. The farmers would be poorer, and the working people in the towns would be no better off, since the employers would lower their wages. What is more, many of them thought that the countryside was the proper place for people to work. These upstart "millocrats" had no feeling for their workers – they exploited the little children, shut people up in the factories, and wanted free trade in corn so that they could pay them less and less. If Britain was kept as a mainly agricultural

82.   The Two Nations. Homes of London poor in 1840.

83. Richard Cobden, standing in the centre, speaking to the members of the anti-corn law league –
a group of serious well-dressed gentlemen.

country, people would be able to earn a decent living, and would work for their "natural" employers, the landowners, who knew their duty and were not merely concerned to make a profit.

So the arguments raged. Some people saw all England's problems as the result of dear bread. Ebenezer Elliott, a Sheffield man, wrote a book of *Corn-Law Rhymes*, which sold by the thousand. They were simple poems, driving home his belief in free trade by showing the results of the taxes on food, particularly bread:

> Child is thy father dead?
> Father is gone.
> Why did they tax his bread?
> God's Will be done.
> Mother has sold her bed;
> Better to die than wed
> Where shall she lay her head?
> Home we have none!

Elliott belonged to an organisation called the "Sheffield Mechanics' Anti-Bread-Tax Society" formed in the early 30's to cam-

paign against the Corn Laws. But before long a more powerful body came into being.

The Anti-Corn-Law League

The Anti-Corn-Law League, formed in Manchester in 1838, led the attack on the "landed interest". At its head were Richard Cobden and John Bright. Both these men were Lancashire manufacturers, who had made their money in the cotton trade. They were helped with gifts of money from manufacturers all over Britain, but particularly from Lancashire and Yorkshire. They used every method of persuasion – meetings, petitions, bills presented to Parliament, and printed propaganda – books, pamphlets,. articles and their own newspaper, the *Anti-Corn-Law Circular*. Among the middle classes their arguments gained immense support. The Chartists viewed the Anti-Corn-Law leaguers with suspicion. Although many Chartists believed in free trade, it is hardly surprising that they did not trust a body which sometimes argued that one of the main things in favour of abolishing the corn laws was that the employers could then pay lower wages. What was perhaps even more important was that the leaders of the League were almost to a man against any reform of the factories. They regarded free trade in labour as being as necessary as free trade in goods, and they strongly opposed any attempt to control the hours of work of children and young people in the factories.

The Free Trade movement was, then, a middle-class affair. It began in Manchester, and it was always strongest there, the centre of England's cotton industry. For eight years it campaigned – earning the hatred of the landowners and farmers, but all the time growing in strength, and all the time teaching the manufacturers a great deal about politics.

The Repeal of the Corn Laws

By 1846 the arguments of the Anti-Corn-Law League were well-known. The Prime Minister that year was the Tory leader, Sir Robert Peel. The Tory party was in the main the party of the landowners, but Peel was always open to argument, and as the years went by, he had come increasingly to think that the Corn Laws were not doing England much good. In 1845 there was a potato famine in Ireland. As long as the Irish poor could live upon potatoes the worst effects of the corn laws had not been felt there. But now, with the potatoes failing, people were starving, while it was still impossible to bring in the cheap grain which might save their lives. Faced with this situation, Peel decided that the Corn Laws must be repealed. In a very impressive speech in the House of Commons, in which he admitted that he had been partly persuaded by the arguments of Cobden and Bright, he proposed the measure, and finally gained the support of his own and the opposition parties for it.

The repeal of the corn laws did not lead to a paradise of cheap bread and better living standards for everyone. In fact, really cheap corn did not begin to come into England until many years later, when it came from Canada and the United States. Although grain prices fell a bit, it was generally true, as it had always been, that if grain was scarce in England, because of a bad harvest, then it was usually also likely to be scarce in the nearby countries from which it was possible to import it.

But the repeal of the corn laws was still important. It was a successful attack on the power of the landowners, and it was a great step forward in the achievement of the free trade, which English manufacturers wanted. It opened up a period in which everything seemed to go right for British industry.

The Great Exhibition

On May 1st, 1851, the Great Exhibition was opened in Hyde Park in London. In a huge building, made almost entirely of glass, manufactured goods of every conceivable kind, from all over the world, were put on display. The Exhibition was a triumph for the middle classes.

The designer of the building was Joseph Paxton, a former gardener, who had become famous as an architect and designer and was knighted for his work on the great glass building.

Hundreds of designers and manufacturers got together to make the exhibition, but the chief inspiration behind it came from Queen Victoria's husband, Prince Albert. Of course, the husband of the Queen could hardly be described as "middle-class". But the upper classes had never liked him, and his greatest success was to win the enthusiasm and support of the manufacturers of England. He went with the Queen to the opening of the Great Exhibition. Queen Victoria walked down a red carpet, between two rows of beefeaters, holding the hand of the 10-year-old Prince of Wales, who was dressed in Scottish highland costume; Prince Albert followed her, dressed splendidly in full military uniform, and Victoria herself was sure that most of the cheers were for him. She wrote two days later to her uncle, the King of the Belgians:

> My Dearest Uncle – . . . I wish you *could* have witnessed the *1st May* 1851, the *greatest* day in our history, the most *beautiful* and *imposing* and *touching* spectacle ever seen, and the triumph of my beloved Albert. Truly it was astonishing, a fairy scene. Many cried, and all felt touched and impressed with devotional feelings. It was the *happiest*, *proudest* day in my life, and I can think of nothing else. Albert's dearest name is immortalised with this *great* conception, *his* own, and my *own* dear country *showed* she was *worthy* of it . . .

The exhibition remained open for six months, during which time six million people from all over Britain and from very many other countries as well, visited it. And although there were exhibits inside the great building from all over the world, it was above all British manufactures that were on show. Furniture, machinery, textiles, goods of every conceivable kind, many enormously elaborate – and you would probably also think enormously ugly – caused people to gasp with admiration. Look at the bed and the table on pages 126 and 127, and you will see the effect of richness and solidness which so many of the things on show gave. Here, they say, is British workmanship. We have the workmen and materials to produce more and more goods – we have people of wealth and position to buy them. England was all set to expand her industry and trade, and there seemed no limit to what she could do.

The Workshop of the World

The second half of the nineteenth century did indeed seem very different from the first. The manufacturers were winning all along the line. They had won over the Royal family and many of the landowning classes. As the years went by, many of the landowners lent their money to industry, and gave up the idea that agriculture ought to be especially protected. The working people, too, stopped fighting the factories. They saw that machine industry was here to stay, and their Trade Unions concentrated on getting shorter hours and better working conditions generally in the factories. There was no longer serious talk of organising co-operative work, or of ending the factory system. Free trade was accepted on all sides. Government after government took off taxes and customs duties on goods of all kinds. Britain became the "workshop of the world" – the greatest manufacturing country the world had ever seen.

The Middle Classes

The third quarter of the nineteenth century – the years between the Great Exhibition and about 1875, were the years of the great flowering of the middle class way of life. In the early days of the Industrial Revolution, most of the factory owners had managed their own firms. But as factories and mills got bigger, and trade spread more and more widely, many more people became rich simply by *investing* money – that is by lending their money for manufacture or trade, and living on the interest which was paid to them. New laws made this a safer thing to do, and gradually the middle class came to be made up more and more of people who had little if any direct connection with manufacturing, except to lend their money. They built themselves comfortable houses a long way away from the mills and factories, they sent their children to be educated at expensive schools, and they spent their money on solid and expensive furniture, silverware, clothes, carriages and goods of all kinds. They had big families, and employed a great number of servants.

In one of Dickens' novels, *Our Mutual Friend*, he describes a man who is the very type of this rich, satisfied middle-class business man, Mr Podsnap. In fact, Dickens invented the word *Podsnappery* for this whole way of living:

> Mr Podsnap was well-to-do, and stood very high in Mr Podsnap's opinion. Beginning with

84.　The Crystal Palace in which the Great Exhibition was held.

85.　Queen Victoria opens the Great Exhibition on May 1st 1851. Goods from all over the world were on show. Notice the fine display of Persian carpets in the galleries on the right.

86. The Great Exhibition of 1851. Apart from the machinery and inventions on show, there were a great many pieces of furniture, and other things for the household. This elaborately ornamented chair, sideboard, fireplace and four-poster bed were among the much admired exhibits.

87.   1851 – in a famous cartoon, Mr Punch is seen showing Prince Albert some of the people who did not appear at the Great Exhibition. It was a former *Punch* journalist, Henry Mayhew, who helped to make known the conditions of the work people of London.

a good inheritance, he had married a good inheritance, and had thriven exceedingly in the Marine Insurance way, and was quite satisfied. He never could make out why everybody was not quite satisfied, and he felt conscious that he set a brilliant social example in being particularly well satisfied with most things, and above all other things, with himself . . .

Mr Podsnap's daughter was very carefully brought up, in the house full of heavy polished furniture – and her early memories were of the reflections of the furniture in her father's shiny boots. On her eighteenth birthday, the Podsnaps gave a dinner party, and brought out all their best silver plate:

Hideous solidity was the characteristic of the Podsnap plate. Everything was made to look as heavy as it could and to take up as much room as possible. Everything said boastfully – "Here

you have as much of me in my ugliness as if I were only lead; but I am so many ounces of precious metal, worth so much an ounce; – wouldn't you like to melt me down?" A corpulent straddling epergne, blotched all over as if it had broken out in an eruption rather than been ornamented, delivered this address from an unsightly silver platform in the centre of the table. Four silver wine-coolers, each furnished with four staring heads, each head obtrusively carrying a big silver ring in each of its ears, conveyed the sentiment up and down the table, and handed it on to the pot-bellied silver salt-cellars. All the big silver spoons and forks widened the mouths of the company for the purpose of thrusting the sentiment down their throats with every morsel they ate . . .

To many people it seemed that the middle class lived only to make money. Business became more and more important and

88. Silver teapot and lace table-cloth, when a typical middle class family takes tea in the garden.

honesty seemed to have been lost altogether.

It was certainly a time when money was being made faster than at any time in our history. During those twenty-five years, exports of all kinds more than doubled, and exports of iron, steel, machinery and coal increased by four times.

Although cheap cotton cloth continued to be the main thing we exported, other things were becoming important. Because Britain had developed the first railways and railway locomotives, the rest of the world came to Britain to buy equipment when new railways were started. This was a good thing for the British iron industry, because iron rails needed renewing every ten years or so, and locomotives and rolling stock every twenty or thirty years. So that British firms were kept constantly busy with orders. British engineers were ahead of the rest of the world, and were in demand wherever railways were

built. With the development of steam ships, British ship-building, which had fallen off a bit as wood got short in the United Kingdom, took on a new lease of life, and built iron steam ships for the whole world. By the 1890's British shipyards were building four-fifths of the world's merchant ships. There seemed to be no end to the countries which wanted to buy British manufactured goods of all kinds.

Merchant shipping had always been important to Britain. Her ships carried most of the world's trade, and here again she was very fortunate during the third quarter of the century. The United States of America, which had been becoming a powerful sea-faring nation, was rent by Civil War in the years 1861 to 1865. It was a long and bitter war, and after it there was a great deal to be done to repair all the damage it had caused to the life and industry of the country.

89. A furniture museum shows examples of the over-decorated taste of the mid-nineteenth century middle classes.

America lost her influence as a great shipping power, and left Britain with no-one to challenge her as ruler of the seas.

Free trade seemed to be helping the growth of British industry. Britain could make nearly everything better and cheaper than any other country, and so could easily sell her goods in most parts of the world. And as more and more people moved into the towns to work in the factories and shipyards, so the farmers were kept busy supplying them with food. British farmers, although not protected by any corn laws, flourished in these years.

Middle Class Culture

"We, of the English middle classes," wrote William Morris in 1881 "are the most powerful body of men that the world has yet seen." Morris himself came from a family whose money had been made by investment. He was sure of a good income all his life, whether he worked or not. By the time he was

writing there were many thousands of English middle class families in the same position. They did not own land or manage country estates. How did they live, and what did they do?

Many English provincial towns grew up in this period, and around the older towns and cities middle class suburbs grew. Here you can still see large houses standing back from the road, usually with gardens in front and behind. These were the houses of the middle class families – large enough to hold the big families and several living-in servants. On the top floors the smaller children lived in nurseries, looked after by a nanny and a nursery maid. The older children probably went to school – the boys to boarding school and the girls to a day school. Father was away most of the day, engaged in some sort of business occupation, or perhaps following a profession, and Mother spent her time in social visits or in some form of charitable "good works".

90. A typical middle-class house. Houses like this were built all over England in the second half of the nineteenth century. This one was actually built in *Shanghai*, but it must have made the English family who lived in it feel very much at home.

W. S. Adams describes a child's life at the turn of the century in a London house:

> . . . a large house with a large basement for the kitchen quarters, and with ninety-seven steps of staircase leading from the hall up to the nurseries and on to the attics at the very top where the three servants, cook, parlour-maid, house-maid slept; and it was these stairs which were entwined with his earliest recollections, whether climbing them laboriously before he could walk them, running fearfully up their shadowed slopes after saying good-night to his parents, or talking to the polite maid who methodically brushed them every morning . . .

His parents went out to dinner parties, or else entertained at home most evenings . . .

Nor was it only adults for whom costly entertainments were provided. The great family festival of Christmas brought scores of presents for the children; the Christmas dinner – its regular menu was turtle soup, cod and oyster sauce, roast beef, roast turkey, Christmas pudding and brandy sauce, meringues, mince-pies, caviare and *paté de foie gras*, dessert washed down with sherry, champagne, port and brandy – . . . the great children's parties with conjuror and always some special entertainment by which his mother just surpassed all the other mothers in the social group. . . .

The family went to the seaside for four weeks in the summer, in a specially chartered horse omnibus "loaded with the dress baskets, trunks, cases and hip bath".

This was the home of a moderately wealthy stockbroker's family. There were richer people living in bigger houses, and many other families lower down the social ladder – families who might have only one maid and live in a semi-detached house in a street and not a square. But the total number of people who came into this category of the Victorian middle class was very large, and made up a new and powerful group.

There were, as we have seen, many Podsnaps among them. The ugliness of Victorian towns and cities and the preoccupation with money-making made many writers and artists protest. But the writers and artists who protested were themselves mostly from the middle class. For all that many of its members were smug and self-satisfied, throughout the second half of the nineteenth century there was a constant debate and discussion going on about the purposes of civilisation. Political and social questions were discussed deeply and at length in scores of periodicals and publications, and many attempts were made to change the worst aspects of society. Novel-writing flourished, and some of the greatest works in English were written during Queen Victoria's reign. Experimental movements in adult education were started, and genuine attempts made to find out more about how people lived in all sections of society. In fact, amongst the mass of the smug, commercial middle class there were always some who were critical, sensitive and enquiring. It was this minority which helped to bring about many of the changes which were to take place in the twentieth century.

Chapter 12

Government in the Middle of the Century

The agitation which led up to the Reform Bill, the Bill itself, and the reorganisation which took place in the political life of England in the years following its passing, the growth of trade and the growing importance of the English middle classes – all these things helped to bring about very great changes in the Government of England.

We have already seen that some political leaders were beginning, in the earlier years of the century, to take more account of public opinion in the country. This process continued in both the main parties, and the old system by which the party leaders were chosen from among a few leading families gradually disappeared. The first Whig government which came after the Reform Bill was a government of the old kind. With its defeat in 1841, and the return of the Tories to power, a new kind of statesman began to come into the lead. Not all at once, of course. It was still much easier to become a political leader in either party if you belonged to one of the powerful families and the Whig Party especially clung to the old type of leadership until well after the middle of the nineteenth century. Nevertheless able outsiders began to appear.

91. The artist, D. Wilkie, in this painting of Queen Victoria's first council in 1837, contrasts the young Queen with the elderly gentlemen who were the real Government of the country.

92. Robert Peel.

Sir Robert Peel

In 1841 the leader of the Tories – or Conservatives, as they were gradually coming to be called – was Sir Robert Peel. Peel was the son of a cotton mill owner – the man who helped to get the first bills through Parliament to protect the factory children. Although the younger Peel did not actually engage in business, the family money had come from the cotton trade, and his associations were very much with the manufacturing classes as well as with the landowning classes. He spoke with a slight Lancashire accent, and he brought into politics many of the qualities of a business man. In fact Gladstone, who started his political career as a member of Peel's cabinet, said he was the "best man of business who was ever Prime Minister". Gladstone also declared that "taken all round", Peel was the greatest man he had ever known. Later on Gladstone became leader of the Liberal party and then Prime Minister, and knew most of the leading statesmen of all parties in the second half of the nineteenth century. If Peel seemed to him to be the greatest of them, he must have had very unusual qualities.

In what ways was Peel a great man? He was not what is called a brilliant man – he did not make witty speeches which were remembered by everyone who heard them. He did not often produce new ideas – he was on the whole opposed to reform, and had to be very certain that reforms were necessary before he would support them. He was above all a great *administrator*. This means that although he was not the sort of person who was very quick or clever at seeing the nature of problems, he was very good at solving them once they had been pointed out. He knew how to organise and instruct the people who worked under him, and how to choose the best people for the right jobs. He was interested in all matters concerned with national finance, and made important changes in banking and taxation.

During his periods in office as Home Secretary and as Prime Minister, Peel several times changed his mind on important questions, and actually took over policies which he had started by opposing. When he was the Leader of the Opposition, he only opposed the Government on matters in which he genuinely thought they were wrong. In the same way, when he was in power, he would accept the views of the opposition if he was persuaded that they were right. His admirers thought this showed great strength of character on Peel's part, but his enemies thought that he simply wanted to stay in power, and did not mind using other people's ideas to help him to do so. Punch wrote:

How wonderful is Peel!
He changeth with the Time,
Turning and twisting like an eel
Ascending through the slime.

But Peel's changes of policy were not just signs that he was a wily politician. The country was changing, and the sort of person and the sort of party which were needed to govern it were changing as well. There were more people in England than ever before, and more wealth; what's more there were more different kinds of wealth. There was no longer simply land and money, but factories, canals, railways, a growing mass of house property of all sizes, as well as a continually-growing volume of manufactured goods of every kind. The 1832 Reform Bill which let some of the new kinds of wealthy people take their part in electing Parliament, was the first *political* recognition of the changes. Politicians like Peel and Gladstone brought new approaches and new methods into the Government. If we compare Peel, for example, with Lord Melbourne we can see some of the differences. Peel always made it his business to be thoroughly well-informed on all matters which came before him. He examined the cases put forward by friends and opponents, and had information of all kinds provided for him. Melbourne was in every way more casual, often leaving things to the last possible moment before dealing with them.

It is interesting to notice that the new men came from the Tory party. The Whigs, who had been the party which actually introduced the Reform Bill, relied on the support which had got them amongst the new voters, and did not trouble too much about improving the quality of their leaders. The Tories on the other hand, as Peel and Disraeli both realised, had to do something to make up for the fact that they had opposed the Bill, and so tried to offer a more effective and vigorous leadership. The Whigs went on under the old sort of "family" system until the death of Melbourne's brother-in-law, Lord Palmerston, but after that their leaders, too, were of the new kind, and the party changed from old-style Whig to new-style Liberal.

Peel, then, represented a more flexible kind of politician than most of his predecessors. In the course of his political career, he changed his mind dramatically on three questions – Cash, Corn and Catholics.

Catholic Emancipation

King George IV, his brothers, and very many of the leading Tories in the House of Commons and the House of Lords were very strongly opposed to the idea of Roman Catholics being allowed to become Members of Parliament, or to hold other important positions in the country. The laws against Catholics were particularly hard on the people of Ireland, where a population that was almost entirely Catholic had to send Protestant members to represent them in the House of Commons.

In 1828 Sir Francis Burdett introduced a Bill into Parliament to repeal the anti-Catholic laws. Some Tories supported him, but Peel voted against it. In the year that followed, however, the situation in Ireland made him change his mind. Led by Daniel O'Connell, the Irish people made a determined effort to force a change in the law. Even people who would anyway not have a vote helped to raise money, and came to huge meetings. O'Connell stood as candidate for Parliament in County Clare in the summer of 1828, and was elected by a large majority. But, being a Catholic, he was not allowed to go and take his seat in Parliament, because that would have meant swearing that he was a Protestant. The excitement in Ireland was enormous. Something like five-sixths of all the British infantry forces were stationed there to keep order, and monster meetings were held all over the island in support of O'Connell. The British Prime Minister, the Duke of Wellington, was afraid that there would be a civil war. Peel, as Home Secretary, came, in his own cautious words, to "a decided opinion that there was less of evil and less of danger in considering the Catholic question with a view to its final adjustment". They therefore agreed to the introduction of a Catholic Emancipation Bill, which was passed early in 1829. But it was passed only because the Whigs voted for it. Many Tories voted against. By the Act, a Catholic could be anything but King, Lord Chancellor, or Lord Lieutenant of Ireland.

Another Act in the same year made the qualification for voting in Ireland the ownership of land worth £10 a year freehold instead of 40/- as it was in England. This was presumably intended to punish the small freeholders for electing O'Connell, but the agitation surrounding the question of Catholic Emancipation had a great deal of effect on the movement for far more radical Reform in England. At the election of 1830 many Tories, including Peel himself, lost their seats, and the Whigs who were pledged to reform Parliament were returned.

The Metropolitan Police

Before we go on to look at the other two "C's" – Cash and Corn, we should mention another of Peel's reforms during his period as Home Secretary. This was the setting up of the Metropolitan Police Force in London.

Until 1829 arrangements for policing towns and villages were made locally. In most places the system was that every person in the village or township was liable to serve a period as unpaid police constable. Many years earlier the system had been modified, so that, instead of serving as a constable, people paid a sum of money each year, and this went to pay for permanent constables. In the towns the richer citizens – particularly merchants and people with valuable property, paid watchmen to guard the streets at night, and to catch thieves where possible. In London, with its thousands of people, this system had been carried further. The West Indian merchants paid for patrols to guard the River Thames and the valuable warehouses along it, and other groups of merchants employed private "thief-takers". But the system only protected property, and was anyway not very efficient. It was the behaviour of the crowds at the funeral of Queen Caroline in 1820, which led to the setting up of commissions to consider the whole question, and eventually, in 1829, to the establishment of the Metropolitan Police in London. They were a force of men trained to enforce the law. They wore blue uniforms and carried truncheons and, to the amazement of the citizens of London, patrolled the streets by day as well as by night. Later, local watch committees were established in provincial towns, with responsibility for setting up police forces. The London police are still sometimes called Bobbies, after Sir Robert Peel.

The Reform of the Banks

One of the things which concerned Peel as Prime Minister was the whole question of money and of banking in England. We have already seen that London had become one of the great banking centres of the world during the eighteenth century. We have also noticed that in order for industry to grow, a great deal of money had to be lent and borrowed. The people who made the great inventions were not usually rich enough to build their own factories, and had to borrow the money to do so. Peel's age was also the great age of railway building. Railways could not begin to make profits until they were built, so for them, too, money to do the actual constructing had to be borrowed.

One of the main reasons why England was the first country in the world to build factories and railways was just that there was so much money in England at this time. Slave-traders, merchants of all kinds, bankers, and improving landowners all had money to spare to lend to industrialists and railway builders.

But since all this lending and borrowing was quite unplanned there were occasional great financial crises. Banks lent money which they did not really have, and went broke. A craze for one kind of industry – for example cotton in the eighteen-twenties, or railways in the eighteen-forties, led people to put far too much money into one particular industry. Very many of them lost their money, when it turned out that there were simply too many cotton mills, or too many competing railway companies, and some had to close down. On top of this sort of

93. The Watchman (*right*) was the nearest thing to a policeman on duty in most towns in the early part of the nineteenth century. London had its special corps of professional police, the Bow Street Runners (*left*), who actually tracked down criminals.

crisis there were very many cases of straight-forward fraud. People set up bogus companies, and "borrowed" money which they had no intention of paying back.

Peel tried to bring in the idea of more central control of all these money dealings. It was clear that as long as they were not controlled at all, people would continue to lose money when there was a crisis, and working people would continue to be thrown out of work when any particular industry received a setback. The measures which Peel took were only a beginning, and were only partly successful. He did succeed in making the Bank of England stronger, and began the slow process of getting all the bank notes in the country to come from one central bank.

He tried to make sure that the banks only issued notes equal in value to the actual gold they had in their vaults, or nearly so. He made investing money safer, by making fraud more difficult. None of these measures did, however, succeed in preventing crises from occurring. All through the nineteenth and most of the first half of the twentieth century, British workers have been faced with the possibility of being thrown out of their jobs by the closing down of large parts of the country's industries, and middle-class people have lost large amounts of money. It is only in very recent times that Governments have found ways of avoiding crises, and of keeping industry of all kinds going, so that most people can rely on regular employment.

The details of the acts by which Peel achieved these results need not concern us, particularly as they were only partly successful. But it should be mentioned that on an important matter of banking policy, the use of gold as the foundation of all money transactions, Peel was persuaded to change sides by the experts he consulted. He changed from being a strong supporter of paper money to being a supporter of gold.

The Corn Laws

We have already seen (Chapter 11) how the agitation of the Manchester industrialists led finally to the repeal of the Corn Laws. This was the most famous occasion on which Peel changed his views. His party, the Tory party, was largely protectionist – that is, they believed that English agriculture should be especially protected by taxes on foreign goods. Peel, as he continued in office, became more and more convinced that free trade between nations was a good thing, and he took off many of the taxes on imported goods. Agriculture, however, had always seemed to be a special case, and for years Peel agreed with the majority of his party that it was right to protect agriculture with the Corn Laws. But (even before the Irish potato famine) Peel was beginning to change his mind. It was always said by the protectionists that if wheat was dear, then the wages of the agricultural labourers went up, so that they were able to buy the dearer bread. Peel had the figures of agricultural wages in several different districts collected, and gradually he became convinced that they did not change as the price of grain rose. If wheat was dear the farmers made higher profits, but the labourers got the same low wages as always, and had to pay more for their bread. In his speech on the subject of repeal in the House of Commons, Peel quoted these figures, and earned the hearty dislike of many of the landowning members of his own party. Very soon after the repeal of the Corn Laws these protectionists in the Tory party saw the opportunity to defeat their leader, and combined with the Whigs to turn him out.

For all his very great qualities as a statesman, Peel was not an easy man to work with. He was gruff and sharp in his manner, and his enemies found him cold and hard. Daniel O'Connell, the Irish leader, said that his smile was like the silver plate on a coffin. It may be, indeed, that his rather brusque personal manner led indirectly to his death; an acquaintance, seeing him out riding on a horse known to be a dangerous "bolter", was too timid of Peel's sharp tongue to warn him. The horse threw him, and a few days later, in June 1850, he died.

Liberals, Tories, and Peelites

After the defeat of Peel, the Whigs took power again, led by Lord John Russell. Russell was the man who had drafted the 1832 Reform Bill, and had become leader of the Whigs after Lord Melbourne. His views were really very little different from those of the "Peelite" Tories.

The years in the middle of the nineteenth century, from about 1846 to 1858 were years in which the old political groupings were breaking down, and the Liberal and Conservative parties of the second half of the century were beginning to take definite shape.

Peel, as we have seen, was a Tory, but was not bound by the ideas of the old powerful landowning class. His actions on the questions of free trade, of reforming the police, of freeing Catholics and other dissenting groups from the disabilities under which they had lived for so long, and of experimenting with new methods of control of banking and finance, were all more in line with the thinking of the manufacturers and traders than with the landowners. After the repeal of the Corn Laws, the Tory party split into two groups – the "Peelites" and the Protectionists. Among the Peelites was a young Tory who had been Peel's President of the Board of Trade, William Ewart Gladstone. Leader of the Protectionists was

Benjamin Disraeli, Peel's chief critic within the Tory party. There was really much more difference of view between Gladstone and Disraeli, both at this time Tories, than there was between Gladstone and the Whig leader, Russell.

William Ewart Gladstone

Gladstone came from the same sort of family background as Peel. He was the son of a rich Liverpool merchant, and had been brought up and educated as a gentleman. He already owned a large country estate. But he brought into politics many of the qualities of his merchant family. It was said of him that although he might be "Oxford on top", he was "Liverpool underneath". After the split in the Tory party he stood for re-election in a new constituency as a "Peelite". He represented this constituency, Oxford University, until 1865, when he stood again in South Lancashire as a Liberal. In 1866 he became leader of the Liberal party.

Gladstone came to stand for English Liberalism. He was a man of very great ability. Like his early leader, Peel, he was a very capable administrator. He had a great interest in financial questions, and was Chancellor of the Exchequer for eleven years, during which time he brought in a series of very famous budgets. The aim of his policy was to make trade more free, so he continually reduced taxes and tariffs on imported and manufactured goods. He also aimed to reduce government spending, and succeeded in doing this by using money more efficiently. In general he, and those who, like him, were coming to think of themselves as Liberals rather than Whigs, did not believe it was necessary for England to have large armies overseas protecting colonies. They thought that free trade was better than trade imposed on an unwilling Empire. They believed, too, that England would acquire greater glory by being the greatest manufacturing power in the world than by having great armies and winning wars. So that the general policy of the

94. William Ewart Gladstone. Tory, then Peelite, and finally the greatest leader of the Liberal Party.

95. Benjamin Disraeli. Novelist and radical Tory, who was to become leader of the Conservative Party and a great supporter of Imperialism.

Liberals of Gladstone's kind can be summed up as – efficiency at home, freedom of trade and manufacture, non-interference in the affairs of foreign countries. Many Liberals also tended to believe that since manufacture was the heart of England's prosperity, then the interests of owners and workers were really the same. They believed that factory workers, if they were allowed to vote, would vote Liberal, and so many of them agreed with giving the vote to working people. We shall see later how these principles worked out in practice, but now let us look at the opposite side of the political scene. What Gladstone was to the Liberals, Disraeli was to the Conservatives.

Benjamin Disraeli

The Peelite split, coming so soon after the defeat over the Reform Bill, was a great blow to the Tories in the House of Commons. Disraeli's great contribution was to gather together the demoralised groupings and to build a new Conservative party from them.

On the face of it, Disraeli was a most unlikely man to become the leader of the land-owning party in the British House of Commons. Although British by birth, his father had been born Italian, of a Jewish family called d'Israeli. Young Benjamin had been educated as an Englishman and a Christian, but his outlandish name, his dark, "foreign" looks and his taste for bright and showy clothes made him a surprising choice for leader of a revived Conservative party.

The qualities which Dizzy (as he was, inevitably, nicknamed) brought into politics, were, however, considerable. His outstanding quality was brilliance. Highly intelligent, he had a gift for witty and effective speech-making which singled him out quite early in his career as an outstanding performer in Parliament. Gladstone, and many of his colleagues amongst the Peelites and Liberals, were thunderous speakers, filling their speeches with Latin and Greek

quotations, and with moral and earnest sentiments. Disraeli scathingly and wittily punctured them, using weapons like ridicule and sarcasm to set the House of Commons and the country outside laughing. Where Gladstone occasionally occupied himself by writing translations of Latin and Greek poems, Disraeli wrote novels. Several of his novels are on political subjects, and both Whigs and Tories found themselves made fun of in them.

It is difficult to sum up clearly what were the ideas in which Disraeli believed. For one thing, what he said in his novels and speeches did not by any means correspond to what he did as a practical politician. For instance he declared his sympathy with the Chartists, and in his novel, *Sybil*, drew an interesting and quite sympathetic picture of Chartists and of factory workers. He was privately sympathetic and helpful to individual Chartists, even to the extent of giving small sums of money to help a Chartist newspaper that was in difficulties. And yet, he did very little when he was in power to improve social conditions. Like the more radical Liberals, however, he believed in the vote for working men, but he believed that they would vote Tory. He was head of the Government which passed the Second Reform Bill in 1867, which began to give the vote to the working people of England.

The New Imperialism

Perhaps Disraeli's main contribution to the political life of the country was his idea of *Imperialism*. We have seen in the early chapters of this book how important the "old Empire" was in the development of English trade and finance. After the American colonies had broken away, and the West Indian sugar trade became less important, the idea of an Empire had rather gone out of fashion. England still ruled over many parts of the world, and gained considerable wealth from her possessions, especially from India. But, as we have seen, the free trade Liberals did not want to spend large sums of money on keeping soldiers abroad guarding colonies, they preferred to rely on Britain's industrial lead to bring money into the country.

Disraeli, however, and the Conservative party under his leadership, loved the idea of an Empire. Not only did it suit the beliefs of the protectionists, who thought that governments *should* control trade, but it appealed to a colourful and romantic imagination. Disraeli was a great believer in the Royal Family. As the century went on, the relief which the British people felt at having a Queen who was respectable and well-behaved, began to show signs of turning into boredom. After Prince Albert died in 1861, Victoria went and lived quietly in Windsor Castle, and would not appear in public. Not unnaturally, the public began to resent the idea of a Queen whom it never saw, who did not perform the ceremonial tasks which had become the chief reasons for having a monarchy. Disraeli rescued the Queen from her unpopularity, and turned her into the most popular monarch in modern times.

In 1876, he introduced a Bill called the Royal Titles Bill. It was a brilliant idea to bring the Queen out of her retirement and to catch public imagination. By this Bill, the Queen was given the title of Empress of India, and the whole idea of a revived British Empire was brought to the fore. Punch, which strongly disapproved both of Disraeli and the Empire, showed him as an Eastern Aladdin, selling the Queen a flashy Oriental crown in exchange for the dignified Crown of Great Britain. But "Dizzy" was right. Popular opinion was ready for a new and romantic idea, and in spite of *Punch* and the radicals, ideas of Empire and the conquest of new colonies caught on in the country as a whole.

96 New Crowns for Old. Disraeli offers Queen Victoria the crown of Empress of India.

Chapter 13
Adaptation and Self-Help

Shops and Shopping in the mid-Nineteenth Century

As long as people lived in villages and small towns, they would buy a lot of the things they needed from their neighbours, from such people as the village shoemaker, tailor, carpenter or saddler. Other things would be bought at markets or fairs – things like pins, needles, buckles, books and writing materials. In between fair and market-days odds and ends that could not be got in the village would be bought from travelling pedlars.

The man with a pack on his back, selling ribbon, lace, tape, thread, needles and pins and such things, was a familiar sight on English country roads until very recent times. The travelling tinker with a horse and cart would travel round the villages selling and mending pots and pans and simple kitchen tools. Working tools might be sold or made by travelling craftsmen, who would stay for a day or two at a farm, getting free bed and board and a small payment, in return for sharpening and repairing

tools, or making new ones. The knife and scissor sharpener, with his grindstone, the man who mended china with small metal rivets, the man who put new rush seats in chairs, all these and others would call at regular intervals and spend a few days in a village before moving on.

As people began to move into the towns, their whole way of living changed, and with it their ways of shopping. Of course, it did not change all at once. Many towns went on having fairs and markets, but they gradually became less important as a way of supplying goods. Shops of all kinds grew up. When both husband and wife worked in a factory, there was less time for making jam or baking bread and cakes, so more things had to be bought from a shop.

The people of the towns came to depend on shops for their supplies of food, clothes and household goods of all kinds. Shops were of many different kinds. Outside London, for instance, there were very few greengrocers – most people bought fruit and vegetables from street markets, stalls in the street, or from men travelling through the streets with carts. In country towns fruit and vegetables still came in fresher and cheaper by cart from the surrounding countryside. But goods such as pots and pans and "hardware" of all kinds which had once been sold by "cheapjacks" travelling from town to town with carts, came, after the middle of the century, to be sold more and more in fixed shops. Railways could bring these things over long distances from the towns in which they were made most cheaply, and the shopkeeper could keep a

97. Pedlars (*left* and *below*). Country people bought ribbons, needles, scissors and other small household goods from travelling pedlars like these men, either at fairs or at their door. Pedlars still visited more remote villages right until the end of the nineteenth century.

good store, while the cheapjack could carry only a cartload.

There were different shops for different classes of people. In most fair-sized towns there were streets of "respectable" shops, which working men or women seldom enter-ed. These would supply people of the mid-dling classes. The upper classes still sent away to London for most of their needs. But ladies of the middle classes began to spend more time shopping. Marketing – that is the buying of food for the household, they would leave to their servants, but shopping for dresses and household equipment they did for themselves. They would drive up to the shop in their carriage, and be given a seat whilst the shopkeeper or his assistant brought out the goods for them to choose from. It was a pleasant thing to do, and, since the number of middle-class families was growing, a profitable business for a good shopkeeper. To keep the good custom, he had to carry a plentiful stock, to be up-to-date with fashion in the goods he was selling, to have a pleasant manner, and to be sure that his assistants were well-mannered, neatly and pleasantly dressed, patient and respectful.

Very different were the shops at the "other end of the town". The shops which mainly served the poorer people had quite different things to think about. For fresh food, the great centre was the Friday and Saturday night street market. On pay-night nearly all the marketing for the week was done, and the seller who got the most custom was the one who made his goods look most attractive, or who shouted their virtues loudest. Henry Mayhew was a journalist, who spent many years gathering information about the lives of the poor people of London in the middle of the century. He describes the colour and noise of a Saturday night street market in Lambeth:

> ... Then the tumult of a thousand different cries of the eager dealers all shouting at the tops of their voices at one and the same time, are almost bewildering. "So-old again" roars

one. "Chestnuts all 'ot, a penny a score" bawls another. "An 'apenny a skin, blacking" squeaks a boy "Buy, buy, buy, buy, bu-u-uy" cries the butcher. "Half a quire of paper for a penny" bellows the street stationer. . . . "Two pence a pound grapes" "Three a penny Yarmouth bloaters", "Who'll buy a bonnet for four-pence?" "Pick 'em out cheap here,' three pairs for a halfpenny, bootlaces". "Now's your time, beautiful whelks, a penny a lot." "Here's ha'porths" shouts the perumbulating con-fectioner. "Come and look at 'em! Here's toasters" bellows one with a Yarmouth bloater stuck on a toasting fork. "Penny a lot, fine russets" calls the apple woman. And so the babel goes on . . .

For the housewife with money in her purse, there was a good choice at the street market.

But, especially in the towns in which there was only one main industry, there were long spells when people had little or no money, even on pay nights. There were also many goods which cost more than could be spared from one week's pay. So shopping for work-ing people was not usually a simple matter of going to the shop and paying for goods across the counter.

Truck and Tommy Shops

One way in which working people shopped in some parts of the country was in what were known as "Tommy Shops". These were shops which were owned by the person for whom they worked. In textile districts these shops had disappeared by about the middle of the century, but in other areas, especially in the mining districts, they were still around in the 1870's. The idea was that the worker got part of his wages as goods. He was either given the goods direct instead of money, or, usually, he was allowed so much credit at the shop which was run by the firm. If the firm was honest, and had the shop just as a convenience for its workers, there was nothing wrong with this system. But usually it was a particularly unpleasant way of doing the workman out of part of his wages.

98. The Market Place of a Lancashire town in
the early nineteenth century.

99. Shopping in a London back street in
1840. Most of the goods on sale are second-hand.

There were no fixed prices in those times,
and the company could set any price it liked
on the goods in the shop. So that if a man —
or woman or child — was forced to spend
several shillings of his wages in his employer's shop, for goods that he could have
got at a lower price somewhere else, it was
the same thing as a cut in wages. Perhaps
even worse was the fact that often these
shops were used to sell off bad goods —
rancid butter or mouldy potatoes, which no
self-respecting shopkeeper would handle.
What was more, in a week in which wages
were short, the Tommy Shop would allow
credit, so that after working a full week, a
miner might find he owed all he earned to
the company shop. If he allowed too big a
debt to build up he might find it difficult
to change his job even if he did get the chance

of better work, and so he would find himself trapped by having been forced to deal at the Tommy Shop.

Credit Shopping and Tally Men

At the root of the problem of working-class shopping was the fact that wages were very low indeed. Most working-class families were in debt even when they were working, and when they were out of work or ill the only way they could live without going into the workhouse was to go further into debt. Only a small number of better-paid or exceptionally clever families lived without credit. For nearly everyone else, pay day always arrived with most of last week's bills to pay, and usually with bills going further back than that.

Once a family were in debt they were tied to the shopkeeper who exploited them in all sorts of ways. In the mid-nineteenth century it was pretty well universally true that all the food the workers ate was adulterated. Chalk, alum, anything cheap and white that could be baked, was added to the flour that made the bread. Tea contained all kinds of other leaves dried, and sometimes coloured to spin out the genuine tea-leaves. Milk and beer were watered – and sometimes cheap crude alcohol was added to the beer to make up the strength which the watering took away. Sand in the sugar, dandelion root in the coffee – there was no end to the adulteration which the housewife had to put up with, once she was caught in the net of credit-shopping. These credit-giving shops were known as "badger" shops.

Clothes were either also bought on credit – often from the so-called tally-men who called weekly for payment, usually a penny a week for every thirty pence spent – or were bought second-hand. There was an enormous turnover of second-hand goods. Pawnbrokers who lent money on goods or clothes, would sell them if they were not claimed back within a certain time. Stolen goods found their way into back-street second-hand shops, servants sold their employers' cast-off clothing. Indeed, however poor you were and however worn the garment, you could usually find someone poorer still who would give a copper for it.

The Early Co-operative Stores

It is against this background of credit buying and the adulteration of food that the early co-operative stores came into being.

As time went by, working people who were in regular jobs, and who would like to buy goods for cash at reasonable prices, found it increasingly difficult to do so. The credit shops did not really want cash sales, when their high prices and low quality might be questioned. The middle-class shops did not always want to supply the small quantities which a working family wanted to buy each week. What was more, the whole atmosphere of some of these shops was one which made it unlikely that a man in working clothes, or a housewife in her apron would pop in in the evening for a small purchase. There are still shops that are rather overwhelming for an ordinary person to go in, but this was much more so a hundred years ago.

We have already seen in earlier chapters that the idea of co-operation had been in the air since the early days of factories (see p. 108). In the second half of the nineteenth century, the idea took on a new lease of life.

The place in which the co-operative shops are usually said to have started was in Rochdale in Lancashire, in 1844. This was actually only one among many which started at around this time, but by the end of the 1850's the number throughout England and Scotland had risen to hundreds. This was partly a sign that the co-operators were hard-working and devoted, for all the early work was unpaid. But what it chiefly shows is that during these years enough working people were earning regular wages which were high enough to enable them to pay for the goods they needed as they needed them. It was for these people, the better-off workers in regular jobs, that the co-ops came

100.   Shopping in a London street market in the early twentieth century.

into existence. For the very poor, who still made up probably the majority of people in the big towns, the tally-man and the badger-shop continued.

The co-ops

What is a co-op? You probably all know that all co-ops give a "divvy" – that is a dividend on purchases. The idea is that each member of the co-operative gets back part of the profit made in the shop. His share depends on how much he has spent in the year. So that the early co-ops were able to sell their members good and pure food, and also to give them back at the end of the half-year a share of the shop's profits. There were four rules which all the successful co-ops adopted. No credit, only pure goods to be sold, a dividend to be given to all members according to how much they had spent, and an agreement that part of the profits should go for the education of members. Each co-

op had a board of directors, elected by all members. This board had to appoint a manager for each shop, watch over all matters concerned with trading, decide what form of education the members wanted and so on. Thus all through the manufacturing districts there grew up co-operative stores, co-operative reading rooms, libraries, choirs, and all forms of social as well as trading establishments. In 1883 the Co-operative Women's Guild was started which gave a particular place for women in the movement. Today your local co-operative store may seem to be only one shop among many others, but in the second half of the last century, the co-ops helped to change the quality of life of a large section of the British people. What is more, they had a good effect on other shops, who saw that they made a good trading profit out of honest trading, and improved their own services in order to compete with them.

Co-operation, then, was one way in which the town workers set about improving their lives after the middle of the century. Another way was the establishment of powerful Trade Unions to improve their wages and working conditions.

The New Model Unions

The idea of Trade Unionism was as old or older than the idea of co-operation. And as with the co-ops, there was a continuous history of attempts, some successful, some not, all through the earlier years of the century. But here again, the low wages and irregular employment of most people in the earlier part of the century had meant that trade unions had usually been short-lived, even the fairly successful ones.

Just as the Rochdale Pioneers Co-operative Society of 1844 is usually given as the beginning of modern co-operation, so the establishment of the Amalgamated Society of Engineers in 1851 is usually taken as the starting date of modern Trade Unionism. Both dates are wrong, in that they were not, in fact, the earliest of their kind, but both dates are useful, as they give an indication of the time when co-operation and trade unionism really began to get under way in their modern form. So they are useful dates to remember.

What was new about the "new model unions"? Probably the most important thing was that they were *national* unions. The Amalgamated Society of Engineers brought together many small unions which had catered for sections of the engineering industry, and provided a secretary and an office for the whole country. The subscription was high – one shilling a week for members. This meant that the skilled men who belonged soon had a fund behind them. This fund was used to pay sick benefit, unemployment pay and old age and funeral benefits, none of which were provided by the government in those days. It also helped to pay the expenses of members who wanted to emigrate, for

the trade unionists believed that it was a good thing to keep down the number of skilled workers in the country. The union was able to insist on only apprenticed men belonging, and to restrict the number of apprentices to be admitted to industry. But above all, the national organisation and the high subscriptions enabled the union to strike for better pay and shorter working hours, with a good chance of succeeding.

The new unions, the engineers, carpenters and joiners, the boilermakers and the iron shipbuilders, set up local as well as national organisations. Trades councils began in the industrial areas, consisting of representatives of all the local unions to discuss local questions, and in 1868 the first national Trades Union Congress met in Manchester. Other industries became organised, and by 1875 the skilled unions which made up the Trades Union Congress had a membership of half a million.

Achievements of the Unions

The great achievement of these new model unions was to see that the skilled workers got a share of the improvements in living standards during the years of growth and expansion. This was not a simple matter. Trade unionists, even highly-skilled men, were often "blacklisted", and found they could not get work in their own localities. Many skilled workers who could have lived in comparative comfort, lost their jobs and had to move to different parts of the country, or to take unskilled work at low wages because they became known as trade unionists.

The new model unions took a big step towards the situation which now exists in industry, where unions are recognised as the voice of the people who work in factories, mines and shops. But they only took the first step, and it was nearly a hundred years before they obtained the full recognition which they wanted.

101.   The Reform Bill in 1867 gave the vote to many working men in the towns. This cartoon in *Punch* suggests that no-one had any idea of what the result would be.

Trade Unions and the Law

One of the things that made the new unions more powerful than the old was their money. But in 1867 they got a shock when a court refused to give legal protection to a trade union's funds. In the case before the court, a trade union, the Boilermakers' Society, was suing the treasurer of the Bradford branch for £24 which he had taken from the branch funds. The judge declared that the union could not recover the money, since trade unions were illegal organisations still, and had no right to the protection of the law. This meant that anyone who happened to have any trade union money in his posses-sion, could have kept it. Of course, the great majority of union treasurers were honest and devoted union members and did not pocket the funds, but the unions were naturally very worried by this judgement.

The years immediately after the 1867 judgement saw a big improvement in the legal position of the unions. A Royal Commission was set up by the Government to look at the whole question of trade union-ism. Its report, and the Trade Union Bill which was passed in 1871 gave trade unions legal recognition and protection of their funds. By the time the Trade Union Act of 1871 was passed, the Second Reform Bill of 1867 had also been passed. This meant that a number of trade unionists had votes, and both the main parties were therefore anxious to gain as much trade union support as they could. In 1871 the Liberal Government passed the act giving the unions legal recognition and protection of their funds. But at the same time, they passed another Act making many kinds of persuasion and picketing by striking workers illegal. In the next election, therefore, in 1874, many trade unionists supported Disraeli and the Conservatives. They were rewarded by two acts passed by the Conservative Government in 1874 and 1875 which made the law much fairer for employed people, and which gave the trade unions greater power to act, by making peaceful picketing and persuasion legal.

So the improved organisation of the unions, together with the fact that many more working people were voting, led both the Conservative and Liberal parties to take account of the unions and pass laws to help them. On the whole, more trade unionists supported the Liberal than the Conservative party and in 1874 two trade union leaders were elected as Liberal Members of Parliament. But many trade unionists were still not happy about the legal position of the unions. They felt that the two main parties were composed mainly of employers, and that, although some employers were sympathetic to trade unionism, and some members of both parties had done a great deal to help, a situation might arise in which the employers and the unions were on opposite sides on an important question, and the unions would have very little chance of being heard in Parliament. It was the need for the working men's case to be presented in Parliament which led in 1901 to the establishment of the Labour Party. From 1871 to 1901 the trade unions kept a committee going to watch the two main parties, and to persuade them to put through laws to protect workmen. Laws to increase safety precautions in mines, to make employers

responsible for compensation of workmen injured at work, to enforce the Plimsoll line on merchant ships to prevent overloading, were all passed partly as the result of pressure from the Trade Union Parliamentary Committee.

The Growth of Democracy

The middle classes had gained, first the vote in 1832, and then an important part in the actual government of the country. There was still a division in the middle classes. One section of tradesmen and small industrialists stayed in the provincial towns and spent their energies in local government, becoming councillors and mayors rather than M.P.'s and members of the Government. Those who actually went in to the House of Commons and into the leadership of the two great political parties were mainly from the very richest families, and were usually men educated at public schools and at Oxford and Cambridge.

The experience of Chartism had shown working people that they could organise their own movements. They had begun to build successful Co-operative and Trade Union movements, and were taking an active interest in local Government.

In 1867 the political experience of the working people was at last admitted, and the Conservative government led by Disraeli passed the Second Reform Bill.

The Second Reform Bill

Although there were many great meetings and demonstrations in the country before the passing of this bill, there was nothing like the excitement which had led up to the first Reform Bill of 1832. Most people believed by 1867 that it was really only a matter of time before all the men in the country would get the vote. This is not to say that there was no opposition. But in the end the bill was passed, giving the vote to all householders in the towns, and to all people living in houses for which they paid more than £12 in rates in the countryside. This meant that there were 938,000 new voters. In the towns many of these were working men, but in the counties the new voters were mainly middle class men. In 1872 the ballot was brought in at last, and from then on all voting was in secret.

The Third Reform Bill

Until the passing of the ballot act, there was not very much point in asking for the vote for all men in the countryside. The village labourers were still so much dependent on the farmers and the landowners, from whom they got their jobs and their houses, that they would never have dared to vote against the party of their employer. After the Ballot Act, however, things were different. The very year it was passed was the year in which a new trade union was started amongst the agricultural workers. They succeeded in many places in gaining wage increases, to the astonishment of the whole country, for most people thought the farm labourers were too ignorant and oppressed ever to stick up for themselves. Under the leadership of Joseph Arch, A Warwickshire labourer of great ability and courage, the Union organised the farm workers all over England. It is difficult to know whether the employers and the old-fashioned parsons were more angry or astonished at this awakening. One bishop urged that union organisers should be thrown into the village horse-ponds, but the result of this and other anti-union speeches was only to strengthen the hold in the villages of the non-conformist chapels. Joseph Arch himself, and many of the other union officials were members of the Primitive Methodist church, and they were quite used to being attacked by bishops.

The Agricultural Workers Union was not able to last through the years of bad harvest and agricultural decline after 1875, but the agitation for the vote continued, helped by radicals and trade unionists in the towns. In 1884 and 1885 two reform acts were passed which gave the vote to householders in the countryside on the same terms as those

102. Joseph Arch – the Warwickshire farm labourer who led the way for better working conditions for English farm labourers.

in the towns. In 1885 Joseph Arch was elected Member of Parliament for North-West Norfolk.

By the end of the nineteenth century, then, most men in England had the vote. Perhaps even more important in the development of a democratic society was the great variety of other forms of activity in which people took part. In the towns and villages, people of all kinds were active on local councils, local school boards, as guardians of the poor, and in many other organisations which helped to affect the way they lived. In the co-ops, trade unions, in many chapels and other voluntary societies, people of all classes used their abilities to help themselves and other people.

But you will notice that all the main reforms of Parliament gave the vote to more and more *men*. By the end of the nineteenth century, there still seemed very little chance of women being admitted to the Parliamentary franchise. In local affairs women ratepayers could vote, they could even be local councillors and members of school boards. But in most organisations they were still regarded with suspicion. Although important steps were being taken to organise women workers, the old-style trade unionists did not want women at their meetings.

Chapter 14

The Organisation of the Unskilled Workers

In England in 1880, there were about twelve million wage earners. Of these, only one million were members of a Trade Union. If wages and conditions of work were to be improved, it was essential that there should be more unions, and that many more working men and women should belong to them. But how was this to be achieved?

Wages at this time were so low, and work was so irregular, that many millions of people did not earn enough to feed their families. It was hardly likely, then, that they would be able to find the money to pay a weekly contribution to a Trade Union, or to buy newspapers or pamphlets which would explain to them about the unions. What was more, in order to get better wages, a union has to be able to call its members out on strike – that is to tell them all to stop work until better wages are paid. How could men, fighting to get a few hours' work a day or a few days work a week, at miserable rates of pay, be expected to give up even that for long enough to make a strike effective? The truth of the matter was that the skilled workers – those who had unions, and who earned enough to pay Trade Union contributions, did not really believe that it would ever be possible to get the unskilled men – let alone the women – into Trade Unions, to "organise" them and to improve their conditions.

The Sweated Trades

At this time many girls and women, and some men, worked at home on "out-work" – working from morning to night, for coppers or at the most a few shillings. To give one example, a woman and her brother, who was too old to get work outside the house, worked at home, sewing buttons on to cards ready for the shops. The buttons and cards were supplied by the factory, and the two workers had to buy needles and thread, sew the buttons neatly on to cards, and return the bundles of cards to the factory. They sat and sewed steadily, from eight in the morning until eleven at night, and earned three shillings and sixpence a week *between them*. Yet they preferred this to going into the workhouse, which was all they could do if they gave up the work.

The Dockers

Outside the home, unskilled workers – strong men prepared to work hard, actually fought in the dock areas for the right to work on the dock unloading and loading ships for 4d. or 5d. an hour – a rate that would give them a wage of about 16/– for a full week. But the worst thing about this sort of work was that men were rarely taken on for a week. Work was given out by the day, or even by the hour, and more time was spent tramping in search of work, or waiting to be called than in actually working. At the London Docks, men waited behind iron bars to be "called on" for work. The bars were necessary to protect the caller-on from the would-be workers:

In a building that would hold very few in comfort, men were packed tightly unto suffocation, like the Black Hole of Calcutta, and this struggling mass fought desperately and tigerishly, elbowing each other, punching each other, using their last remnants of strength to get work for an hour or half-hour for a few pence. Such struggling, shouting, cursing, when one man, younger than the rest, would throw himself bodily on the heads of this close-packed, struggling mass! For what? The possession of a ticket which, at the best, would afford four hours' labour for a wage at its highest of no more than sixpence an hour. And the men, old and young, fought for those few shillings as men fight for life. Coats, flesh, even ears were torn off. Men were crushed to death in the struggle. The strong literally threw themselves over the heads of their fellows, and battled with the milling crowds to get near to the rails of the "cage" which held them like rats – human rats who saw food in the ticket . . .

This description of the dockers fighting for work was written by a man who was a docker himself. Ben Tillet first came to the docks as a very young man of about nineteen. By then he had already been at work twelve years. He had started as a labourer in a brick-yard at seven years of age, working a full week cutting and carrying clay for one shilling and sixpence. He had run away from this to join a travelling circus, where he had worked in and out of the ring for little more than his keep. Next he had joined the Royal Navy as a boy sailor. There were no clothes or shoes in the stores small enough to fit him, but small and young as he was, he had learned the craft of seamanship in the navy, and later had joined the merchant navy. Now, after some years at sea, he wanted to work on shore, and joined the vast crowd of the London unskilled labourers. For the next few years, he worked on the docks, and when he could not get any work ashore, he went back to sea. He was a tough, intelligent man, and although he had had almost no schooling, he taught himself to read, and began to try and understand the world he lived in. Although, as he improved his education and got to learn new skills, he could have moved out of dockland into a more regular and comfortable job, he was never able to forget what he called the "horrible nightmare of the dockers' poverty". Every job he was on,

103. Ben Tillett.

he found himself acting as spokesman, trying to get better conditions.

A Dockers' Trade Union

In 1887, Tillett was working in a tea warehouse, heavy work moving tons of tea up and down stairs. In the evenings, after his day's work, he would sit up at his books, trying to teach himself Latin and Greek. He thought that he must educate himself if he was to help his friends and workmates to get out of poverty and distress. But things began to move around him. The employers decided to try and lower the wages paid for unloading the new supplies of tea, and the men working in the tea warehouses decided to call a meeting and try to form a Trade Union. Ben Tillett was known to be a good hand at putting a case, so he was taken to the meeting by his fellow-workmen. He was a small man, and his friend, a great hefty Irish labourer,

F
153

104. Mrs Besant, who wrote about the condition of work of the girls in the match factories.

105. Some of the girls from Bryant & May's match factory who struck for better pay and conditions in 1888.

was afraid that he would not be heard, so he lifted him bodily on to a table in the middle of the room in which the men were gathered. And there, standing up on the table, supported by the powerful Irishman, Tillett spoke, impeded by a stammer which always affected him when he was nervous, and put forward his suggestions for forming a Trade Union of Dock Labourers. As a result of that meeting, he was appointed secretary of the newly-formed union.

This was in 1887, and for the next two years Tillett and a few others worked to try and get the dockers' Trade Union going. It was a hard job. Not only did the employers oppose them – sometimes hiring gangs of toughs to break up their meetings and to attack the speakers, but the members of the older Trade Unions, the skilled men, far from helping the new union, sneered at it, and did their best to discourage people outside from helping. Even the dockers themselves, underpaid and overworked as they were, did not always see who were their friends, and union speakers at the dock gates sometimes found themselves attacked and shouted down by the very men they were trying to help.

The difficulties were great, but Tillett persisted. And gradually things improved. Some of the older union leaders saw that the organisation of the unskilled must in the end help them as well, and they began to help with money and with advice. Other people who were sympathetic to the hard life of the dockers helped as well. Clergymen who had churches in the dock districts, writers and journalists who came and saw for themselves how the people were living, teachers and doctors who got to know the districts, all helped the union organisers to let other people know how bad things were.

The Match Girls' Strike

In 1888, Mrs Besant, a woman who was already known for her interest in the way people really lived, wrote some newspaper articles about the appalling conditions in which the girls worked who made matches. She hoped that her description would make someone come forward to help the girls, but to her surprise they decided to help themselves. They read what she had written, and decided to stand it no longer, but to come out on strike at once. Mrs Besant helped them to raise £400, and this was enough for them to stay off work until their employers agreed to give them more wages, shorter hours, and cleaner and healthier conditions of work.

The success of the match girls was a great encouragement to other unskilled workers. There were plenty of jokes about match girls striking, but there was serious work afoot as well. In 1889 a union was formed by the London gas labourers. These men did some of the hardest and most unpleasant work in the big towns, working long hours amongst the choking fumes of coke and gas. Their leader was Will Thorne, a labourer himself, who, when he first began to organise the union, could not read or write. The first thing the gas workers wanted was an eight hour working day, and they declared that they would go on strike to get it. But even without a strike, the employers agreed, and the union had its first victory.

So two groups of unskilled workers in London – both among the worst-paid and worst-treated had succeeded in improving their wages and working conditions. Now the possibilities began to seem brighter for others. In August, 1889, there was a small dispute between some dockers and their employers in one of the big London docks. Rather than give in, the dockers remembered Ben Tillett and his little tea-warehousemen's

106.   A meeting of the striking dockers at the gates of the East and West India docks. Speaking to the men is John Burns – in the front of the platform holding a paper.

union, and came to him for help and advice.

The Dock Strike of 1889

This was the beginning of the Great Dock Strike – a strike which was called to insist that all dock workers should be paid at least sixpence an hour. Ben Tillett sent a telegram to his friend Tom Mann – an engineer with a great gift for organising and for speaking. Tom was a man, Tillett said, who "combined the qualities of whirlwind and volcano", and he threw himself into the job of organising the strike, of getting food supplies for the men and their families, and of raising money. As the strike went on, many other helpers joined the headquarters. John Burns, another engineer, who had at first been doubtful about a strike of unskilled workers, joined in as a speaker and organiser. For five weeks the dockers held out. Money came in from all parts of the world, and from sympathisers from all classes. From Australia nearly £30,000 was sent.

And in the end, the union won. The men returned to work, with a guarantee of 6d. an hour, 8d. for overtime, and with some improvements in the way of working and being paid.

The dockers had won a great victory for themselves and for other unskilled workers. But many people began to realise that although the unions could help to keep wages up, and to see that working conditions in their own industries did not get too bad, there were a whole lot of things which were too big for the unions to handle. One of these was the length of the working day. There were other things too. At this time sick people had to pay a doctor for attending to them, so that the very poor people often went without a doctor's care when they needed it, or called the doctor too late. There was no unemployment pay for men who could not find work, no sick pay if they were off sick, no old age pension, no family allowances. The unions could help the unskilled worker while he was at work, but they could not do much to help him face the problems of sickness, unemployment and old age.

A New Political Party

It was problems like these which made many people think that the old political parties were no longer enough. What was needed, they thought, was a new political party which would send working men to Parliament, men who would try and get laws passed to keep working hours down to eight hours a day, to provide social services and insurance for all people against sickness, unemployment and old age. Soon after the Dock Strike some of the new men were elected to Parliament for the first time. In 1892 three seats were won by working men. The new men in Parliament were John Burns, one of the leaders of the dock strike, Havelock Wilson, a leader of the sailors' trade union, and Keir Hardie, a miner from Scotland.

Although the modern Labour Party was not formed until 1901, it was really the entry of Keir Hardie into Parliament which marked the beginning of modern labour politics. The people of West Ham, in London, who had elected him, were so pleased to have their M.P. in that some of them escorted him to the House of Commons for the first time in a charabanc – a kind of large horse-drawn coach often used for workmen's outings, with a brass band playing on the top. Keir Hardie wore his usual clothes: his best suit and a cloth cap. The top-hatted M.P.'s already in the house were horrified. Perhaps their horror helps us to understand why it was necessary to have working men in the House of Commons, and not just thoughtful and radical-minded gentlemen in silk hats, as most of the earlier radicals had been. Hardie was an M.P. for only three years this time. He came back into the house again after four years' absence in 1899. But he succeeded in shocking the members on more than one occasion. It is worth describing one of these occasions – the most famous, to show again

107. During the dock strike, the dockers organised regular processions through London to collect money.

how very different his outlook was from that of the rest of the M.P.'s.

On 23rd June 1894, the Duchess of York had a baby. On the same day there was a dreadful mining disaster in South Wales, when 260 miners were killed. The next day, the President of France was assassinated. On 25th June, Sir William Harcourt speaking for the Government, moved that a message of sympathy should be sent to France on the murder of her President. Hardie rose and asked whether a message of sympathy was going to be sent to the families of the men who had been killed in the mining disaster. "Oh, no", was Sir William's reply, "I can dispose of that now by saying that the House does sympathise with these poor people." Hardie was so furious at this offhand attitude, that he protested by voting against sending a message of congratulation to the Duchess on the birth of her baby. Hardie's fury at the refusal of the Government to send sympathy to the miners' wives was nothing to the rage which his action in opposing the congratulations to the Duchess aroused in the rest of the House. One reporter wrote: "I've been in a wild beast show at feeding time ... I've been at a football match when a referee gave a wrong decision ... but in all my natural I've never witnessed a scene like this ..." The Victorian gentlemen who made up the House of Commons could not understand Hardie's rage at the slighting of the miners' families. And Hardie had not been prepared for their fury at his slighting of a Royal Duchess. This complete lack of understanding on both sides shows very clearly the great differences

157

between classes in England at the end of the nineteenth century.

The story of the growth of the Labour Party would take us beyond the time to be covered by this book. But as the century ended, there was in England a sizeable group of people, Socialists and Trade Unionists, who were determined to form a new party, to send working men to Parliament to work for improved social services, and if necessary to make important changes in the way the country and its industries were run and owned.

108.   A typical election poster in support of Keir Hardie, the first Independent Labour Member of Parliament.

VOTE FOR

Home Rule.

Democratic Government.

Justice to Labour

No Monopoly.

No Landlordism

Temperance Reform.

Healthy Home

Fair Rents.

Eight-Hour Da

Work for th Unemployed

KEIR HARDIE

Printed and Published by F W. Scrose & Co. [L.S.C.], 151, Barking Road, Canning Town, London, E.

Chapter 15

Britain and the World Overseas

Europe in the mid-Nineteenth Century

The most important thing that was happening in the countries of Europe and the United States of America during the nineteenth century, was that these countries were becoming *industrialised*. For centuries nearly all their peoples had been living in the countryside and spending their lives in raising food and in carrying on hand crafts in their homes or workshops. Now towns were growing rapidly, industry was being concentrated into factories, work was becoming linked with machines. More and more of the people were living and working in towns. Britain was the first country to become industrialised, and to face the problems which this process brought with it. Most of the events in this book have been the reactions of the people and of the government to the changes brought about in England by rapid industrialisation.

These changes were also going on in the rest of Europe – very slowly in some countries, more quickly in others. As we saw in England, industrialisation needs good communications – roads, railways, canals. Goods have to be moved quickly and freely. It also brings into importance a new class of people – the *entrepreneurs* – that is the people who find the money for new factories, organise the sale and manufacture of goods and make use of the new techniques of production – machinery and new sources of power. In an industrial society, money becomes as important as land, and the men who deal in goods and money become as important as the men who own the land.

So that as the countries of the world moved towards industrialisation, they faced the same problems that Britain had faced – the need for better transport and communication systems, the need for freedom of trade, the breaking down of old restrictions on the movement of goods, and the demand by the middle classes – the industrialists and *entrepreneurs* for a share in the governments of their countries. Towards the end of the century, the leading countries of Europe were also looking for new places to sell the goods that their factories produced and for new sources of supply of foodstuffs for the people living in their towns: this resulted in the building up of world-wide empires from amongst the non-industrialised countries of the world.

In England, we have already seen that one of the great political struggles at the beginning of the nineteenth century was for the middle classes to get political rights, and that they achieved this with the 1832 Reform Bill. We also saw that free trade, and the prevention of government interference with industry were the main political aims of the middle classes. In Chapter 16 we shall see how Imperialism developed in England.

The rest of Europe saw similar movements taking place. Because of the different histories of the different countries, the actual form of these developments varied from place to place. There is no space here to examine the exact details of each country's history, but as we look at the relations which Britain had with the rest of the world, and particularly with her neighbours in Europe, we can understand them better if we keep certain broad principles in mind.

Liberalism

Broadly speaking, liberalism was the name given to the various movements in Europe which were aimed at including the middle classes in political power. Very often the liberals wanted a system very like the British, by which the King ruled together with an elected parliament. Some liberal movements were closer to the American republican idea, or took their programmes from the early days of the French revolution of 1789.

Nationalism

Along with the desire for more democratic forms of government, went the idea of nation states based on language and a common culture. This usually meant one of two things. Many countries, such as Greece, Poland and the countries of the Balkans, had their own languages and a long history as nations. By the nineteenth century, however, they had become absorbed into one of the three great European Empires – the Russian, the Austro-Hungarian or the Turkish. They were treated as subject countries, not allowed to use their own languages or to practise their traditional religions, and certainly not to develop their own independent trade or industry. This sort of nationalism, then, meant the breaking away of small nations from large empires, and setting up their own independent governments. On the other hand, there were two peoples, the Italians and the Germans, who had their own languages and history, but who, by this time, were divided up into a number of small states, some independent, some within one of the great empires. For them nationalism meant coming together as a single nation. There was, of course, a great deal in national feeling which had nothing to do with industrialisation or trade, but both these strong economic movements worked to break up the old system and re-arrange the map of Europe. The old empires

wanted to keep the smaller nations backward, and the fragmented state of Italy and Germany made trade and communications unnecessarily difficult.

The attitude of Britain

Britain, after 1832, was well on the road to industrialisation. What she looked for in her relations with other countries was peace and the maximum possibility of free trade, particularly the keeping open of sea routes. She did not want to see any power in Europe grow too strong and so become a threat to peace. Where there was no danger of war, on the whole British people, including many people in the government, had a lot of sympathy with those people in Europe who wanted to copy the British constitution.

Throughout the middle years of the century, from 1830 to 1865, British foreign policy was controlled, with only a short break, by Henry John Temple, Lord Palmerston.

Lord Palmerston

Palmerston was an Irish peer, and so did not have a seat in the House of Lords. For 58 of the 81 years of his life he was a member of the House of Commons, and for 48 of those years he was a member of the government. He was originally elected as a Tory, but changed to become a Whig under the leadership of Lord Grey because he supported the Reform Bill. Like many of the Whigs who helped to pass the 1832 Reform Bill, he considered that that Bill represented the last word in reform. To the end of his life he was strongly against giving the vote to any wider section of the people, and since he dominated the Whig party it was only after his death in 1865 that the question of more reform was seriously considered by the party as a whole.

In home politics, therefore, he was in effect very conservative, believing that the political system had reached perfection and should not be changed. Abroad, however, he was in favour of change, if it brought

109. Lord Palmerston making the ministerial statement on Dano-German affairs in the House of Commons 1864.

foreign governments more into line with the British system. Thus he was often to be found sympathising with and even helping liberal and nationalist movements in Europe, even when they actually involved revolutions, as they did in many countries in 1848.

For most of his period of office, Palmerston was foreign secretary. Almost his first act on becoming foreign secretary in 1830 was to recognise the independence of Belgium, which, as we saw in Chapter 8 was in revolt against Holland. In the final settlement, the Treaty of London in 1839, Britain and the other major powers of Europe guaranteed the independence and neutrality of Belgium.

1848

In 1848 there were revolutions in France,

Prussia, Austria, Hungary, Bohemia, Italy and France. All were inspired either by liberal or nationalist feelings, or by a combination of both. In the long run, the events of that year were to have a great effect on the history of Europe, but the changes which the revolutions brought about were mostly short-lived at the time and by the end of 1849 the revolutions had been crushed, or the new governments had slipped back into the old ways of ruling. In the years in which Italy was struggling to become a united country, Britain, under Palmerston's guidance, insisted on the policy of "Italy for the Italians". In particular in the years 1859–60, the British fleet protected Garibaldi, the Italian revolutionary leader, in his exploits in Sicily and Naples and British diplomatic pressure prevented either the Austrians or the French intervening in Italian affairs.

Eastern Europe

In Eastern Europe, where industrialisation had as yet made little progress, the three old European Empires were having trouble with their subject peoples. It is ironical that, although the great powers of Western Europe were already becoming rivals for world trade and were soon to become rivals for the actual control of vast areas of the world, they were provoked into war in 1853 as they were on a world scale in 1914 by events in the European backwater of the Balkan states.

Turkey, Russia and the Balkans

The Turkish Empire had existed in South Eastern Europe for more than three centuries. During those years the Christian people of the Balkan countries had been ruled by the Moslem Turks. Now, however, the Turks were not able to keep an effective force in all the countries under their rule. Nationalism was strong among the Balkan peoples, and Russia, the leader of the Christians in that part of Europe, made it clear that she would enjoy helping her smaller Christian neighbours to shake off the Moslem yoke.

But international affairs are rarely simple. The Austrians, unsure of their own Empire, were not prepared to let Russia take over control of the Turkish possessions, for fear she should become too strong. What is more, Britain was not happy about Russian expansion. If Russia moved into the Balkans, why should she not also move in the other direction, and challenge British rule in India? So, throughout the middle years of the century, Britain had looked anxiously at Eastern European affairs.

In 1853, the situation got suddenly much sharper. It was now clear that Turkey must soon leave her European possessions, and

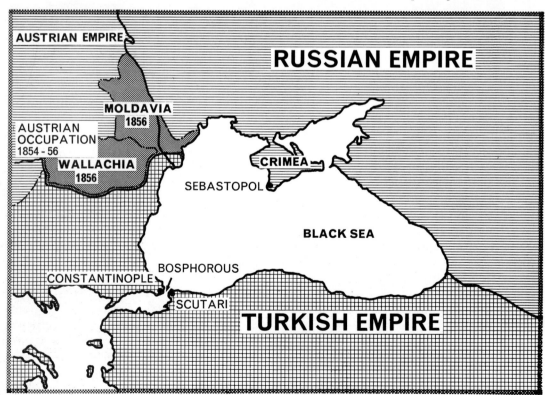

the Czar "sounded out" the British ambassador to Russia about the possibility of Britain and Russia coming to an agreement on the division of the Turkish Empire. This proposal was rejected by Britain and the Czar was left to carry on his own negotiations with Turkey.

Crimean War 1854–1856

In March 1853, the Czar of Russia made two demands to the Sultan of Turkey. One was that the holy places in Palestine (which was part of the Turkish Empire) should be cared for by Russian monks. The other was that the Czar should be recognised as the protector of all the Sultan's Christian subjects.

Neither of these demands looked sufficiently grave to provoke a major war. But all Europe was watching the situation. In France a new Emperor calling himself Napoleon III had just attained power, and was anxious to impress his countrymen. He declared that the Holy Places should be looked after by French monks of the Roman Catholic church, and expressed himself so strongly on the subject that he encouraged the Sultan to stand up to Russia. The British ambassador in Constantinople also encouraged the Sultan to believe that he would have British support. As a result, when Russian armies marched into two Christian provinces, the Sultan declared war on Russia, and began one of the most futile wars in world history.

From 1854 to 1856 Britain and France were at war with Russia, in a campaign which was fought in that part of southern Russia called the Crimea. The outstanding thing about the whole campaign was the extraordinary inefficiency with which it was fought.

British and French troops were badly led and badly equipped. Food was in short supply, medicines almost non-existent. The clothes with which the troops had been issued were quite unsuitable for the bitter climate of the Crimean winter. When new supplies were sent, they did not arrive or were unsuitable. On one famous occasion a load of badly-needed boots arrived for the British forces which turned out to be all for left feet. The French and British commanders could not agree on the conduct of the war, and in any case they were for the most part elderly veterans whose ideas were long out of date. The famous charge of the Light Brigade at Balaclava was the result of a mistaken signal; Tennyson celebrated the

110.   The Charge of the Light Cavalry Brigade, 25th October 1854.

111. Florence Nightingale (left) with her sister.

bravery of the soldiers in his famous poem:

> Forward the Light Brigade
> Was there a man dismayed?
> Not tho' the soldier knew
>   Some one had blundered:
> Their's not to make reply,
> Their's not to reason why,
> Their's but to do and die;
> Into the valley of Death
>   Rode the six hundred.

But the bravery had been pointless, the death of so many men made no difference at all to the result of the battle.

The news from the Crimea was sent home by *The Times* newspaper correspondent, W. H. Russell. He was one of the first men to take on the job of going with the armies into the battle area, and of sending back news of them. He was very critical of the lack of care from which the troops suffered, and of the appalling lack of efficiency with which supplies were handled.

At the beginning of January 1855, he wrote back:

While our friends at home are disputing about the exact mean degree of cold of the Crimean winter, and are preparing all kinds of warm clothing, which at some time or other will come out to the men, our army is rapidly melting away—dissolved in rain. At the present date there are no less than 3,500 sick men in the British camp before Sebastopol, and it is not too much to say that their illness has, for the most part, been caused by hard work in bad weather, and by exposure to wet without any adequate protection . . .

Two days later:

. . . The cavalry division lost about sixty horses during the night; and I dread to think of the number of our noble soldiers who will receive their *coup de grace* from this weather if it lasts . . . out of one division alone 150 men were taken out of the trenches to the hospital tents, seized with cramp and half frozen, not so much perhaps from the cold, as from the want of proper clothing and inability to move about to circulate the blood.

Readers of *The Times* were shocked and horrified by Russell's reports. In the poor streets of London, where *The Times* was not often read, the same story was told by the sellers of penny ballads:

> All you who sleep on swan's down, in
>   happiness and ease
> Remember our poor brothers whose very
>   blood doth freeze
> Who lie there in the trenches, sick, hungry,
>   stiff and dumb
> The life-blood of our country, to muddy
>   beds they come.
>
> From Balaclava harbour into the town they
>   went
> To draw the carts and cannons their own
>   poor backs were bent
> They bore it uncomplaining, then came the
>   silent night
> So many saw the sunset, so few the morning
>   light.
>
> I heard a maiden crying "O, hearken to
>   my tale,
> My father lies and slumbers in Inkerman's
>   cold vale

164

112. W. H. Russell, *The Times* correspondent
at the front.

113. Bashi-Bazouks – the Turkish mercenary
soldiers who were the spearhead of the Turkish
army.

My brother, he lies wounded beyond
recovery –
No Christ can cure the wounded who fell
in Skutari . . . ''

The effect of the news of all this confusion in England was considerable. There was an important section of British opinion which thought in any case that the war was not necessary. The Manchester businessmen, led by the cotton manufacturer and free-trader John Bright, thought that the whole Eastern Question could be solved peacefully. They regarded the war as a waste of money and manpower and an interference with trade. Richard Cobden declared that the war had brought with it "10 per cent income tax and 0 per cent benefit to mankind". But the idea of the war was popular with the country as a whole. The radicals welcomed an attack on Russia, the most reactionary power in Europe. But they, too, were appalled at the conditions under which the soldiers had to fight. The war showed up the inefficiency of the British Army and many reforms resulted from this. Probably the best-known were the reforms of the nursing services associated with the name of Florence Nightingale.

Florence Nightingale

Florence Nightingale was in her early thirties at the time of the Crimean war. Born into a wealthy family, she had already shown herself to be awkward and self-willed. She had refused to lead the idle life of an upper-class young lady, and had gone to Paris and Germany to study nursing methods and to train as a nurse. She had already begun a campaign to improve hospitals in England, and had gathered a small number of nurses trained in her methods when the stories began to reach England of the Crimean horrors. She approached the Secretary of State for War, Sidney Herbert, who agreed to allow her to take a group of thirty nurses to the war area. The story of her courage and intelligence in nursing the sick and wounded men and reorganising the hospitals is well-known. In after years, the campaign in the Crimea came to be remembered not for the names of great military or naval commanders, but for the name of Florence Nightingale, "the Lady with the Lamp".

Results of the Crimean War

The war ended in the spring of 1856. By the Treaty of Paris which followed it, the Russians agreed to give up their claims in the Holy Land and as protector of the Christians in the Turkish Empire. Responsibility for both these matters was given to a joint guarantee by the main European powers. Provisions were agreed that the River Danube should be open for European shipping and that the Black Sea should not be used by Russia as a naval base, but should be open to the merchant ships of all nations. These last two points very much lessened the power of Russia in the Balkans, at a time when Turkey's power was anyway falling off. It meant that the Balkan states could consider establishing themselves as independent nations, free of both Turkey and Russia.

Results of the War in England

The war had certainly lessened the power of Russia. But Britain had lost 22,000 men and spent £50 million pounds to achieve this result. The "cotton-spinners" thought the results had not been worth the cost, and many others came to agree with them. But the Crimean war did have another important effect. For one thing, after the experience of the Crimea, the system of granting commissions in the army was reformed. It was never again possible for control to rest with men whose only qualifications for leadership were money and influence. We have already mentioned the effect of Florence Nightingale on army nursing. She used her experience in later life to improve nursing generally. What was more, she had established the important fact that women had more to contribute to the welfare of the country than simply their roles as wives and mothers.

The Balkans after 1856

To the people of Western Europe, Russia seemed to be the enemy. Her government was a dictatorship, Jews and other minorities were persecuted, the press was censored, and in general she stood for everything that was anti-democratic in European politics. But for the people of the small countries of Eastern Europe, she was their only real hope of escaping from Turkish rule. And Turkey was just as harsh and cruel a ruler as Russia. She was also a Moslem power. And as Turkey got weaker, so she became more vicious. She had made various promises to respect the religious beliefs of her Christian subjects, but she soon began to persecute the Christians in the small Balkan powers.

In 1875 there was a revolt in Herzegovina (now part of Jugoslavia) when the local people first refused to pay taxes to Turkey and then defeated a Turkish army that was sent to punish them. In 1876 the Bulgarians also refused to pay their taxes to Turkey, and murdered more than a hundred Turkish government officials. The Turkish government was afraid that this would lead to similar outbreaks all over the Balkans, and indeed two other of the small countries there, Serbia and Montenegro (now also part of Jugoslavia) actually declared war on Turkey.

The Bulgarian Atrocities

The Turkish Empire was weak and inefficient. It could not put down all the revolts by force, and so decided to make an example of Bulgaria. A force of mercenary soldiers, the Bashi-Bazouks, was sent into that country to put down the rising and to punish the Bulgarians.

On June 23rd, 1876, the London newspaper, the *Daily News*, published the first account of what had happened in Bulgaria. The Turkish mercenaries had run wild, torturing and murdering men, women and children. In one town alone, twelve thousand people had been slaughtered, and their corpses left in heaps to rot.

The ordinary people of England were horrified by the news. John Bright, the Liberal leader, said that news of the Bulgarian atrocities caused "an uprising of the English people". There were meetings in all the main towns, called by Trade Unions and Trades Councils, to protest. Gladstone, who was living in retirement whilst Disraeli was Prime Minister, came back into public life and attacked Turkey. In speeches and in pamphlets, he led the country-wide campaign for Britain to force the Turks out of the Balkan countries. In one famous pamphlet on the Bulgarian massacres, he wrote a phrase which has gone down in history:

> Let the Turks now carry away their abuses in the only possible manner, namely by carrying off themselves . . . one and all, bag and baggage, shall, I hope, clear out of the province they have desolated and profaned . . .

Both Russia and Turkey are a long way from Britain. And yet, the quarrel between the two empires caused more excitement in England than almost any other event in the second part of the century. The Crimean War seemed to have actually achieved very little. If Turkey was forced out of Eastern Europe, Russia was there ready to move in. To the ordinary people of England both these great empires seemed cruel and dangerous. The Liberals were opposing Turkey, saying that it was absurd for England to try and bolster up the vicious rule of the dying Empire. But the Conservatives were for supporting Turkey as a weapon against Russia. As the quarrel got fiercer, many people on the Conservative side thought that we should again, as we had done in the Crimean war, join Turkey against Russia. At any rate, they said, we should not be caught out again, as we had been then, without proper arms and properly trained soldiers. On the music-hall stage a star

114. "The Great McDermott" – the music-hall singer who brought a new word into the English language with his song – "We don't want to fight, but by Jingo! if we do – "

called the Great McDermott made a great hit with a new song:

> We don't want to fight, but by Jingo, if we do,
> We've got the ships, we've got the men, we've got the money too

Because of this song, the war party were nicknamed "the Jingoes", a name they accepted. And ever since then the word "jingoism" has been used to mean a particular sort of warlike patriotism.

The Russo-Turkish War

In 1877 Russia declared war on Turkey. The war went on for a year, by the end of which time Turkey was defeated. England did not join in, nor did the other great powers of Europe, but after the end of the war, they refused to agree to the peace settlement, imposed on Turkey by Russia, and called another conference. At the conference, the Congress of Berlin, Disraeli prevented the Russians from destroying the Turkish Empire, but Britain herself took Cyprus from Turkey.

The Russo-Turkish war and the two conferences which followed it did not end the matter. In fact, the various problems in Eastern Europe helped to cause the First World War in 1914.

British Foreign Policy in the Nineteenth Century

After Waterloo, Britain was only involved in one great European war in the nineteenth century – the Crimean War. Beyond Europe she was involved in a number of colonial conflicts, some of which are described in the next chapter. Britain did not intervene in some of the great struggles of this period such as the American Civil War or the war between Prussia and France in 1870–1, nor did she become a member of any of the alliances between the great powers of Continental Europe. As we have seen, she did intervene in some of the nationalist uprisings – in Italy, Belgium and South America for instance – but only when her sea power could be used effectively and especially where her own trading interests were involved.

Chapter 16

Britain and the Empire

We saw, in Chapter 5, a little about the "old" British Empire. With the loss of the American colonies and the ending of the slave trade, the Empire became an unimportant part of English politics. Britain continued to defend trading posts and to send armies and governors overseas, but most politicians saw the Empire as a responsibility rather than a source of profit. By the end of the nineteenth century, however, the British Empire had become the country's greatest glory, and Great Britain had become the world's strongest Imperialist power, drawing millions of pounds in profits from the world's largest empire. How did this change come about?

Imperialism

The last quarter of the nineteenth century has often been called the "Age of Imperialism". All the great powers of Europe developed overseas Empires in this period, and the ideal of free trade between nations gave way to the reality of protected trade within empires.

From time to time in the history of the period we are studying, we have come across problems of *historical interpretation*. These are questions on which historians disagree fundamentally. Some disagreements are about the facts of history, and some about the meaning of the facts. We saw problems of this sort, for example, in the question of why the population in Europe began to rise so enormously in the second half of the eighteenth century, and the question of whether the working people were better or worse off during the years of the industrial revolution than they had been before it began. The question of Imperialism is another example of a problem on which historians of today disagree, and one about which people living at the time also had serious disagreements.

Was the Empire profitable? Did it benefit the people of England? Was it built up in order to make profits, or was it built up in order to help backward peoples, or did it just grow up by accident?

We do not have clear answers to any of these questions. Of course, the empire was very profitable indeed to some people. Millions of pounds in profits poured into England in the years between 1870 and the first world war, and huge fortunes were made. But this money went directly to only a section of the population. In order for these profits to be made, the country as a whole had to pay for large regular armies to conquer and protect the colonies, and to keep down the native people. English soldiers were always in action, and many thousands died on active service in various parts of the world.

The Case against the Empire

The Liberal free-traders were on the whole against the building up of an empire. They did not like the need for continual wars, and for the maintenance of a huge army and navy. They tended to believe that all countries should be left to develop in their own time, and to object to the attempts by the great powers to overcome and keep down the less developed countries. They thought that countries like Canada and Australia that had been settled by Europeans should be allowed to become independent countries, to "drop off" the tree of the Empire, like "ripe plums". The great example, they thought, was the United States of America. Here was a country which had started out as a group of colonies. British people had gone out and settled in America, and had been helped by British money and arms to defeat the native Red Indians. Then they had developed their own agriculture and industry, and finally their own government. When they felt ready for independence, they had broken away from Britain, and ever since they had traded on equal terms with the "mother country". The result of the American experience, said the Liberals, showed that free trade between equal powers was a better way of doing business than the forced trading of a colony with a powerful mother country. They looked forward to the time when all the existing colonies would become independent, and they did not want Britain to acquire any new colonies.

The Liberals' main objection, then, to the Empire was that it was expensive and unnecessary. They were joined by radicals of all kinds in the early part of the nineteenth century when they objected also to the cruelty with which the native populations in the conquered territories were treated. Ernest Jones, a Chartist leader, wrote about the Empire on whose colonies "the sun never sets, but the blood never dries . . . ". Respect for the peoples of the colonial territories tended, however, to get less as the century advanced and Imperialism became more popular. In many places Christian missionaries who had gone out to convert the natives to Christianity protested against the brutalities of the conquering armies, and stood up for the rights of the conquered peoples, but in general, neither the possessions nor the traditions of the original inhabitants were respected by the conquerors. Even if education was provided, as it was in parts of British India, it was education in British ways, British language and British religion. The history, culture and language of the Indian people themselves were neither taught nor understood. So that as well as being wasteful and unnecessary, the Empire was seen by its opponents as being brutalising for the men who had to conquer it and for the people who lived in it.

The Case for Imperialism

But the free-trade Liberals and those who thought like them about the Empire were in a minority by the 1880's. By then many people, including radicals like Sir Charles Dilke and Joseph Chamberlain, who were republicans and in favour of very radical social policies in England itself, were enthusiastic about the idea of a world-wide empire for Britain.

What were the main arguments in favour of an Empire?

In the main they can be looked at under three heads, *economic* – that is, the empire as a source of wealth, *political*, the empire as a source of national prestige, and *ideal* – the empire as a source of adventure and excitement. All these three ideas overlap and intermingle, so that by the end of the nineteenth century, it was taken for granted by probably the majority of British people that the empire was a good thing for a whole mixture of reasons, which they did not examine too closely.

Let us look briefly at these three defences of the Empire. First, the economic. There is no doubt that throughout the years, wealth had poured into England from the Old Empire. India alone had supplied millions of pounds. But it was always arguable that the cost to the country as a whole was greater than the profits, which only went to a small section of the people of England. After 1880 Britain and the other European powers began to take over Africa, and to stake out claims in countries with difficult climates and without a great deal of natural wealth. Many modern scholars consider that the profits made from these territories were never worth the cost of conquering them. Certainly the United States, which did not have a great empire in the sense in which the European powers had, grew in wealth at least as fast as the colonial powers in the same period. Britain did, without doubt, gain economically from the Empire. She was able to buy very cheap raw materials – mainly foodstuffs and minerals, and she was able to sell her manufactured goods to her colonies, and to prevent them from buying manufactured goods from other countries. But it could be argued that she might have achieved much the same results by trading agreements with the backward countries, without the expense of conquering them and keeping an army and government services in them. But, once the "grab for Africa" had started, the economic motive became entangled with the political.

The political motive saw the achievement of a great empire as a sign of national greatness. All the old rivalries of the great powers in Europe were reflected in the desire to dominate the largest possible share of the world, whatever the cost. The major European powers annexed land in Africa and in the Far East, and had also to conquer and control areas nearer home which were important as routes to these colonies. The Middle East became important both as an area for colonial development, and as part of the route to Africa and the Far East.

The ideal view of the empire recognised that it was a source of wealth and of national greatness, but saw it also as more than that. The empire was a great civilising mission, and through her ownership of so many lands, England would bring civilisation, learning and Christianity to the backward peoples of the world. Charles Kingsley expressed it when he wrote of:

> brave young England longing to wing its way out of its island prison, to discover and to traffic, to colonise and to civilise, until no wind can sweep the earth which does not bear the echoes of an English voice.

In this view of the matter, the Empire was an inspiration and a safety-valve. The unemployed workman in a crowded city would find his ugly life more bearable when he thought of himself as a citizen of the world's greatest empire. And the great open spaces of the empire provided a challenge for the more adventurous or discontented inhabitants of these overcrowded islands.

The Growth of the Empire

So much for some of the ideas about the empire. Let us now look briefly at the actual territories concerned.

The break-away of the North American colonies in 1783 left England with two particular problems. One was what was to happen to the people who had fought for the British side. For many of these life in the United States was no longer possible after the American victory, and between 40 and 60 thousand of them moved northwards into Canada. Canada was still a British possession, but most of the people living there were in fact French, until this large influx of British.

The other problem was that, until the break-away of the American colonies, the British government had been accustomed to transport long-term convicts there. Fortunately for the operation of British justice, Captain Cook had, a few years earlier, reported the discovery of the eastern coast of Australia, which he had called New South Wales. In 1788 the first shipment of convicts was sent there from England. From that date until 1868 men were transported to various parts of Australia for criminal offences.

So the loyalists of Upper Canada and the convicts of New South Wales formed the basis of two of England's greatest overseas settlements. As the years went by, many thousands of other people from Britain joined them, especially when rich strikes of gold were made in Canada and Australia.

In 1839 Britain annexed New Zealand, and already in 1820 British settlers had

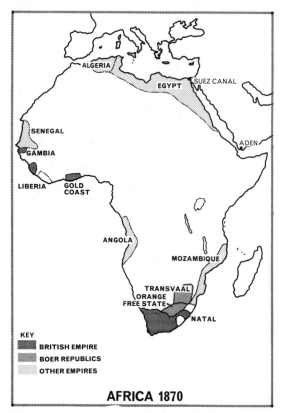

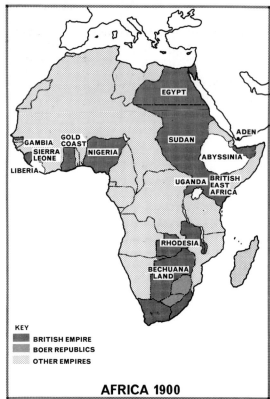

founded a small settlement in South Africa, where they existed as a minority amongst the Dutch settlers.

Thus, all through the earlier years of the nineteenth century there was a flow of British emigrants going into Canada, Australia, New Zealand and parts of Africa. At the same time, by a process of expansion which seems inevitable in any Empire, British rule in India was spreading. The East India Company ceased to have a trading monopoly after 1833, but remained as the government of India until 1858.

The Grab for Africa

Until the last quarter of the nineteenth century, British possessions in Africa had been largely *strategic*. That is, they were seen as necessary posts to protect and simplify the passage of British ships to India and the Far East, rather than as sources of wealth in themselves. They, and the posts of other colonial powers, were situated along the

northern coast of Africa, at scattered points on the Western coast, and around the Cape of Good Hope, which latter was the area of the greatest amount of actual settlement in Africa. All the vast interior of the African continent was known as "the Dark Continent", and was almost entirely unknown to the white peoples.

Beginning in the 1870's, however, came what was known as the "grab" or "scramble" for Africa, and during the last years of the century almost the whole continent was divided up between the great powers of Europe.

During this period, the British Empire was increased by around 5,000,000 square miles, and 90,000,000 people; France took over some 3,500,000 square miles and 40,000,000 people; Germany got 1,000,000 square miles and 17,000,000 people; Belgium, in the Congo, got not far short of 1,000,000 square miles and 30,000,000 people; Portugal got 800,000 square miles of Africa

The dark shaded area on the map was governed directly by the East India Company in 1857. The lighter areas were ruled by Indian princes who had signed treaties with the British. During the mutiny most of the princes remained loyal to their alliance and some sent troops to help the British.

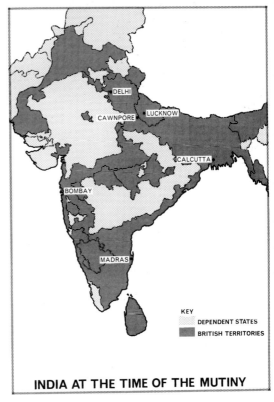

INDIA AT THE TIME OF THE MUTINY

KEY
DEPENDENT STATES
BRITISH TERRITORIES

and 8,000,000 Africans. From being a dark and unknown area, the African continent became the hope of adventurers, explorers, speculators and investors throughout Europe.

It goes without saying that all these annexations were not accomplished without continuous fighting. The series of colonial wars which accompanied the process of grabbing need not be listed here. But Britain fought two major wars in the Empire before the end of the nineteenth century – the so-called "Indian Mutiny" of 1857, and the Boer War of 1899–1901.

British Rule in India

In 1857, Britain had been in control of India for one hundred years. She had taken control first from the French and then from various Indian rulers, and now ruled over the greater part of the continent.

India was the greatest source of wealth within the Empire and during the first hundred years of British rule, had been sending a regular tribute of three or four million pounds in trading profits to England each year. Because a trading company had controlled the policy of Britain in India during those years, the results of British rule had been strongly to favour British trade. The Indian cotton textile industry had been destroyed, to allow Manchester cotton goods to be sold in India. Labour had been diverted from raising grain and other food crops to raising opium, sugar, indigo and tea for export. No railways were built in India until after 1850, and then it was the need to transport raw cotton for export to England and also the possibility of reducing the number of British troops in India which finally prompted the government to encourage the building of a railway system. The Indian railways were started on a large scale in 1853. The money for the building came from investors in England, but they were guaranteed by law a return of five per cent on their money. They were to get this return

115. India was a rich source of trade and profits. The scene in Calcutta harbour in 1860 shows British merchant ships waiting to load.

116. The building of the Indian railways was the source of a great deal of profit to British shareholders. This station at Hyderabad is an example of the grand scale of much of the work (right, top).

117. Rebel sepoy soldiers attack at Delhi in 1857.

even if the railway did not make a profit, as the Indian government agreed to raise the necessary money by taxes.

The construction of the Indian railways took millions of pounds from India which went in dividends to the British who had invested money in the projects. The benefits to India from the railways were of a longer-term nature. It became easier to maintain law and order when troops could be moved quickly about the country. Many old customs died out as the country was opened up, ideas as well as people were able to move more freely. And probably the greatest contribution of all was that the railway opened the way for the possible abolition of famine, by providing for the speedy movement of food supplies.

Within British India there lived many different nationalities and many different religions. Some of the cultures and religions were very much older than the culture of Britain or the Christian religion. But Englishmen of the nineteenth century did not, in the main, consider that they had anything to learn from the ancient cultures of the East. One feature, therefore, which was common to most of the men who went out to rule India was a total disregard for the way of life of the people over whom they exercised authority. As British rule became more widespread, and more families came out to join the men who served in the army and the administration, more and more Indians became servants to the white men, and more and more Indians were enlisted to serve in the army. In the early days of the Indian army, soldiers were enlisted to serve under their own officers, but by the middle of

the century this practice had been done away with, and the Indian army consisted of Indian soldiers with British officers and non-commissioned officers.

By 1857, then, the picture was of a great continent of two hundred million inhabitants, of whom only a few thousand were white; but the white minority controlled every position of power within the British-controlled areas, and it was their culture and language which were taught at all schools, and their religion which was officially recognised and encouraged. A historian who lived through the years of the mutiny described the total lack of understanding which existed between the Hindus – one of the main religions in India – and the British:

> To many a man fresh from the ways of England, the Hindoo doctrines and practices appeared so ineffably absurd that he could not believe any human beings were serious in their devotion to them, and he took no pains to conceal his opinion as to the absurdity of the creed, and the hypocrisy of those who professed it . . .

It never occurred to the English that their own habits and beliefs might appear absurd and hypocritical to people raised in a different culture, and so they added a complete lack of sympathy or understanding to the indignities of conquest.

The Indian Mutiny of 1857

Many Indians believed that they were due for deliverance from British rule in 1857, because of prophecies that the rule would last for one hundred years. There was almost certainly a great deal of preparation, about which little is known still, for a rising in the early months of 1857. The rising when it did come began in the army, and for this reason the civil war which followed has been called the "Indian Mutiny". But it was on a far greater scale than this name would suggest.

You have probably heard the stories of the grievances which sparked off the army revolt. It was supposed that cartridges issued to the troops had been greased with fat from cows or pigs. Since the cartridges had to be bitten off, this went against the religious practices of two of the major religions, for the Hindus were not allowed to eat the meat of the cow, which was sacred, and the Muslims were forbidden to touch pork, which was considered unclean. There were also changes in the conditions of enlistment, and soldiers were being faced with the possibility of being sent to service overseas in Burma, which again clashed with the rules of their religion.

The offending cartridges had been in use for some weeks before the mutiny proper occurred. Complaints by the soldiers were first punished by disbanding the regiments and sending the soldiers back to their villages. In May 1857, however, soldiers at Meerut, who had refused to use the cartridges, were court-martialled and eighty-five troopers were sentenced to ten years' imprisonment. The day after these sentences had been passed, the three Indian regiments at Meerut shot their English officers, broke open the gaol, released the imprisoned men and set off for Delhi, the ancient capital of India.

This was the outbreak of a civil war. Soldiers acting in this way were not simply mutinying, they were declaring war upon the British. Throughout the summer of that year fighting took place throughout central India, Oudh and the Ganges valley. The Indians, after a century of submission to the white rulers, seem to have been very much in awe of the British troops, and often failed to attack small forces of British, even when they might have had a very good chance of winning. The successful battles were mainly led by Indian princes, for there was not a united nationalist movement. Victories for the Indians were often followed by outbreaks of fighting amongst the different groups and religions. The Hindus, who were the most prominent amongst the rebels, were very much disliked by some of the other religious groups, particularly the poorer ones, and the British were able to raise armies from amongst the Sikhs and Muslims to oppose the mainly Hindu Indian armies.

This lack of unity of purpose amongst the Indians themselves, was probably the main reason for the British victory. The British were overwhelmingly outnumbered, but they were efficient and daring soldiers, who seized every opportunity to attack, and took advantage of any divisions amongst their enemies. The war was fought with great brutality on both sides. At Cawnpore British military prisoners were murdered, and later the women and children of the garrison were also murdered before the defeated forces of the Indians retreated. On the British side, too, there was a grim record of brutality. The chaplain of a British regiment recorded his horror after the seige of Delhi, when

> A general massacre of the inhabitants of Delhi, a large number of whom were known to wish us success, was openly proclaimed. Blood-thirsty boys might be heard recommending that all the native orderlies . . . in our camp should be shot . . .

Lord Roberts, later commander-in-chief of the British forces in the Boer War, was a young lieutenant during the Mutiny, and he wrote home to his mother:

> We have come along this far, doing a little business on the road, such as disarming regiments and executing mutineers. The death that seems to have most effect is being blown from a gun . . .

By 1858 the rebellion was over, and British rule was firmly restored. But a legacy of bitterness remained which was never wiped out. Before 1857, many Europeans believed that it would be possible for Britons living in India to come to terms with the Indians, and through education and understanding, to make a permanent civilisation there. After the Mutiny this solution never seemed possible, and the Indian national movement which grew up during the later years of the ninetecnth century, grew up as a movement aimed at forcing Britain out of India.

South Africa

Most of the colonial wars of the nineteenth century were wars between white would-be conquerors and the peoples who were native to the colonial countries. This was true in

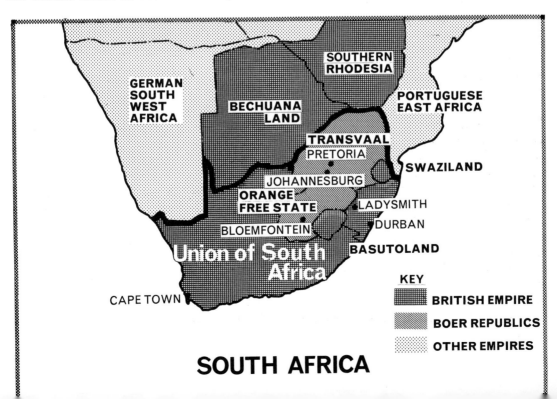

SOUTH AFRICA

118. Boer soldiers.

most of Africa where, apart from a certain amount of friction with the French in North Africa which did not burst into actual war, Britain was mainly concerned either with suppressing nationalist movements, in the North, or with driving back the fierce tribes in the interior and in the South. In one part of South Africa, however, Britain was faced with the added complication of a population of hostile settlers of Dutch origin, the Boers.

Boer is the Dutch word for farmer, and these men were the descendants of the original settlers of the Cape province in South Africa, who had been Dutch. During the Napoleonic wars Britain had annexed the Cape, to protect her sea route to India, and had later paid compensation for it to the Dutch. During the first half of the nineteenth century there had been various quarrels between the Dutch settlers and the English, and eventually many of the Boers had moved out of British territory altogether, and had set up two independent Boer states, called the Orange Free State and the Transvaal. Here they farmed in their own way,

and had elected governments of their own.

Relations between Britain and the Boer republics were never good. There were various reasons for this. Britain had an organised military force in South Africa, whilst the Boers did not, and on more than one occasion British troops defended the Boers against attacks from the Africans. In spite of this military help, the Boers did not want any political control by Britain. In 1880 this led to the first Boer War. In the course of the Zulu war a year earlier, Britain had annexed the Transvaal, and the Boers rose in protest against this. They attacked and wiped out a British garrison, and as the result, they were again given their independence.

As long as the main occupation of the settlers, British and Dutch, was farming, the quarrels between them were fairly simple. But a new element had entered the picture when diamonds were discovered in various parts of the district, and big strikes of gold were made. Quite a different kind of settler came to South Africa. More and more terri-

178

tory was annexed or "protected" by Britain, until by the middle of the 1890's the two Boer republics were surrounded by British and British-controlled territory.

Cecil Rhodes

Foremost amongst the new wave of British settlers was Cecil Rhodes. He, more than any one other person, stands for the nature of British Imperialism at this time. Immensely rich — ·he made a tremendous private fortune out of South African diamonds — an active and ardent politician — he was Prime Minister of the Cape Colony in 1895 — he carried his ideas about Imperialism much further than the mere accumulation of wealth or the gaining of political power. He had dreams of an Africa completely ruled by Britain. Like many of the great imperialists of the period he hated women and had no time for the ordinary ideals of family life. He had those qualities about him which make great leaders — he seems to have inspired enormous devotion among his followers, and to have been a popular Prime Minister, in spite of his dictatorial and domineering tendencies.

Paul Kruger

Leader of the Boer republics was their president, Paul Kruger. He was an old man, fanatically hostile to Britain and all things British, especially to the commercialism of men like Rhodes. He wanted the Boers to be left in peace with their families to farm their land; he was not prepared to admit that the people who came into the territory to dig for diamonds and gold had as much right to be there as the farmers. Since most of the people associated with the mines were British and German they were called Uitlanders — foreigners — and, although they were very heavily taxed by Kruger's government, they had no votes and no right to take part in the government.

The Jameson Raid

In 1895 Rhodes organised a scheme to take over part of the Transvaal for Britain. An

119. Paul Kruger, leader of the Boers.

agent of his, Dr Starr Jameson, organised a semi-military police force, and gathered it together on the Transvaal border. Rhodes meanwhile had spent a great deal of money in organising a revolt amongst the discontented Uitlanders in Johannesburg. His plan was that as soon as the rebellion began there, the police would march in from Bechuanaland to make sure that the Boers did not come in from the farms outside Johannesburg. Together the rebellious Uitlanders and the police would force the Boer government to allow at least a British sector around the mining areas of Johannesburg.

Unfortunately for Rhodes, and for British ambitions in the district, the plan misfired. The Uitlanders included a good many Germans, and they were not unnaturally suspicious of Rhodes' plan to bring them under British rule. They gave away details of the proposed rebellion to Germany, whose government was sympathetic to the Boers. Then Dr Jameson, instead of waiting until the rebellion took place, decided to

120.　An incident in the Boer War — an artist's idea of an early and unsuccessful attempt to relieve Mafeking.

act anyway, and rode into the Republic of the Transvaal at the head of about five hundred "police". He had no excuse – there was no rebellion, no need to help British subjects. His raid looked like a piece of straightforward and unprovoked aggression. The Boer military forces surrounded the raiders and compelled them to surrender. The British government had to pretend that they were quite unaware of the plans of Jameson and Rhodes, although there is good reason to believe that the colonial secretary, Joseph Chamberlain, did in fact know of the plan. The German Emperor sent a telegram of congratulation to Kruger.

The result of the Jameson raid was to arouse suspicions of Britain in other European countries; especially in Germany. It also gave the Boers confidence in their opposition to Britain, and so helped to cause the second Boer War.

The Second Boer War 1899–1902

Apart from the Indian Mutiny, which had been fought mainly by the forces stationed permanently in India, Britain had not been at war since the Crimean War. She did not at first consider a possible clash with the Boer farmers as being a major war.

Kruger, on the other hand, did not underestimate his enemy. For three years after the Jameson raid he kept up negotiations with Britain, although it became increasingly clear that there was no possibility of reconciling the two views. At the same time, however, he made sure that the Boer forces were being trained, and arms were being bought. The main leaders of the proposed rising in Johannesburg had been arrested and sentenced to death. Kruger commuted their sentence to the payment of enormous fines, and with these he bought artillery, Maxim guns, rifles and ammunition. Then, when he felt he was ready, he chose the time for the conflict by invading Natal and the Cape, and immediately besieged the British garrison towns at Ladysmith, Mafeking and Kimberley.

In defence of the British unpreparedness, it may perhaps be said that the previous wars in Africa had been fairly easily won. But now the enemy was not a tribe of Africans armed only with primitive weapons, but a force of determined Europeans, fighting over a country they knew well. The British Army, wearing scarlet uniforms, made easy targets in the open country. Most of the British troops were infantry, whilst the Boers were mounted. With greater freedom of movement, greater knowledge of the country and bigger and better-equipped forces, the Boers inflicted a series of crushing defeats on the British in the first few months of the war.

In England interest in the Boer war was greater than anything that had occurred in the past. Two years before, the Diamond Jubilee of Queen Victoria had been a veritable pageant of Empire. Through the streets of London a great parade had passed, including people from every part of the Empire, Africans and Indians in traditional costumes as well as military uniforms of all kinds. At last the Imperialism which Disraeli had tried to encourage amongst the English people had taken root, and there was an enthusiasm for the Empire among all kinds of people which was something quite new in English history. During the Indian War of 1857, a German visitor to London had noticed that only the upper and middle class people were interested in the news of the war. He thought the working people of England were unpatriotic and quite unconcerned about the fighting in India. Now, however, the working people were ardently interested in the war in Africa. The defeats which the Boers inflicted on the British forces in the early months of the war produced violent anti-Boer feelings. Ordinary working-class lads with no military training or military family traditions volunteered to fight in South Africa. Ironically, it was the appalling state of health of the majority of these volunteers which brought home to the authorities the dreadful state of poverty and undernourishment in which the people of England's great cities were living.

Opposition to the War

But although there is no doubt at all that the Boer War was thoroughly popular with

121. David Lloyd George – a Welsh lawyer with great powers as a speaker, who was a leading opponent of the Boer War.

most English people, there was a minority which determinedly opposed it. A few Conservative and considerably more Liberal politicians attacked it from the beginning. They maintained that it would have been perfectly possible for Britain to maintain a friendly attitude to the Boer republics, and to press for reforms of the regulations governing the Uitlanders. They found it difficult to believe that England needed to go to war to enforce the right to vote of a number of miners in South Africa, when no women had the right to vote in England, and the working people had only had that right for fifteen years. They maintained that the whole campaign was a plot by the gold and diamond firms to get British soldiers to establish their right to exploit the whole of

Southern Africa. Outstanding amongst the Liberals who opposed the war was a young Welshman, who had entered the House of Commons for the first time in 1890.

David Lloyd George

David Lloyd George was to be one of the most important – and one of the most war-like – politicians of the first half of the twentieth century. The main story of his political life belongs outside this volume. But his activities during the Boer War were a very important part of his career, and they also throw an interesting light on the changes in public opinion which took place during the war.

The first stage of the war saw an explosion of "jingoism" in England, as we have seen. The defeats inflicted on the British forces during the early months only increased this. For Lloyd George and others who opposed the war the public at large had nothing but hatred. They were labelled "Pro-Boers", and were in constant danger of actual physical violence.

Lloyd George maintained his opposition to the war by speaking at a series of great public meetings in the major towns of Britain. Although the halls were always full of supporters, they were also surrounded by gangs of opponents – in Glasgow Tory students, in Birmingham supporters and employees of Joseph Chamberlain, colonial secretary and one of the founders of the firm of Birmingham Small Arms Ltd. On at least one occasion Lloyd George was lucky to escape with his life.

At the beginning of 1900, the war entered its second phase. British reinforcements had been rushed to South Africa, and Lord Roberts was sent in as supreme commander. In February Kimberley and Ladysmith were relieved, and in May the town of Mafeking was at last relieved. The celebrating and rejoicing which took place in London on the night on which the news of the relief of Mafeking reached England was so wild that it introduced a new word into the English language. "Mafficking" is still used to describe uncontrolled mob celebrations, in which drinking and lighting bonfires play the major part.

In June 1900, Roberts went on to capture Pretoria, the capital of the Transvaal, and the war seemed all but over. The Boers had withdrawn entirely from the provinces they had invaded, and their armies were scattered.

The British forces had triumphed, and many people felt that peace had been achieved. The military High Command, however, insisted on unconditional surrender by the Boers, and the war continued. This was the time chosen in England by the government for an election – the first so-called "khaki election". They thought that their popularity would be at its height as the result of the victories in South Africa.

Lloyd George, and those who thought like him in the House of Commons, had to face the electors, and justify their anti-war views in order to get re-elected.

At a famous meeting at Nevin, in his constituency of Caernarvon Boroughs, Lloyd George faced a hostile audience and explained to them why he thought the government should make peace terms with the Boers. He ended his speech with the words:

Five years ago, the electors of the Caernarvon Boroughs gave to me my strip of blue paper, the certificate of my election, to hand to the speaker of Parliament as your accredited representative. If I never again represent the Caernarvon Boroughs in the House of Commons, I shall at least have the satisfaction of handing back to you that blue paper with no stain of human blood on it.

The audience leaped to their feet and applauded, and within a few days Lloyd George was again their member of Parliament.

The change in Wales was representative of a change that was taking place all over Britain. The war government was returned, it is true, but it was not swept in with the overwhelming majority it had hoped for.

Public opinion was becoming more critical, the war fever was dying.

The final stage of the war, a year and a half after the Khaki election, brought many people into sympathy with Lloyd George and the other objectors.

The Independent Labour Party Opposition

From the very beginning, the war had been opposed by the young Independent Labour Party, and its leaders, Keir Hardie, Bruce Glasier, Ramsey MacDonald, Philip Snowden and a number of others. These were the people who were working for the representation in Parliament of the working people by a party of their own. They were united in agreeing that the South African War could not bring any good to the people of Britain, and they expressed their sympathy for the Boer farmers fighting for their country. This attitude, of course, got them branded as "Pro-Boers" in the early part of the war, and they lost a great deal of support among the working people. Keir Hardie, particularly, their most able speaker, was subjected to the same sort of violence as Lloyd George, and spoke with him on many of the same platforms.

By 1900, however, the I.L.P. was beginning to get more support for its attitude. In the spring of that year, the I.L.P. together with representatives from Trade Unions and other groups, met to discuss the setting up of a Labour Representation Committee, to see that working men were put up for Parliament. Before they could get the committee working properly, however, the election came along. Lloyd George's victory in Wales showed that the Liberal electors were moving away from unquestioning support for the war. Further south, at Merthyr Tydfil, an even more striking victory was recorded. Keir Hardie was returned as candidate of the Labour Representation Committee. Richard Bell, a railwaymen's leader, was returned as L.R.C. candidate at Derby.

Hardie's return in 1900 was not his first entry into the House of Commons (see

122. Keir Hardie, a Scottish miner, was the first Independent Labour Member of Parliament. His clothes, manners and accent were as strange to the members of the established parties as his politics.

Chapter 14). But its importance now was that, from that year onwards the Labour representation in the House of Commons remained and grew. It was no longer a matter of the odd Radical or Socialist slipping in, but a solidly based party was at last established. The story of the growth of the Parliamentary Labour Party begins in 1900 – in the middle of the South African War. It was partly the split amongst the Liberals on this question of Imperialism, which enabled Labour to emerge as an anti-imperialist party.

The Last Stage of the War

With the British victories of 1900, the war

entered its final phase. The Boers split up into small groups, and fought a long-drawn-out guerilla campaign over country they knew well. This kind of war has become well known in modern times, and so have some of the methods with which the British tried to defeat it.

The Boers formed small fighting groups, called Commandos, lightly armed and swift-moving. They fought by making quick raids on military centres, and then slipping away into the protection of the countryside and the villages. In order to deal with these groups, the British set up "concentration camps" – barbed wire compounds in which the families of suspected guerrillas were imprisoned. It was calculated that twice as many Boer women and children died in these camps, as Boer soldiers were killed in the fighting. The British also burnt farms and destroyed crops in order to force the Boers into surrender.

This last long-drawn-out struggle lasted eighteen months after British victory had been assured. Critics in England and even more people in other European countries, maintained that if Britain were to offer generous peace terms, the war could be ended and much suffering avoided. Finally, on 19th May 1902 peace was signed at Vereeniging.

Peace Terms

The terms of the Treaty of Vereeniging were: Britain annexed the Transvaal and the Orange Free State, that is they became member states of the British Empire. But they were given a guarantee that they would soon be allowed to elect their own government. This right they got in 1907. Afrikaans, the form of Dutch spoken by the Boers, was to be the official language in the two districts, and a grant of three million pounds was made to help repair the damage done to lands and farms during the last stage of the war.

The war had lasted thirty-one months. It had cost two hundred and fifty million pounds. Twenty-two thousand British soldiers had died – five thousand on the battlefield, the rest from wounds or disease. The victory which had looked so assured at first, had been won at very heavy cost.

The Rest of the Empire

You will see from the map on page 185 that, in concentrating on India and South Africa, we have failed to mention a whole number of other parts of the British Empire as it was by the end of the nineteenth century. The forms of government which made up the empire at this period were in the main three, so let us summarise the position under these three heads.

The Dominions

Britain had by the early twentieth century, three great dominions. These were the "ripe plums" of which earlier Liberals had dreamed – that is areas which had been settled and conquered by British people, and which had developed their own independent governments. *Canada* had become a dominion by being granted her own independent government, in 1867. Canada was by then a federation of four provinces. Others were added later, and modern Canada now consists of ten provinces.

Australia became a federation of provinces in 1900, and became a dominion with her own central government in 1901. *New Zealand* did not become a dominion until 1907.

The Colonies

In 1887, the year of Queen Victoria's Golden Jubilee, a Colonial conference was held when many statesmen from the Empire were in London for the Jubilee. After that regular conferences were held, usually about every four years, known as the Imperial conferences. At these meetings the prime minister of England attended, and the prime ministers of the dominions, together with the Secretary of State for India and the Colonial Secretary. This illustrates the difference between the various parts of the Empire at that time. The dominions had their own governments, and their own prime ministers. India and the rest of the Empire were represented by members of the British Government.

India was a special case, and was ruled under its own laws and constitution. But it was always regarded as a part of the English government, and very few Indians took any part in the government of their country during the nineteenth century. The other colonies, in Africa, the West Indies and the Far East, had no local government at all, but were ruled by officials sent out from Britain.

Between the colonies, ruled from Britain, and the dominions, with their own governments, came the protectorates. These were areas in which the great powers exercised control without taking over the entire government of the country, and with the view to leaving at any time, if they felt satisfied that a stable government existed with whom they could deal. Egypt and the Sudan became protectorates of Britain jointly at the end of the nineteenth century. Both were areas of no great natural wealth, but with importance as routes to other parts of the empire. With the encouragement of the Egyptian authorities, French engineers designed and built the Suez canal, which was opened in 1869. To begin with, the shares in the canal were held mainly by French capitalists and by the Khedive, the ruler of Egypt. In 1875, however, the Khedive went bankrupt, and Disraeli bought his shares on behalf of the British Government, for £4,000,000. This gave Britain a controlling interest in the canal. Thus she had good reason to want to see a stable government in Egypt, and one that was sympathetic to the countries of Europe whose shipping used the Suez canal for the route to the Far East.

Each country in the British Empire would need a book to itself, if we were to try and describe all that happened there during this period. All that has been possible has been to try and indicate some of the ways in which the possession of a great empire overseas affected the lives of the people of the British Isles. There are many excellent books in which you can read a fuller account of some of the dramatic and exciting events which coloured the history of Britain's imperial expansion. There is, however, one imperial possession which we have not looked at yet in this chapter, and which does stand in a very special relationship to England. This is Ireland.

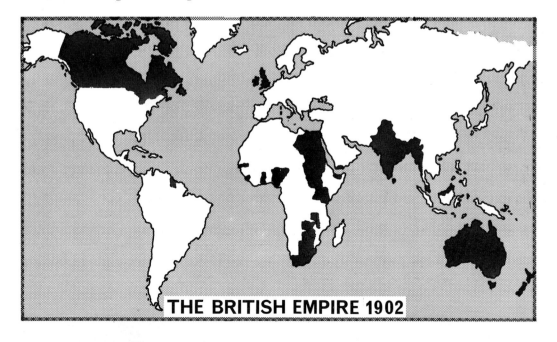

THE BRITISH EMPIRE 1902

Chapter 17
Ireland in the Nineteenth-Century

The Act of Union of 1800, which we described in Chapter 6 made Ireland as much a part of England's government and administration as Scotland and Wales. But the Irish never accepted this situation as the Scots and the Welsh people did. Both Scotland, and to a greater extent Wales, felt some dissatisfaction at being ruled from Westminster. Nationalism was strong in Wales during the nineteenth century, and the demand for a Welsh parliament and the right to much greater local control by the Welsh people was never absent from Welsh politics for long. But this nationalism was of quite a different order from that of Ireland.

The nationalism of the Irish was intensified by the fact that the great majority — about three quarters of the Irish people — were Catholics, and England had spent two and a half centuries trying to keep Catholics out of any sort of participation in the government of the country. For more than a quarter of a century after the Act of Union it was not possible for the Irish people to send a Catholic to represent them in the House of Commons. So although they were allowed one hundred Members of Parliament, these had to be chosen from amongst the small minority of Protestants. Catholic emancipation was achieved — as we saw in Chapter 6, in 1829. Before it was actually granted there were years of struggle and organisation in Ireland, in which the small freeholders and voters among the Catholics raised money to enable Daniel O'Connell, the leader of the movement for Catholic emancipation, to get finally into the House of Commons. But the Act which granted Catholic emancipation also took away the right to vote from the smaller freeholders. The qualification was raised from 40/-, which was the figure for the countries in the rest of Britain, to £10. So it was not until after the 1832 Reform Bill, when Ireland was brought into line with the rest of Britain, that a strong group of Irish nationalists was elected to Parliament.

A major grievance amongst the Irish Catholics was that the official Church of Ireland was the Established (Protestant) Church, to which very few Irishmen belonged. But whether they belonged or not, they had to pay tithes to the local rector, who often did not live in the village and seldom if ever visited it. So the poor peasants and small farmers, many of them living on the very edge of poverty, had to support two churches out of their meagre incomes.

During the years in which England had tried to deal with the "Irish problem", many measures had been adopted by successive English governments which had had an effect on the *economic* life of Ireland — that is on her industry and agriculture. English farmers and manufacturers had always urged the Government to keep Ireland from competing with England, and both her agriculture and her industry had suffered. Protestant landlords had been "planted" amongst the Catholic peasantry at various times since the seventeenth century. Many of these landlords were from English families, and kept their ties with England, often living most of the year away from their Irish property. Even those who were more Irish in sympathy found their social life and their natural sympathy and friendships among their fellow-Protestant landowners, rather than among the illiterate Catholic peasants who worked their land.

Disraeli once described the troubles of Ireland as "an alien Church, a starving peasantry, and an absentee aristocracy". These three basic problems were still unsolved by the end of the century, although various efforts had been made to solve them.

Attempts to Repeal the Act of Union

From the time of the Reform Bill onwards, there was a continual attempt by Irish members sitting in the House of Commons to get the Act of Union repealed by legal, constitutional methods. The first measure introduced by Feargus O'Connor, when he was elected as a Chartist, was a motion for the repeal of the Union. It was always open to the House of Commons to approve a motion for repeal, and many such motions were presented. But even the hundred Irish members were not unanimous in wanting it. Some were Protestants from the northern counties who were afraid of being swamped if they lost the protection of England. Many Irish also felt a deep loyalty to the Crown. Daniel O'Connell himself, the leader of the group of Catholic M.P.'s, who was more than any one man responsible for the passing of Catholic emancipation, was a strong royalist, with a great affection for the "darling little Queen". He even refused to allow money to be contributed to the Repeal Association by supporters in France, because they were republicans. O'Connell wanted self-government, but not complete separation from England.

Until 1844 the movement for repeal, under O'Connell's leadership, tried the methods of persuasion. They held huge meetings and demonstrations, but in spite of their totally unmilitary nature, O'Connell was arrested in 1844 and tried and imprisoned for the offence of trying to alter the constitution by force.

Armed rebellion against England had failed in 1798. Now peaceful persuasion seemed to have failed as well. Both were to be tried again before the century ended, together with a third way of working, when the Irish members in the House of Commons found themselves in a position to play off the two parties in the House against each other, and to win some of their points by allying themselves with first one and then the other of the evenly-balanced major parties.

Before this happened, however, Ireland was to go through her greatest agony. To understand it we must look briefly at how the "starving peasantry" actually lived.

The Irish Peasantry

The enormous population increase which occurred throughout Western Europe in the last quarter of the eighteenth century was very marked indeed in Ireland. But whereas in England it coincided with an Industrial Revolution which created a demand

123.   Distress in Ireland.

124a and b.   Scenes from Ireland during the Great Hunger which followed the potato famine of 1845 and 1846.

for workers, Ireland had almost no in-dustry. Many Irish workers did leave their country and go and work in the English factories and on building roads and railways, but for the great majority of those who re-mained in Ireland there was only the land to support them. They did not even have the resources of the English villagers. Irish farms by the beginning of the nineteenth century were so small that there was no work for day-labourers. Either the Irishman had to be able to rent a piece of land, or be starved. There was no Poor Law until 1838, so that without land he could only keep himself alive by begging.

We have already seen that most of the land was actually owned by absentee land-lords. A few great estates were run well and the tenants helped to farm efficiently. But such good estates were extremely rare. On most, the rule was that the tenants were given no aid or encouragement to efficient farming. Most tenancies were "at will" – that is, the tenant could be turned out at any time by the landlord. Improvements made by the tenant became the property of the landlord as soon as he left the property, and he was given no compensation for any money he may have spent on improving the land or the buildings.

The results of these various circumstances can easily be imagined. Very few farmers had enough land to do more than grow a few potatoes to feed their own family and live-stock. They might keep a pig, a few chickens or even a cow, though by no means all families managed this. As the children grew up, the parents had either to turn them away from home, or to divide up the small family plot of land into even smaller plots on which the children and their families could live and grow food. More than half the popu-lation in the 1840's lived in one-roomed houses built of mud and roofed with turf, and their animals lived in the same house. Their diet was potatoes and milk or butter-milk, their houses were heated with fires made from peat or turf.

When the 1841 census was taken, the population of Ireland was shown to be well over eight million. Disraeli declared that Ireland was the most densely populated country in Europe. And all these millions depended on the potato. No other crop could have been grown under Irish con-ditions. The bread on which the English labourer lived could not be grown in such small areas. It could not be cultivated with only a spade, as the potato could, nor could it be so easily prepared. Visitors to Ireland were horrified by the poverty in which the people lived, but they were also impressed by the beauty of the Irish peasants, and by their fine physique. When the Irish came to Eng-land for work, employers welcomed them for the heaviest jobs. The combination of fresh air and potatoes was obviously a good one in many ways.

The Great Hunger

In 1845 disaster struck. A new disease attack-ed potato crops all over the world, and in a matter of weeks well over half the Irish potato crop was ruined. There had never before been a failure on this scale, although local crop failures had occurred from time to time, causing considerable hardship. But the 1845 famine was of a hitherto unimagin-ed severity. We have seen, in Chapter 11, that it was a major factor in leading Peel to press through the repeal of the Corn Laws.

The horror of the Irish famine was in-creased by the fact that whilst people were dying by the thousand, food was being ex-ported from Irish ports. The operation of Free Trade was such a sacred idea that the British Government was not prepared to prohibit the export of food from Ireland. Thus wheat, grown on the few large and prosperous farms, was exported; sometimes the ships carrying it actually crossed the path of ships coming in from American and English ports carrying meal for the relief of the famine, paid for with money collected in England or America. But the food which

125. Pursuit of the Fenians in Tipperary, 30 March 1867.

went out greatly exceeded that which came in, and the Irish had reason for describing the famine as an "artificial" one.

In all, something like two million people "disappeared" from the Irish population in the famine year and the year that followed. Some died of hunger, some left their homes and sailed to England or America. Of those who emigrated many died on the voyage or on arrival. Weakened by hunger, they were unable to stand the hardships of the long sea voyage, or to resist infection.

In 1847 it was calculated that over 100,000 emigrants left Ireland for Canada. 17,000 died on the voyage, mainly from typhus, and a further 20,000 died in Canada before the end of the year. Another 25,000 were treated in Canadian hospitals. At Grosse Island, the quarantine station for Quebec, a memorial stands to the people who died at the emergency hospital there in 1847, including four of the doctors. The inscription reads:

In this secluded spot lie the mortal remains of 5,294 persons, who, flying from pestilence and famine in Ireland in the year 1847, found in America but a grave.

Young Ireland

It is hardly surprising that the people of Ireland were not in any position to take part in a rising in 1848. A nationalist group, Young Ireland, did make an attempt at a rising, in that year of nationalist risings throughout Europe, but it was on a small scale, and failed utterly. The leaders were arrested and sentenced to death, sentences which were later commuted to transportation for life. From their convict settlements in Austrialia, several of the Young Ireland leaders later escaped to America, to join the growing Irish community there.

There were by the second half of the nineteenth century a very great number of Irishmen living and working outside Ireland – chiefly in England and the United States. Many of them had been forced to leave Ireland because of their anti-government activities. In America many Irishmen became rich and successful, and although some of them made a new life and forgot about the problems of Ireland, for most of them the idea of Irish nationalism remained very strong. In 1858 some of them started a society called the Fenian Brotherhood, whose aim was to work for the overthrow of British rule in Ireland.

The Fenian Brotherhood

With a headquarters outside Ireland, and with plentiful funds collected in the United States, a new kind of Irish nationalist movement emerged. The Fenians carried on a sort of guerrilla activity in England and in Ireland. Military centres were raided for arms, explosions were organised. Lives were lost as the result of the Fenian outrages, and Irishmen were executed. There seems, however, to have been no really united leadership to the movement; what was more, after a few years of existence, the Brotherhood was denounced by the Roman Catholic Church. Since for many Irishmen the Church was a great tie with their native country, this undoubtedly kept much support away from the Fenians. What they did achieve, however, was the keeping of the question of Irish nationalism in the open. No one in England could forget that the Irish were profoundly discontented.

The Politics of Home Rule

The continued distress in Ireland, kept before the British partly by the activities of the Fenian Brotherhood, began at last to lead to political action in the last quarter of the nineteenth century. Two men were in the

126. Charles Stewart Parnell, leader of the Irish Party in the House of Commons. He was driven out of politics because of his involvement in a divorce case, and the cause of Irish Home Rule lost one of its greatest leaders.

lead in this period – one was Gladstone, leader of the Liberal party and Prime Minister of England from 1868 to 1874, from 1880 to 1885 and again in 1886. He knew that the Irish question would be one of the most difficult ones he would have to solve, and is said to have made the statement when he was first asked to become Prime Minister – "My mission is to pacify Ireland". He gradually came to the view that Home Rule was the only solution for Ireland, and by his belief in this principle, and by his attempts to get it accepted by Parliament, he split his own party, and kept the Liberals out of power for ten years.

Charles Stewart Parnell

The other outstanding figure in the politics of the Home Rule movement was the Irish M.P., Parnell. He was elected in 1875, and for the first time really tried to organise

127. Charles Stewart Parnell speaking at an open-air meeting at Limerick in 1879.

the Irish members in the House of Commons. Of the one hundred Irish members, about 80 were usually Irish nationalists. Parnell organised them to make the most of their numbers. When the two major parties, the Liberals and the Conservatives, were fairly evenly balanced in the House of Commons, the Irish were able to decide how important votes should go. As well as using their numbers to put pressure on the other parties, they also used various methods to disrupt the business of Parliament. The process which the Americans call *filibustering* was used very effectively. Irish members would go on talking in debates on unimportant matters, so that the business of the House of Commons was held up and the whole programme put out by days at a time. It was because of this trick that the modern practice of taking a vote on a Parliamentary motion whether or not the debate has been finished, came into use.

In Ireland itself Parnell encouraged activity to protect the tenants. One way in which this was done was that if a landlord evicted a tenant for no good reason, or if another farmer took over the land of a tenant who had been unjustly evicted, they were isolated. No one in the district would speak to them or trade with them, work for them or have any social relations with them at all. The first landlord to be treated in this way was called Captain Boycott. He had the unenviable distinction of having added a new word to the English language, the word "to boycott".

Clearly Parnell was a leader of imagination and great ability. In the House of Commons he formed an alliance with Gladstone and the leaders of the Liberal party, and helped to convince them that the only answer to the Irish question was complete Home Rule.

Gladstone never succeeded in persuading the whole of the Liberal party to support Home Rule. He died, and the century ended, with the question not settled. Before Gladstone died in 1898, he had seen the

Home Rule Bill passed by the House of Commons, but it had been thrown out of the House of Lords. The Lords managed to prevent its being passed, although it was in the end one of the questions which led to a reform of the House of Lords, and the limiting of their powers. But this lay many years in the future. As far as the nineteenth century was concerned, Gladstone had failed in his mission. Ireland remained discontented, although Gladstone had been able to effect some reforms, such as the disestablishment of the Irish Church – that is the abolition of tithes and the placing of the Protestant Church on the same footing as the Catholic and Nonconformist Churches in Ireland. He had also passed various Land Acts which gave some protection to Irish tenants. But by this time such reforms fell so far short of what the Irish actually wanted that they had little effect.

In 1890 the Home Rule movement suffered a severe blow when it lost its leader, Parnell. In that year, he was cited as co-respondent in a divorce case by another member of the Irish movement, Captain O'Shea. Although it had been well known that Parnell and Mrs O'Shea had been living together as man and wife for some years before the divorce, the fact of its being made public caused the official Liberal leaders to throw up their hands in horror, and to demand Parnell's resignation. The attack was led, with the hypocrisy which was all too typical of the Victorian age, by a Liberal who was himself living with a woman to whom he was not married. Parnell's own followers, many of whom were, of course, Catholics who did not recognise divorce, also demanded his resignation. Parnell fought hard to retain his position, but was finally driven out of the leadership of the Irish party. He died within a year.

By the end of the century, then, Ireland seemed no nearer to self-government. The Liberal party had split – an important section of it, under the leadership of Joseph Chamberlain, joining the Conservatives in protest against Gladstone's Home Rule policy. The small but growing Labour Party was in support of Home Rule, but within Ireland itself there was a movement amongst the Protestants of the northern provinces to remain part of Great Britain. There was little sign of a quick solution to the question, and it was indeed to remain unsolved for many more years to come.

Chapter 18

Women in Nineteenth-Century England

We have already noticed in passing that the very great political reforms which took place throughout the nineteenth century had almost no effect on the position of women. The century closed with a queen on the throne but not a single woman in either house of Parliament. Women could not vote for Members of Parliament, and there were no women in the top posts of the Civil Service. But there was a movement in existence which was working for a change in the law to admit women to the vote and to participation in the government of the country at all levels.

The position of women was probably worse in the nineteenth century than it had ever been in England. This sounds a very strong statement, so let us examine it more closely. Of course, standards of living for all classes were going up during the century, and in this sense it is true that women as well as men were benefiting. Mothers were less likely to lose babies and children by the end of the century than ever before, and were less likely to die in childbirth. They could expect to live longer than their parents and grandparents. In all these ways life was better, even for the poorer families.

But life had in many ways got worse for women during the century. In the working classes they were the worst-paid section of the workers and after a day at the factory or mill still had the responsibility of feeding and clothing the family and keeping the home decent. In the middle classes, far from having two jobs, as so many working women had, they had no job at all until they married, and even then, the richer their husband the less they were expected to do. For the unmarried girl whose family, though middle-class, was not rich, there was very little chance of earning a living. Almost the only job she could take was that of a governess in a richer family. Otherwise, if she did not marry she had to live with a member of her family who had married; there she helped with the household, but had no real place and often no money of her own. Higher up the scale, the girl from a well-off middle class family had to waste her time until she married – education in any but a very limited number of subjects was not considered suitable for young ladies. After her marriage she might have to superintend her household, but all the work would be done by servants and all the important decisions taken by her husband. In the upper classes, where money was getting more and more plentiful, girls and women spent their time in social occupations which anyone with any intelligence found intensely boring, paying calls on each other and taking tea. In earlier centuries the women of wealthy households had had far more responsibility in the organisation of the household, the education of the children and the supervision of some parts of the management of their husband's estates than they had in Victorian times. The fashion was for women to be decorative and stupid, and they became increasingly to be regarded more as part of their husband's property than as people in their own right.

"Why", wrote Florence Nightingale,

"have women passion, intellect, moral activity – these three – and a place in society where no one of the three can be exercised?"

The story of the emancipation of women as a whole – the gaining of the vote and the right to take part in making the laws of the country – belongs to the twentieth century. So too does most of the story of women at work – the fight for equal pay and the right to do skilled as well as unskilled jobs in industry. What was achieved in the nineteenth century was some progress in the rights of women to be educated, to enter some of the professions, and to own property and have some legal rights to the custody of their children. These matters mainly affected women of the upper and middle classes, as very few working women had any property, or were in a position to benefit from the right to receive higher education.

The Case of Caroline Norton

Many of the legal disabilities from which women suffered are illustrated by the case of Caroline Norton, which took place at the very beginning of Queen Victoria's reign. Caroline herself wrote "I have learned the law respecting married women piecemeal, by suffering every one of its defects of protection", and her case does indeed illustrate very clearly many of the ways in which women suffered when they were in conflict with their husbands.

Caroline Norton was the beautiful and talented wife of the Hon. Richard Norton, to whom she had been married at the age of nineteen. The marriage was not a happy one, and they quarrelled frequently. Finally Richard took their three young children away from the house to the home of a relative, and refused to let Caroline see them. Caroline went back to live with her own family, and then discovered her legal position as a married woman. She had absolutely no right to see her children, let alone to have them with her. The house and furniture, much of which she had contributed on her

marriage, all belonged to Richard, as did all her other property. Not only this, but when she wrote some books to earn money, Richard claimed the profits on them – and proved that he had the legal right to any money she earned. When her character was attacked in print, she found that as a married woman she had no right to sue for libel, as a married woman had no status in law apart from her husband.

As the result of the activities of Caroline Norton and those who helped and supported her, a law was passed in 1839 which gave the timid beginnings of the right of

128. Caroline Norton (*left*) whose case began the reform of the laws controlling the property of married women and the custody of children.

129. Elizabeth Garrett, the first woman doctor to practise in England.

custody to the mother of children under seven, and of the right of access to older children. From that date on various other acts were passed, although it was not until 1925 that wives were given equal rights to be guardians of their children with their husbands.

The laws about property and children must certainly have kept many women tied in marriages which were unhappy. Until these laws were changed, a woman could only leave her husband if she was fortunate enough to have a family who would take her back and keep her. An unmarried woman without property of her own was if anything in a worse position. She must rely on being kept by members of her family, or try and earn a living in one of the very few positions which were open to her.

The Governesses

If you have read *Jane Eyre*, or any books about the Brontë sisters, you will have some idea of what the job of a governess was like in the nineteenth century. Above the servants, but not on an equal footing with members of the family, she was a lonely member of the household, often overworked and usually underpaid. "Punch" published a satirical advertisement for a governess in the middle of the century, which was rather too near the truth:

Wanted, a young lady who has had advantages, for a situation as governess. To sleep in a room with three beds, for herself, four children and a maid. To give the children their baths, dress them and be ready for breakfast at a quarter to eight. School 9–12 and half-past 2–4, with two hours' music lesson in addition. To spend the evenings in doing needlework for her mistress. To have the baby on her knee while teaching and to put all the children to bed. Salary £10 a year and to pay her own washing.

This was invented, but in 1862, a speaker at the Social Science Congress told how she had had 810 applicants for a "respectable" job with a salary of £15 a year.

The brothers of these girls would be trained to be lawyers, doctors, teachers, or would enter into family businesses of various kinds. The girls, however, had no training for any such work, and no chance of getting any.

The Reformers

The women who took the lead in changing things were mostly from rather unusual families. In spite of the general middle-class attitudes to women, there were a number of families in which the father helped his daughters to become educated, and in which the girls were treated equally with the boys. It was girls like this, who had had the advantages of education themselves who usually led the movement to get the same advantages for others. Most of the leaders in the women's movements had fathers or husbands who agreed with them and helped them.

There is a pleasant story about three of the most famous women in the movement, Emily Davies, Elizabeth Garrett and her younger sister, Millicent Garrett. The two older girls were discussing all that they would like to do to improve the position of women, and Emily Davies said:

. . . Well, Elizabeth, it is quite clear what has to be done. I must devote myself to securing higher education, while you open the medical

130. Girton Girls. Some people wondered what the effect would be of having young women in a university. Would it make a difference to the behaviour of the men students? Would they take up tea drinking instead of beer drinking, as this cartoonist seemed to think?

profession to women. After these things are done, we must see about getting the vote.

And then she turned to the little girl who was sitting quietly on her stool and said:

You are younger than we are, Millie, so you must attend to that.

Emily Davies did achieve her aim. Before she died in 1921, all the English universities had admitted women as students, and hundreds of girls every year were awarded degrees. Elizabeth Garrett became the first woman doctor to practise in Britain, although she had to get her degree in France, and young Millicent became one of the leaders in the movement for women's suffrage which was growing in strength by the end of the century.

The Education of Young Ladies

In many ways the question of girls' education was the most important one. As long as they were brought up to be incapable of using their minds, it was only too easy for those who opposed them to argue that women were incapable of serious thought, or of training for a profession. The old system of education for children of well-off families, which took place mostly at home, was changing in Victorian times for a pattern in which boys went away to boarding school while they were quite young. So the chance for girls to be educated with their brothers, at least until the brothers went away to University, was lost, and in the absence of the boys a special sort of female education was provided. A novelist described this education:

They were very highly educated – that is to say they could do everything that is useless – play, draw, sing, dance, made wax flowers, bead-stands, decorative gilding and crochet work; but as to knowing how many ounces there are in a pound of tea, or how many pounds of meat a person should eat in a day, they were utterly, entirely and elegantly ignorant... Not one of them could write a letter without a copy, and they were all very uncertain in their spelling – though they knew to a day when every king and queen began to reign, and could spout all the chief towns in the kingdom...

The aim of the education of these girls was, in the words of a contemporary book on *The Wives of England* to produce wives with just enough knowledge to be good listeners when their husbands spoke:

It is the privilege of a married woman – wrote the author of this work – to be able to show by the most delicate attentions how much she feels her husband's superiority to herself –

not by mere personal services... but by a respectful deference to his opinion, and a willingly imposed silence when he speaks...

It is hardly surprising that girls like the Garretts, brought up in a family in which they were given the widest possible education, and by a father who respected his daughters' opinions as much as his son's, should be angry at the futility of the education which was usually offered to girls. But it was not only women who objected. Many of the more intelligent men of the time protested against the subjection of women.

Perhaps the most eloquent supporter of the freedom of women was the philosopher John Stuart Mill. With relentless logic he argued that if women were not capable of entering the professions and of working at men's jobs, then there was really no objection to their being educated. They would soon show in practice that they could not do the work. The fact that they were forbidden to try showed that they might

131.   Lady students took part in sport as well as work. This is the cricket team of a London University Women's College in 1887.

very well succeed if they were allowed to try.

The eighteen-seventies and eighteen-eighties saw the opening of University education to girls at Cambridge, London and Oxford Universities. The battle was a long-drawn out one – fought by a group of determined students, helped by many sympathetic men teachers at the universities. By the end of the 'seventies women were even admitted to the medical schools. Here the battle had been fiercest, for the idea of women doctors aroused horror in many quarters. Queen Victoria herself was outraged at the idea:

> To propose that they should study with men – things which could not be named before them – certainly not in a *mixed* audience – would be to introduce a total disregard of what must be considered as belonging to the rules and principles of morality.

By the time the women's colleges got going, and women were enabled to take University courses, two or three first class girls' schools had been opened. In the early years of the century girls had been educated either at home, or in schools of the sort described by Charlotte Brontë in *Jane Eyre*, schools whose teachers often had no particular qualification to teach and who were concerned more with the moral character of the pupils than with the training of their minds.

In the last few years of the century, then, it was possible for girls to be educated up to the standard of men's education. But this was only for those whose families would allow it and could afford it, and long after education for girls was possible, most girls were still kept from getting it by the deep prejudice which existed against education for women. It was either considered "unwomanly" for girls to go to college, or, more often, it was feared that people might think that parents who allowed their daughters to go to college did so because they were not able to support them properly. And it was one thing to go to

132. Women at work: the London Telephone Exchange in 1883.

college, even to get qualified in a profession. It was another and more difficult step to be allowed by your family and by the men already in the profession to practise it.

Nevertheless, by 1900 there were a small number of women doctors, factory inspectors and research workers in various fields. There were many more educated women doing unpaid work, as members of school boards or local government committees, and bringing trained minds to the work instead of the vague goodwill which their mothers and grandmothers had brought into their "charitable" activities.

The Lower Middle Classes

The effect of the opening of the professions to women was to be felt more in the twentieth century than in the nineteenth. But the general breaking-down of the prejudice against young ladies working was beginning to show by the end of the nineteenth century in the greater range of jobs which they were able to do. In the middle of the century the position of governess had seemed to be the only one open, but by the end things were changing. The census figures show, to take two examples, no nurses listed in 1861. In 1891, 53,057 are listed. In 1861 there are no female clerks listed, in 1891, 17,859. New inventions like the typewriter and the telephone were especially suitable for girls to handle. These girls did not always earn a living wage. It was assumed still that unmarried girls lived at home, so any of the young clerks or teachers who were daring enough to set up house away from their families often had to live on very little.

But the possibility of doing work outside the home, and of being independent was there, and a great change was beginning in the way women lived.

The Suffrage

It was only to be expected that girls with a university education would begin to ask why they were not allowed to vote. Throughout the nineteenth century the vote had been in

133a and b.   Parlourmaids (above) and housemaids (right). At the end of the century more girls were getting educated and doing interesting jobs. But still there were more women working as domestic servants than in any other job.

the forefront of politics. First the middle class, then the working class had fought to gain it; as each class became admitted to the franchise, so Parliament had begun to consider its problems, to recognise its rights. But women were classed with children, lunatics and sailors in being considered not fit to take part in politics. When laws that especially concerned women were before Parliament they had to be supported by the few men members who were sympathetic to women's views.

There were always a few M.P.'s who did believe in votes for women. At the time of the passing of the Second Reform Bill in 1867, John Stuart Mill, who was a Member of Parliament as well as being a philosopher, proposed an amendment giving the vote to women, and eighty members supported him. Three years later came an even more encouraging vote. A bill was introduced which passed its first reading by 124 votes to 91. But when Mr Gladstone, the Liberal leader, made it clear that he did not approve of the idea of votes for women, giving no

reason but simply saying "It would be a very great mistake to carry this Bill into law", most of the Liberal supporters changed their minds, and the Bill was defeated on its second reading by 106 votes.

Gladstone's opposition meant that there was very little chance of getting the law changed. While some Conservative members were in favour of women's suffrage, more support existed amongst the Liberals. But as long as Gladstone remained leader of the Party, favourable votes were always turned into unfavourable ones by his intervention.

By the end of the nineteenth century the movement for women's suffrage was growing all through the country. Although it had mainly started amongst middle-class women, it now had support from all classes, including factory girls from Lancashire and the small but increasing number of women Trade Unionists. Amongst men politicians, too, there was growing support. Many of the new I.L.P. leaders were strong supporters of women's equality and therefore of votes for

women. Perhaps the most outstanding of these was George Lansbury, later to be leader of the Labour Party in the 1930's. But, by 1900, New Zealand was the only country in the world in which women had the vote, and English women had another eighteen years to wait before the first of them were given the right to vote.

The Others

In looking at things like women's education and the laws about children and property, we have, of course, been concerned with only a minority of women. Changes in the law which they brought about – for example the Married Women's Property Act of 1882 which gave women some rights to own property, and the Married Women (maintenance in case of desertion) Act of 1886, which gave women the right to claim maintenance without first being forced into the workhouse, certainly improved the position of women of all classes. Other gains in the way of educational improvement, the right to have custody of the children of a broken marriage, and the improvement of the position of divorced wives, have been of great benefit to all classes in the hundred years or so which have passed since they were achieved. But at the time such questions hardly touched the majority of English women. In fact, the women who became doctors or university teachers were only able to do so because there was a vast army of domestic servants to attend to their housework for the most minute wages. Over a million women worked in domestic service by the middle of the century – more than the whole number of women textile workers. They had no Trade Unions, and their wages were never enough to give them any sort of independence. In addition, thousands of outworkers, dressmakers, milliners, makers of matchboxes, toys, fancy goods of all kinds, worked at home, often helped by their children or old relatives, for wages which never amounted to more than a few shillings a week. The workers for women's suffrage may, however, have felt – and rightly – that the case of the great number of exploited and underpaid women who worked in British cities at this time would have been treated with greater urgency by politicians if women had all been voters.

Chapter 19

Children and their Education

We have no means of knowing how many people in England could read and write in the eighteenth century. There are ways of guessing. For example, you can look at the signatures, in the Parish registers of churches, of people getting married. Some historians have worked through a selection of such registers, and by counting how many people put crosses instead of their signatures, have arrived at figures for the percentage of people who could write. But this sort of counting is not very reliable. If writing is a sign of superiority, many wives would make a cross, even if they could write, to show their husband's superiority over them. Some people may learn to sign their name, but not be able to write anything else. In any case, an inability to write does not necessarily mean an inability to read. Many managers of Sunday schools and charity schools thought that people ought to be taught to read, in order to read the Bible for themselves, but not write. Books and newspapers were so expensive in the eighteenth century that we cannot tell much from the numbers of books and papers sold.

What we need to guard against is the idea that until full-time education at schools was made compulsory for all children, very few people could read or write. This is certainly not the case.

Eighteenth-Century Schools

As with many other social questions, there is good reason to believe that education for the poor got worse in the early part of the

134.   A village dame school in the early nineteenth century.

nineteenth century. When most people lived in villages, and most people worked at home, it was in many ways easier to give simple instruction to children than it was when people lived in big cities and both parents, and sometimes the children as well, worked all day out of the home. For the village child there were three kinds of instruction that he might get. He – or she – would certainly learn about his parents' trade, or in the case of girls, about household jobs of all kinds, in the home, or by going out with the parents to their work at certain times. He might also learn reading and writing at home, especially if there was work, like weaving or spinning, which could be carried on at the same time as some simple teaching.

Many villages, probably most villages, would have some kind of a *dame school*. This was a school kept usually by an old lady, at which children were taught to read and write and do simple sums for a very small charge. Such a school might be little more than a baby-minding service for children too young to work or to help at home, but it could lay the foundation on which later education could be built. We have many descriptions of this sort of school, some rather horrifying, some rather charming. The poet Crabbe describes a dame school at the turn of the century:

> Yet one there is, that small regard to rule
> Or study pays, and still is deemed a school:
> That where a deaf, poor, patient widow sits
> And awes some thirty infants as she knits –
> Infants of humble, busy wives, who pay
> Some trifling price for freedom through the day

Many years later, in the middle of the nineteenth century, Charles Kingsley in the *Water Babies* drew a picture of a village dame school in Yorkshire, and of the old lady who was so kind to the little chimney sweep, Tom.

> At her feet sat the grandfather of all cats; and opposite her sat, on two benches, twelve

or fourteen neat, rosy, chubby little children learning their chris-cross row . . .

The dame school was not likely to give much in the way of serious education, yet it could give an important start to a child who was naturally bright and inquisitive.

Apart from the dame schools there were other day schools of a rather similar kind, but intended for older children. Here, too, the teachers were not likely to have much in the way of qualifications. One such school in Yorkshire was kept by a weaver who could not go on with his trade after an accident to his arm. There were also in very many villages schools attached to the Church, where the vicar's wife and daughters taught the local children to read and write as well as giving them religious instruction. In fact, very many people with a little money which they wanted to put to a good charitable use invested it in the education of the village poor children. It is not possible to say how many children in the eighteenth century got some sort of elementary education – enough to get them over the first hurdle, that of learning how to read. All we can say is that probably more children did get a year or two at a day school than we sometimes think.

Elementary Education in the Nineteenth Century

As people moved more and more into towns, and factory work became more common, the pattern of education changed. In the factory districts two patterns emerged. One was the system of part-time education. The other was the Sunday School movement.

Sunday Schools

Among the originators of the Sunday Schools was Robert Raikes, a newspaper owner of Gloucester. He spent a lot of money in organising schools for the children who worked all the week at the local pin factories. His lead was soon taken up, and in 1785 a national committee was founded to set up Sunday Schools all over the country. The

135. John Pound, founder of Ragged Schools educated many hundreds of poor children in his lifetime.

aims of these schools were religious. The committee consisted of half members of the Church of England and half of representatives of the nonconformist churches. Among the rules were these instructions – "Be diligent in teaching the children to read well ... Neither writing nor arithmetic is to be taught on Sundays."

Some historians have suggested that the Sunday School movement was the beginning of genuine popular education. But it might also be considered to have held back the beginnings of real education for the factory children. There is no doubt that many people who were worried about the conditions in the early factories were especially worried by the fact that the children had no chance to receive any education. But many of the people who had to do with the factory children thought that it was more important that they should receive moral and religious instruction than that they should learn to read or write. Thus Mr Rickards, one of the first Factory Inspectors to be appointed, wrote suggesting:

> That every young person from ten to eighteen, after entering a mill, should be compelled to attend a Sunday-school regularly. It is only, as it appears to me, by a systematic education of this nature, long and uninterruptedly continued, that the vicious habits of this population can be corrected.

A rather different sort of education was given at the factory and other part-time schools.

Day Schools for the Factory Children

When Lord Althorp's factory act was passed in 1833 (see Chapter 9) one of its provisions was that all children at work in the factories must have some education. Every employer was required to demand proof from a child, before he took him on for work, that he had

had at least two hours' education each day of the week before. But this proved unworkable. Some employers took the matter very seriously, and there were examples, particularly in large firms, of factories with schools on the premises where a regular schoolmaster was employed. At Todmorden, in Lancashire, at the works of Fielden Brothers, a school was set up for the factory children, at which one of the office clerks acted as schoolmaster. The children paid ½d. a day for their instruction, and in 1837 there were a hundred children attending the school. Since there was apparently only one master, this may account for the fact that a report on the school a few years later commented on the fact that very few of the children could write. Three out of four could read, but only one in ten could sign their names.

Fielden Brothers were unusual, however, in having a factory school at all. In his first official report after his appointment under the 1833 act, the factory inspector for Scotland reported that not a single mill-owner there enforced the rule about schooling. Mr Rickards, inspector for Yorkshire and Lancashire, in his report, said that it was quite impossible for the employers to enforce the rule, and that he therefore had stopped asking about it. As we have seen, some employers did provide schooling, others made a gesture in that direction – by calling a cellar a "schoolroom", and a workman who was not doing anything else at the time, a "schoolmaster". Most of the factory masters ignored the question.

It would have been very difficult for an employer to insist that his children should do two hours school work a day. Very few industrial districts had even the sort of day schools we described earlier, and even if they had, they would not be likely to be open after an eight-hour day had been worked at the factory. And if they were, they would not necessarily want ragged, dirty, tired little factory children coming along for lessons. When the Commission on Factory Labour

was hearing evidence, they often asked people, clergymen, employers and workers, what they thought about education for the factory children. One employer complained that he could not get the children to stop in after work and go to school:

> There is no school at this mill; there was one, but ... the children did not attend, and it was given up; but they are going to re-establish the school, and to lock the gate to force them to attend.

But perhaps one of the saddest pieces of evidence given to the Commission was from a little Scottish girl, Betsey Faulkner, eight years old, who was solemnly sworn in, and who said that

> ... she sweeps the spinning-flat, and is sair tired at night; that she goes to school, but has never any time to play ... she cannot write.

It is hardly surprising that, on the whole, the people who were trying to make things better for these children were more concerned that a child who was "sair tired" should have time to play after her work than that she should learn to write.

The Half-Time System

As more schools became available, and hours became shorter, an attempt was made to combine work and school by the introduction of the half-time system. Children of ten, eleven, or twelve, when they had reached a certain standard at school, were allowed to work half-time in the mill, and to come to school for only half the day. As they were supposed to prove that they could pass certain tests in reading, writing and arithmetic before they were allowed to work, it usually happened that the brighter a child was, the younger he could leave full-time schooling. This system went on until well into the present century in the factory districts of the north, and there are many people still living in the West Riding of Yorkshire and in Lancashire who started work while they were still under school-leaving age as "half-timers". There were plenty of examples of people who used the education they got in this way as a foundation, and educated themselves as they got older. But for the majority of children, especially when they began on the half-time system at a good deal below the legal age, learning must have been almost impossible. Joseph Wright of Bradford went to work half-time at the age of seven at the Saltaire Mill, near Bradford, in 1860. Wright was a man of very great ability, who later was to become Professor of Comparative Philology at the University of Oxford. Saltaire was one of the most enlightened mills of its time, with good provision for meals and rest for the people who worked there. The school would be likely to be as good or better than most factory schools – indeed it was one of the very few provided especially for half-timers. Many half-timers went to ordinary day-schools and had to take their chance with children who went full-time to school. Nevertheless, young Joseph learnt very little there:

> When I left school (he wrote many years later) I knew very little more than when I first went. I knew the alphabet and had a smattering of elementary arithmetic, and I could recite, parrot-like, various Scriptural passages, and a few highly moral bits of verse; that was almost precisely the extent of my educational equipment after three or four years of schooling. Reading and writing, for me, were as remote as any of the sciences.

Half-time education was of very little use. Still less valuable was education given to these children after a full day's work. A serious programme of education for all children could only succeed when child labour was made entirely illegal.

We have already looked at the very cheap schools to which people without much money might send their children by day. In the last chapter we saw that many families employed governesses to teach the girls and little boys. What happened to these children when they grew old enough to need more in the way of instruction than the governess,

136. Exhausted factory children mostly learnt very little at Sunday school.

with her limited knowledge, could teach them?

At the end of the eighteenth century, the rich boys would probably have a tutor. Education was still in those days mostly given at home. Many young clergymen, waiting for appointments, would work for a few years as private tutors. Writers and scholars who did not have enough money of their own to live on, sometimes worked as tutors. As the education of a young gentleman was not considered to be complete without a tour of Europe, the tutor often had the chance to travel as part of his job. They were generally held in much higher regard than governesses, better paid, and treated as members of the family.

A middle-class family which could not afford a tutor for its sons might still be able to employ a clergyman or someone else with a good education to teach the boys for a few hours each week. But it was boys of the middle classes who were the pupils of most of the secondary schools that existed.

Endowed Schools and Private Schools

Until the beginning of the twentieth century, all secondary schools in this country were either endowed schools or private schools. Private schools then, as now, were schools set up as a business. They provided education for which parents paid, and they varied as much as any other sort of business. Some were cheap and bad, some were expensive and good. Some were undoubtedly expensive and bad, of the kind described by Dickens in *Nicholas Nickleby*. Here, at "Dotheboys Hall", set up in a remote part of Yorkshire, boys were sent who were not wanted at home. Parents or guardians who wanted them out of the way did not worry too much about the fact that Mr Wackford Squeers, who ran the school, was himself hardly educated at all, or that the food on which the boys were fed was scarce and nasty. But most private schools in the earlier years of the century were probably not only for boarders. Boys living nearby would go to school each day, and boys who lived in the country might sleep at the school during the week and go home at week-ends. Usually these schools were run by one headmaster, often a clergyman. He would be assisted by teachers or monitors who might have very little special qualification. Modern children would find some things about these schools strange and unpleasant. In some, beating or caning was the regular punishment, although this was not the case in the better schools.

Henry Solly, who wrote his autobiography in the 1890's, remembered a typical middle-class childhood in the 1820's. He was one of a large and happy family who lived on the outskirts of London, at Leyton in Essex, and until he was eight and a half years old, he had lessons at home with his sisters. Then he went as a day boy to a school two miles away, riding each way on a Shetland pony. After six months as a day boy, he became a weekly boarder, coming home on Sundays. Life at school became much tougher as a boarder, with bullying, fighting and teasing going on all the time, and making an unpleasant contrast with the happy life at home. At this particular school the staff did not beat the children – in fact there was only one occasion on which a boy was flogged in front of the whole school, for stealing, during Henry Solly's five years there. But the atmosphere was one of cruelty, among the boys themselves rather than between teachers and boys. The boy who had been flogged, for example,

> instead of being removed, from this school, as he should have been, was, at his father's request, kept there during the rest of the half-year, and (by a refinement of inconceivable, though unintentional cruelty) 'sent to Coventry', all the boys being forbidden to play with or to speak to him. And when the masters were out of the way, I repeatedly saw some of my school-fellows showing their righteous indignation at his crime by baiting him, in the most cowardly and barbarous manner . . .

There were no organised games or physical training lessons for the boys. All their games seem to have been organised amongst themselves, though they were provided with hoops, bats and balls.

The education at this school (at which Benjamin Disraeli was also a pupil) was entirely classical. That is, the boys learnt Latin and Greek and Ancient History, spending most of their time on Greek and Latin grammar. This they learnt with great thoroughness,

> But alas! that is the limit of praise to be given to the actual tuition provided at this school,

while any supervision of the *morals* of the school seemed out of the question, though it was no worse in these respects than most other schools of the day; I fancy rather better, in fact, than the great public schools. But as for mathematical teaching, book-keeping, history, science or literature, this was simply non-existent or despicable...

At the age of thirteen, Solly changed schools, as his first school closed down. He was sent for three years as a boarder to a school at Hove, in Sussex. By this time he was old enough to enjoy being a boarder, and as this school introduced some mathematics and poetry as well as classics, he learnt a good deal more.

After three years at Hove he became a student at the newly-founded University of London. Here he studied mathematics and classics and philosophy for two years, for which he was awarded a certificate. At this time only Oxford and Cambridge universities could give degrees, so students at London had no letters after their names when they had finished their courses.

We have looked at the education of one middle-class boy in a little detail. The Sollys were a well-off family, who had enough money to send all their children, boys and girls, to good private schools. They were a family in which affection and co-operation were much more important than punishment, and they tried to see that their children were educated in the same spirit. There were very many families of this kind in England, and the need for more schools and universities to teach them soon became clear. The Solly family were Unitarians – that is, they were nonconformists. For this reason the children were not sent to one of the endowed public or grammar schools which almost all taught only the doctrines of the Church of England. They could also not go to Oxford or Cambridge Universities, since to enter these institutions, tests had to be passed, which included membership of the Church of England.

Endowed Schools

Although many of the schools which we now call public schools were in existence in the early years of the nineteenth century, they were not a bit like the schools which have the same names today. For one thing, only two of them, Eton and Winchester Colleges, were entirely boarding schools. The rest, together with many other grammar schools, were endowed schools for day pupils, some of which took boarders as well.

"Endowed" schools were schools which had been founded by a gift of money some time in the past. Some had been founded by individuals – often by money left in a will. Some had been founded by organisations – guilds of tradesmen or religious orders. Usually these schools had been founded for the education of poor children in a neighbourhood – at a time when the education of the better-off took place at home. They were almost all "grammar" schools – founded to teach Greek and Latin grammar, and very many of them had been founded to teach the poor "children", not specifically boys. By the end of the nineteenth century most of these schools were boarding schools, taking pupils from all over the country. They were for boys only, almost entirely for the children of rich families, and they taught modern languages, mathematics, and many subjects as well as Latin and Greek grammar.

The Public Schools

One writer on educational history has said that the state of the public schools in England between 1750 and 1840 was worse than at any time since King Alfred – eight hundred years before. He may have been exaggerating, but some of the conditions which were revealed when serious enquiries began to be made in the second half of the nineteenth century would seem to support his view. One famous school, for example, had endowments which brought in £500 a year. This was the salary which was drawn by the headmaster – quite a handsome one for that period. But in 1868 there had been no pupils at the school for 30 years. This sort of situation existed in many places. In return for their salaries, many of the schoolmasters did a minimal amount of teaching in Latin and Greek grammar. If they taught other subjects, they charged extra for them. They were able to justify this by showing that the original endowments had been for "grammar" schools. But when it was pointed out by local citizens that the original endowments were also for "free" schools, or for teaching "poor" children, the schoolmasters were able to prove that "free" in this case meant "free from too much outside control" and that "poor" meant "hard up" or "in need of financial assistance", which could apply to almost anyone.

During the first half of the nineteenth century, the endowed schools had been becoming increasingly boarding schools and had been charging fees which put them into a fairly high social class. The sort of private school which Henry Solly and his brothers attended probably gave a much better education in this period.

By the middle of the century, however, it was becoming clear that if England was to keep her lead as an industrial power, she was going to have to see that her children, in all classes, got a very much better general education. France, and even more Germany, were drawing ahead in the provisions they were making for education. As usually happens in England, the changes which did come about came partly from individual experiments within the schools, and partly from outside pressures, from the government and from public opinion.

Among the public schools, three outstanding headmasters had transformed their own schools by the time that the government began to show an interest. These were Thomas Arnold of Rugby, Samuel Butler of Shrewsbury and Edward Thring of Uppingham. All three of them took over schools which were of the ordinary endowed grammar school type, and brought in changes in the subjects taught and in the organisation of the school. Arnold and Thring especially stressed the importance of organised games for schoolboys, and it was while Arnold was headmaster of Rugby that the game of Rugby-football was evolved.

All three headmasters also broadened out the syllabus, and tried to provide a good education for boys of differing abilities. Edward Thring wrote:

> Every boy is good for something. If he can't write Iambics or excel in Latin prose, he has at least eyes and hands and ears. Turn him into the carpenter's shop, make him a botanist or a chemist, encourage him to express himself in music, and if he fails all round, here at least he shall learn to read in public his mother tongue and write thoughtfully an English essay.

If you have read *Tom Brown's Schooldays*, you will have some idea of what Rugby was like under Thomas Arnold. There was still a great deal of brutality amongst the boys – bullying, even "roasting", of the little boys by bigger and more powerful lads. But compared with the great brutality which existed in most of the public boarding schools, the atmosphere in these new model public schools was healthy and cheerful.

The improvements of individual headmasters, the competition from the private schools, and the general demand for better standards of education led the government to show an interest in the 1860's. In 1861 the *Illustrated London News* voiced some of the questions which were beginning to concern people:

> No Latin or Greek may make Master Jacky a dull boy: but Latin and Greek without anything else go far towards making Master Jacky a very dullard. Parents are beginning to feel this, and to ask whether a skinful of classical knowledge, with a little birching thrown in for nothing, be an equivalent for the two hundred a year they pay for the education of a boy at Eton. It is true that young hopefuls of the aristocracy *may* learn French, German,

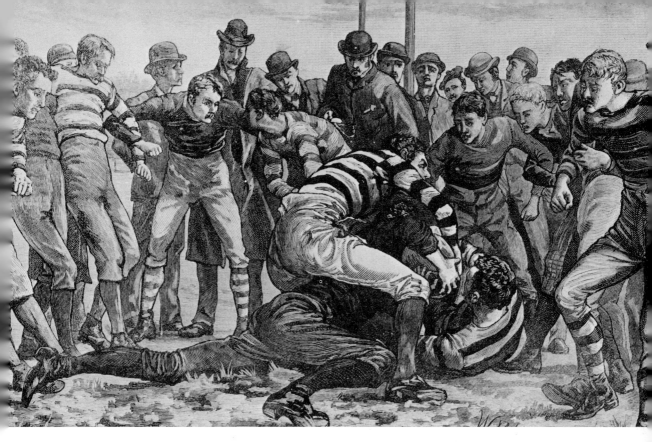

137. Rugby-football in the mid-nineteenth century.

drawing, and mathematics at public schools . . . but these branches of polite education are treated as 'extras' and charged for accordingly . . .

The result of this and similar complaints was a Government Commission, which was set up to examine the education given at the seven leading public schools, and which made recommendations for it to be broadened and brought up to date. The schools were left independent, provided that they modernised themselves.

After the major schools, the government began to investigate the smaller public schools and the other endowed schools. The result of the two Commissions was in general a widening of the syllabus at most of the endowed schools, but it was left to the governing bodies of the schools to carry out the improvements; the Government did not interfere.

We have looked at the private and public schools first, in this survey of English educa-

tion, because they were the schools which actually existed, and were educating children in the middle years of the nineteenth century. They only educated a small minority of the nation's children, of course. But as a wider educational system grew up, it grew up beside these schools, and to some extent in imitation of them.

The Government and Elementary Education

We have seen that the attempts to educate the factory children, either on Sundays or after work, had had little effect. A few people tried to interest the Government in plans for education, indeed, in 1833 J. A. Roebuck moved in the House of Commons "that this House proceed to devise a means for the universal and national education of the whole people". He got very little support for his idea. But that year was the first in which the Government did grant some money for popular education. It granted £20,000 – not very much, considering that in

138.   A view of Rugby school in 1841.

the same year it granted £50,000 to improve the Royal stables. Nevertheless, it was a first step which began the long process by which the Government gradually took over responsibility for education.

The development of education in England has always been confused by the religious issue. More than in any other country, the question of who should give the children their religious teaching has come before the question of their general education. The first body which set out seriously to provide free or very cheap education for poor children in the nineteenth century was the British and Foreign Schools Society, founded by a group of nonconformists in 1811. This was soon followed by the National Society, set up by the Church of England to promote education. These two societies collected money, and used it to set up schools at which free or very cheap education was given to poor children. The church schools were more widespread in the country districts, while the nonconformists tended to build in the towns. The schools which they set up were not under any sort of outside control, and many of their buildings were tiny and insanitary. Nevertheless, there they were, and when the Government did make its £20,000 grant, they were ready to receive it.

It is a sad thing in many ways that elementary education should have started in this way. By 1833 the air was full of ideas about education. Many experiments had been tried, in Switzerland, Germany and in England in the education of young children. At New Lanark, Robert Owen had run a school for the children of the factory workers which was a show piece, attracting visitors from all over the world. Here he had used pictures, music and dancing to introduce children to a lively and imaginative view of the world. He had forbidden parrot-like learning, and encouraged questions and discussion. Punishments were forbidden and there were no individual prizes. Instead the children were encouraged to help each other, with their reward the satisfaction of achievement. The results were praised by everyone who visited the school. But the great majority of British children were not given the benefit of Owen's experience. The two bodies who did undertake the education of the poor children were not concerned with educational theories, but in the main, only with seeing that the children's religious education followed the right course.

In 1837 the House of Commons appointed a committee to consider "the best means of providing useful education for the children of the Poorer Classes in large towns throughout England and Wales". They found that in Leeds only one child in forty-one was attending school, at Birmingham, one in thirty-eight, in Manchester one in thirty-five. But their report did not have much effect at the time.

In 1861, however, when another Commission reported a situation very little better, it appeared that some determined Government action was needed. But the attitude of many members of the Government towards the education of the poor was still that it was a necessary evil. The member of the Government responsible for education, Robert Lowe, wrote

> the lower classes ought to be educated to discharge the duties cast upon them. They should also be educated that they may appreciate and defer to a higher cultivation when they meet it, and the higher classes ought to be educated in a very different manner, in order that they may exhibit to the lower classes that higher education to which, if they were shown it, they would bow down . . .

It was still to be nine years before an education act was passed to remedy the conditions which the 1861 Commission had revealed. In this period a new system was introduced by which a school could qualify for Government grants. This was the system known as "payment by results". Each school receiving a grant was to have a yearly examination, at which the school inspectors examined each child in the "three R's". If he passed, and if he had attended school regularly, the school would get a grant for him. Under this system, the Government grants to the school societies began to go down. In order to qualify for the grants, teachers had to be careful not to waste time on "non-essential" subjects, like drawing or music – or even history or literature, and concentrate on getting every child in the class up to scratch in reading, writing and arithmetic. Some people criticised the Government for introducing the system, but Lowe replied:

> Those for whom this system is designed are the children of persons who are not able to pay for their teaching; we do not profess to give these children an education which will raise them above their station and business in life – that is not our object . . .

Education and the Vote

In 1867, the second Reform Bill gave the vote to many working men in the towns. The whole question of education now became even more important. In 1869 a body was set up called the National Educational League. One of the leaders of this league was Joseph Chamberlain of Birmingham, a young radical manufacturer, just beginning to take an active interest in politics. The League soon gained wide public support, including that of many of the Trade Unions. The Education League and the Trade Unions wanted schools in which there would be no religious instruction, and they wanted at least a good primary education for all children. In 1870 an Act was passed by Gladstone's government which brought that goal a good deal closer.

The Education Act of 1870

The Education Act which was passed in 1870 was a compromise. It did not, as is sometimes thought, provide for free compulsory education, but it did open the door to it.

The "voluntary" schools, that is those

139. When primary education became compulsory in London, school attendance officers had the job of rounding up truants and non-attenders.

set up by the churches, were allowed to continue, helped by government grants, and subject to inspection by the Government. Where no voluntary school existed, a school board was to be elected by the ratepayers, whose function was to build and run a school. The money for the new schools was to come partly from the Government, partly from the local rates, and from school fees, which were not to be more than ninepence a week. Boards could allow pupils to attend free if they thought the parents could not afford the fee. They could also make school attendance compulsory by a local by-law. Religious instruction in the Board schools was to be "non-denominational" – that is, it was not to be the teaching of one particular branch of Christianity. School boards could, if they liked, decide that no religious instruction was to be given. Where it was given, it must be either first period in the morning or last in the afternoon, so that parents who wished to could withdraw their children. This clause allowing parents to withdraw their children from religious instruction applied to any school which had a Government grant, including the voluntary schools.

The 1870 act laid the foundation of modern primary education. In 1880 school attendance was made compulsory; in 1891 parents could choose whether or not they paid fees, although fees in primary schools were not completely abolished until 1914. In 1902 the School Boards were abolished, and the schools came under local education committees. But the two kinds of school, the "voluntary" and the state-provided have remained, although there have been a number of changes in the way in which they have been financed, mostly in the direction of more Government and rate help to the voluntary schools.

Secondary Education

The period covered by this book ends with an Education Act, in 1902, which gave local education authorities powers to provide secondary as well as primary education. But the development of this belongs to the twentieth century. The achievement of the nineteenth was the establishment of a national system of primary education, and the great reduction of ignorance and illiteracy. But that this was not going to be enough can be seen from the statement of the delegate from the London Trades Council, giving evidence before a Royal Commission on education in 1887:

> We believe (he said) that the children of the poor ought to be able to rise from the elementary to the secondary schools, and on to the universities ... all educational facilities ought to be equal and open to all classes ... We feel that it is necessary to have all the roads to

education open, free, and unfettered to the people.

The Universities

Just as the public schools changed during the century from stagnant out-of-date places into thriving and lively institutions, so the old Universities also underwent a revolution. New subjects and higher standards of tuition and lecturing brought them more into line with the needs of the nineteenth century. Oxford and Cambridge enlarged and modernised themselves, and in 1870 abolished the religious tests, so that students who were not members of the Church of England could obtain degrees.

The need for higher education, however, had been felt by the nonconformists and others to whom the old Universities were not open. Colleges had grown up in the main centres, particularly in the North of England, and by 1902 England had six universities and Wales one. The English six, moreover, included a federation called Victoria University, which soon split into the separate Universities of Manchester, Liverpool and Leeds.

Technical Education

It might be thought that a country whose industry was such a source of pride would take especial care to instruct its children and young people in technical subjects. But in fact technical education did not really begin to develop in England until the last few years of the nineteenth century. The commission which reported on the subject in 1884 showed that England had lagged far behind Germany and America in this matter. Technical colleges providing day and evening classes in trade subjects and courses in mathematics and technical drawing began to grow up in the North and in London during the last years of the century, but it was not until more education was available for all children in the national system that many people were able to take advantage of these courses. In the main, technical education

was still carried on in industry itself through the apprenticeship system for most young people.

Some Results of the Educational Changes

A national system of compulsory education, then, had been established in England by the 1880's. In 1901 *The Economist* looked back approvingly on the thirty years' progress, and summed up the reasons for it:

> Our public education system as adopted in 1870 was the outcome of agitation on the part of two classes – the intellectual class who saw that we were very nearly the worst educated nation in Christendom, and the commercial class, which saw that our markets were threatened by competitors unless we took up in earnest the task of providing our children with the key of knowledge.

It may be that by the end of the nineteenth century the "commercial class" and even the "intellectual class" were congratulating themselves that the children of England had been provided with the "key of knowledge". For the people actually engaged on the job of providing it, however, the thirty years after 1870 had been a period which had been, in the words of Margaret McMillan "not only discouraging but very puzzling as well". Margaret McMillan was one of a group of people who were interested in education primarily from the point of view of the child, rather than from the point of view of national policy. And for teachers and others who had to deal directly with the children, the first results of the new school system must have been very depressing. Charles Booth, who made a detailed study of the life and work of the people of London in the 1880's, wrote about the "puny, pale-faced, scantily clothed and badly shod children".

> these small and feeble folk may be found sitting limp and chill on the school benches in all the poorer parts of London. They swell the bills of mortality as want and sickness thin them off, or survive to be the needy and en-

feebled adults whose burden of helplessness the next generation will have to bear.

Many people on the school boards, and many teachers felt that they were wasting their time trying to educate hungry children. It was not until the early years of the twentieth century that the first victories of these people began to be won, and school medical services and free school dinners began to be introduced.

Some of the first results of the new education system, then, were social. For the first time, many people in local government and in educational circles saw hundreds of poor children gathered together, and got an idea of the vast amount of illness, malnutrition and poverty that existed in the great cities. Children came to school in rags – or, at the other extreme, in so many clothes that they could hardly breathe – "While examining one little girl in the poorest school," wrote one of the first school doctors, "after loosening the dress I found three bodices and a pair of corsets, then another old velvet dress which fastened at the back. At that point I gave up in despair and did not persist in the examination of the child". The same doctor found many of the children in London and Liverpool stitched into their clothes for the winter. These children obviously needed so much more than instruction in the three R's that it was often difficult to know where to begin. Many of the ideas of social welfare which developed in the twentieth century arose out of discoveries about actual poverty made in the classrooms of the first elementary schools.

The Reading Public and the Cheap Press

It has often been said that one of the results of free education was the cheap newspaper. The *Daily Mail*, started in 1896, was a "popular" paper, selling at $\frac{1}{2}$d. a copy, and reaching a sale of 989,000 copies a day by 1900. But although the number of people buying it was very much larger than the numbers who bought the more expensive papers earlier in the century, it was still only a tiny fraction of the adult population, and was almost certainly mainly shopkeepers, clerks and people higher up the social scale than working people.

Chapter 20

The End of the Victorian Age

The last quarter of the nineteenth century has been called the period of the Great Depression. British industry was meeting competition from the more modern industries of America and Germany, and the result was a fall in the prices which we could get for our goods. But in spite of this, for most people in England, these years were years of prosperity. Industry was still expanding. Food and raw materials were being imported at lower prices because of new techniques in shipping. From 1880 onwards refrigeration and cold storage methods were used to bring in cheap meat and dairy products, and earlier the development of railways and steamships had made possible cheap grain from Eastern Europe, the United States and Canada. For British agriculture this sort of competition was indeed disastrous, but England was by this time no longer a mainly agricultural country. The advantages of cheap food were felt by many millions, while the disadvantages of low prices for British farm products were felt by a far smaller number.

The last twenty years of the nineteenth century were probably the most generally prosperous that Britain had ever known. Consumption of basic foodstuffs – meat, butter, sugar and tea – was going up steadily, as was the consumption of tobacco and beer. Money wages for those in regular employment were rising, and even more important, real wages – that is what could actually be bought with the money – were going up even faster.

Poverty

In an atmosphere of generally improving living standards, of mass-produced furniture for working-class as well as for middle-class homes, of falling prices and rising wages, some of the real facts about poverty at last became known.

140. Street scene, Newcastle 1880. By the second half of the nineteenth century the majority of English people lived in towns. Children like the little girls in this picture grew up with no other playground but the city streets.

141. A "sweater's den" around the turn of the century. The poorest people in the cities had to work in crowded and unhealthy conditions to earn a mere living.

The pioneer in the study of the life of the poor was Charles Booth, a Liverpool ship-owner who decided to finance an enquiry into how the poor in London actually lived. He employed research workers who spent nearly twenty years compiling volume upon volume of material on all aspects of life in London. The final volume appeared in 1903, but by that time he had already published ample material to show that one third of the population of London were living in poverty. A similar survey, carried out at about the same time by B. Seebohm Rowntree in York, showed an almost identical figure there. Both reports took a standard of poverty to be one by which families could not provide enough food and clothes to keep their members in health. Booth's figures were collected between 1887 and 1892, a period of average trade, and the York figures were collected in 1899, a year of especially good trade and very little unemployment. The London report showed

30·7 per cent of the total population of London were living in poverty, and the York one 27·84 per cent.

Probably these figures show an improvement on conditions which had existed earlier. Nevertheless, they shocked many people. One thing which the surveys did show was something well-known to working people, but something which had never been fully realised by politicians and educated people looking for solutions to the problem of poverty. People were poor not just because they worked in low-paid jobs, but because the way of life of working people meant that they must expect to be living in poverty at certain times in their lives. Thus a working-class baby would be born into a situation of poverty, and stay in it until he was old enough to leave school. Then as he and his brothers and sisters went to work, the family income would go up, and the family would be living above the poverty line, as long as most of them were healthy

218

and in regular jobs. Then when he married and began to have children himself, he would be living in poverty again until the children were at work, or until his wife could return to work. Then, provided his health was good, he could expect a better standard of living until he got old, when he would once more sink below the poverty-line. However hard he worked, the ordinary labourer was more or less bound to live in this way. If he was exceptionally good at managing his affairs, he might save a little money for illness or old age, but he would be very unlikely indeed to be able to put by anything like enough to cover the ordinary emergencies of illness or temporary unemployment.

This new knowledge about poverty set the pattern for most of the social reforms which were to take place in the next fifty years. Ideas like family allowances, free medical services, school dinners, unemployment insurance, old age pensions, are all attempts to try and eliminate the areas of poverty in people's lives. Gradually the Victorian ideal of self-help began to be replaced by ideas of social help – or using some of the country's resources to help people at the periods in their lives when they are least able to help themselves. But all this belongs to the future.

The death of the Queen

On January 22nd, 1901, Queen Victoria died. She had collapsed a few days earlier after an hour's interview with Lord Roberts, in which she had shown the greatest interest in his victories over the Boers in South Africa. She had retained her interest in affairs of the country, and in particular in the Empire, until the last. Her death was a shock to everyone in the country. Many – in fact most – of the people of England could not remember a time when she was not on the throne. In the sixty-four years of her reign she had completely changed the way in which people looked at the monarchy. She had not always been popular, but as she grew older

142.   Queen Victoria, with her son, Edward VII, her grandson, George V and her great-grandson, the Duke of Windsor.

143.   A Victorian family group.

her popularity increased, and her death had the air of a national tragedy. The *Annual Register* wrote that "The feeling of forlornness which pervaded the country, was alike in its diffusion and its depth of a kind such as has not been known in England since the death of King Alfred a thousand years before . . ."

Victorianism

By the time the old Queen died, the word "Victorian" was used by everybody to describe the years of her reign. We still use the word today. For many years it has meant all that was stuffy, pompous, humourless, "correct" and restrictive. Victorian ladies wore tight corsets, crinolines and elaborate

144.   Edward VII as Prince of Wales. His way of life and his interests were in strong reaction against the narrowness of his mother's court and family life.

hair styles. They drank weak tea, and swooned and had the vapours at the slightest provocation. Victorian gentlemen wore top hats and mutton-chop whiskers, worked in the City and exercised the strictest and most tyrannical control over their families. Victorian children were members of large, overdressed families, were "seen and not heard", and played only sedate games like Happy Families or hoops. If we look at this picture, we can see that the typical "Victorian" image is that of a middle-class family. Although we know that this is nothing like a complete picture of the age, nevertheless, it may well be that the popular caricature, like all good caricatures, has brought out the most important thing about its subject.

Certainly the picture that many people wanted England to present was made up of four virtues which were of a very middle-class kind. Hard work, serious-mindedness, respectability and self-help have been called the main elements of Victorianism. But if everybody had agreed with this picture, perhaps it would not have been so necessary for writers and preachers to insist on it. The fact is that the nineteenth century was full of richness and variety, and very many people lived by values which were not "Victorian" in this sense at all.

Edward, Prince of Wales

There were on one hand, plenty of rich people – in the upper and in the middle classes, who saw no reason for hard work when they had all they needed to lead a life of pleasure. Although Queen Victoria herself presented the picture of a hard-working lady, busy with matters of state and interested in all that concerned the country, yet she would not allow her son, Edward, the Prince of Wales, to take a regular part in her work. So it was hardly surprising that Edward used most of his time and energy in spending money and in enjoying himself. Indeed, some historians date the end of the Victorian period not at the death of the old queen, but some twenty years earlier, when the Prince of Wales, became the leader of upper-class "Society" and began to introduce new ways of behaving. In his social life, he had a far wider circle of friends than the narrow court circle which surrounded his mother. He was interested in many forms of sport, particularly in blood sports of all kinds and in horse-racing. He travelled widely, not only in other countries but throughout Great Britain, and helped to bring the monarchy more into touch with the ordinary life of the country. He also began the custom of meeting working-class and radical leaders personally. There are several accounts in the reminiscences of Labour and Trade Union leaders of visits to the Royal Household. And although it may seem logical to us today that the head of the State should meet leaders of all kinds, it was certainly a new and shattering experience for some of the nineteenth-century Trade Unionists to be entertained by Royalty. Henry Broadhurst, the stonemason who became a Liberal M.P., spent three days at Sandringham, during which time the Prince of Wales poked the fire in his bedroom. He left, he afterwards wrote, "With a feeling of one who had spent a week-end with an old chum of his own rank in society, rather than one who had been entertained by the Heir Apparent and His Princess . . ."

Non-respectable people

Edward, then, was breaking down the Victorian picture of royalty as remote and infinitely respectable. He encouraged by his example an attachment to pleasure and to sports which did not accord with the ideal of serious-mindedness. At the other end of the social scale there were many millions of people who had little opportunity to practise the virtues of respectability or of self-help. Many labourers lived a hand-to-mouth existence which encouraged them to make the most of any good fortune and not to try and plan for the future. Only the better-off members of the working classes,

people like engineers and skilled workers in the building trades, could hope to gain a position of respectability through hard work and careful saving. The drudgery of the work which many people were forced to do – the lower-paid domestic servants, dockers, miners, and all kinds of casual labourers – often led them to look for escape by drinking or gambling.

But it was not only the poorest and most desperate who opposed the ideals of "respectability". In the songs from the pubs and Music Halls we can see how the town-dwellers made fun of the search for "respectability" like *Knocked 'em in the Old Kent Road*. In the countryside, in spite of the flow of people into the towns, and the ending of many of the old forms of social life, there was a whole range of beliefs, customs and culture which did not fit in all with the middle-class ideal. When, in the second half of the nineteenth century, musicians began to be interested in English folk-songs, and to go out into the villages to collect examples of these songs, they found that the words were often very shocking. In the notes to editions of folk-songs, the editors found themselves explaining that they had had to re-write the words, since the originals were "very indelicate", "too coarse for reproduction" or "impossible to print". Fortunately for us, some of the collectors, including the greatest of them, Cecil Sharp, noted the original words in their notebooks, and today we can see that most of the songs which shocked the Victorians did so by a simple honesty and lack of prudery, and not from coarseness or obscenity.

The Protesters

Even within the middle classes, there were always voices which protested against the worst aspects of Victorianism. Writers like Dickens attacked the hypocrisy of "Charity" and the inhumanity with which the poor and the defenceless were treated. Thomas Carlyle and John Ruskin wrote against the pre-occupation with money-making, and the

145. Marie Lloyd – the popular music-hall singer, whose cheerful and vulgar songs made no attempt to please "refined" Victorian taste.

attempt to reduce everything in life to things which could be bought and sold. William Morris rebelled against the appalling ugliness of the life in Victorian cities. As we have seen, Trade Unions and Co-operative Societies tried to keep alive the ideals of working together against the "self-help" ideal of "every man for himself". Although the general picture of English towns was one of unplanned squalor the idea of town planning was being discussed. In the city of Birmingham, under the leadership of Joseph Chamberlain, a programme of slum-clearance and radical planning had already been started in the 'seventies. Here the idea of a town planned with all its citizens in mind had begun to take shape, and to set an example which was to be widely followed in the twentieth century. In London, which had doubled its population between 1851 and 1901, local government machinery had been completely reorganised in the last ten years of the nineteenth century. A beginning had been made on the wide programme of social provision, in housing, health and education that was to be carried out in the new century.

1902

We end, in 1902, with a new king on the throne, and a new century barely begun. The Conservatives are in power, within three years of the end of a twenty-year term of office, the result of the split in the Liberal party over the question of Irish Home Rule. The Boer War has ended, and the country is at peace. To many people it must have seemed as if the new country, coming after a hundred years of social and political change, was bringing in a period of calm and peace. Very few can have foreseen the violence of events which were to come within a very few years, and to make the first quarter of the twentieth century as dramatic and full of change as any time in the history of the country.

Glossary

The meanings given here for the words listed are the meanings in which the words are used in this book. They are not always the only meaning of the word. Where a fuller explanation is given in the text, the page is given in brackets by the word. Some of the unusual words come in descriptions or quotations about trade and industry, especially the textile industry. Where the meaning is a special one for an industry, the name of the industry is put in brackets.

ABDICATE: give up power or an important office, e.g. the crown.

ABSENTEE: a landowner or office holder who lives away from his estate or work.

ABSOLUTE MONARCHY: rule by a king who has no Parliament, but rules as a dictator.

ADMINISTRATION: management, often used to mean the government.

ADMINISTRATOR: manager – some one who is capable of organising (p. 134).

ADULTERATED: false – mixed with poor ingredients.

AGITATION: commotion, disturbance, debate, discussion.

ALLOTMENT: small piece of land let out to be cultivated.

ALMSHOUSE: house built by charity for poor people to live in.

ALUM: a white mineral salt, very cheap, sometimes used to adulterate food.

AMALGAMATED: mixed together, joined, combined.

AMITY: friendship.

ANNEXED: added to existing territory or possessions.

APOTHECARY: old word for druggist or chemist.

APPRENTICE: some one who is learning a craft or trade, and is bound to stay with the master who is teaching him for a certain number of years.

AQUEDUCT: a bridge built to carry water (p. 42).

ARBITER: judge or umpire, some one appointed to settle a quarrel.

ARCHITECT: man who designs buildings.

ARISTOCRAT: member of a ruling class of nobles.

ARTISAN: mechanic, skilled craftsman (p. 3).

BADGER SHOP: shop which allows people to owe money, and sells bad goods at high prices.

BALLOT: secret voting – usually by making a cross on a piece of paper and putting it into a box so that no one can see how the vote has been given.

BARONET: lowest rank of the hereditary peerage.

BARRICADE: a barrier – usually one set up in a street during street fighting.

BASTILLE: a famous French prison which was attacked at the beginning of the French Revolution of 1789. In England the name was given to the workhouses set up after the 1834 Poor Law Amendment Act (p. 102).

BEEFEATER: a Yeoman of the Guard, member of the ceremonial guard at the Tower of London.

BLACKLIST: a list which was passed round

amongst employers with the names of members of Trade Unions to prevent them from getting jobs.

BLASPHEMY: speaking or writing against God or against Christianity.

BOBBIN: spool for holding yarn.

BOROUGH: town with the right to send members to Parliament.

BOYCOTT: send to Coventry, bring pressure on some one by ignoring them.

BRUSHING: (textile) raising a nap on cloth by brushing with wire or other stiff brush.

BUDGET: yearly estimate of government spending made by the Chancellor of the Exchequer.

BURGESS: Member of Parliament for a borough.

CANAL: artificial waterway for inland navigation.

CARDING: (textile) brushing raw wool with wire teeth to prepare it for spinning.

CARICATURE: funny or satirical picture of a person or thing, exaggerating certain aspects.

CASUAL LABOURER: man who works when he can get work, and does not have a regular job.

CAUSEWAY: pavement or raised footpath.

CENSUS: official count of the people in a country (p. 17).

CHAPLAIN: a clergyman who works for a private household or for a school, prison or other institution.

CHARCOAL: Partly burnt wood, used where great heat and little smoke are needed.

CHARABANC: long horse-drawn carriage with benches on for trips and outings.

CIVIL RIGHTS: the rights of a citizen.

COLONIES: settlements in overseas countries which are still governed directly by the mother country (p. 170).

COMBERS: (textile) men who prepare worsted yarn for spinning, by combing the raw wool into long slivers with heated metal combs.

COMMERCE: trade – the selling and exchange of goods.

COMMISSION: used here to mean a group of men given responsibility by the Government to enquire into certain definite questions (p. 100).

COMMITTEE: group of people appointed or elected to do a particular job – often the leadership of a party or movement.

COMMITTEE STAGE: between the second and third readings of a parliamentary bill, the bill is considered by a committee of the house, and changes may be made in it.

COMMON: land which belongs to the whole village.

COMMUNICATIONS: connections between people or between places. So can be roads railways etc. or written or spoken words between people.

COMMUNITY: body of people living together.

COMMUTE: change – usually to make a punishment less severe, sometimes to change one sort of payment for another.

COMPENSATION: something given as a recompense, for example money given to some one who has been injured.

COMPULSORY: forced, obligatory.

CONCESSION: something admitted or allowed.

CONSTITUENCY: the people who elect a member of Parliament, or the place in which all the electors live, and which the member represents.

CONSTITUTION: way in which a country is organised – its system of government.

CONSTITUTIONAL: in agreement with the political system by which the country is governed.

CONTEMPORARY: people living at the same time, books or newspapers published at the same time.

CONTINGENT: part of an army, or of any organised crowd.

CONVENTION: an assembly of people meeting together like a parliament, but not summoned by the king.

COOPERATION: working together for the same things.

CORN LAWS: the laws which controlled the import of corn in the early nineteenth century (p. 121).

CORRUPT: rotten – influenced by bribes.

COUP DE GRACE: finishing blow – the last stroke needed to overthrow something.

CREDIT: belief, trust, ability to pay money.

CRINOLINE: wide hooped petticoats used to make dresses stand out (p. 220).

CRISIS: turning-point, moment of danger or anxiety.

CRITIC: some one who makes a judgement, usually some one who makes an unfavourable judgement.

CUIRASS: waistcoat (p. 88).

CUSTODY: care and guardianship of children (p. 145).

CUSTOMARY: usual, according to the ways of the country.

DEIST: some one who believes in a god, but not in any one religion.

DEMONSTRATION: show of force, by large numbers of people, to press for a particular object.

DESOLATE: alone, sad, dreary.

DESPOTISM: the rule of one man over a whole society.

DICTATORSHIP: also means the rule of one man, but here usually a man who has taken over the government in a time of crisis.

DISABILITY: a thing, often a law, which prevents people from doing something.

DISSENTER: member of a sect that has separated itself from the Church of England.

DIVIDEND: share of profits, usually in return for having lent money.

DOFFERS: (textile) the worker who changes the empty bobbins for full ones on a power loom.

DOMESTIC SYSTEM: industrial system in which the actual work is done in the workers' own homes.

DOMINION: overseas possession which has its own government, but which still comes under the British crown (p. 170).

DURATION: length of time for which something continues.

ECONOMIC: to do with industry and trade.

EFFIGY: portrait or model, usually of a person.

ELECT: choose, usually choose by voting.

EMANCIPATE: set free, usually from legal disabilities.

EMIGRATE: leave one country and settle in another.

ENDOWED SCHOOL: school which is set up by gifts of money or bequests in wills and not by government grant.

ENTREPRENEUR: some one who buys and sells or lends money for industry, not usually the person who actually manufactures the goods.

EPERGNE: centre ornament for a dinner table.

ENCLOSED: here, meaning fenced in and hedged fields in place of open fields and commons.

ESTABLISHED: official, recognised as legal.

EVICT: turn out, usually to turn out tenants from houses or land.

EXCLUSIVE DEALING: a manner of influencing electors by shopping only at shops owned by voters who vote your way (p. 118).

EXPLOIT: use or work for your own advantage.

FALLOW: uncultivated land.

FANATICAL: filled with too much or mistaken enthusiasm, usually used of religions.

FILIBUSTER: delay and obstruct.

FINANCE: money, often applied to government taxes.

FLAX: plant from which the thread for making linen cloth comes.

FRAMEWORK-KNITTING: a method of knitting stockings on a frame, instead of cutting and making up the stockings from cloth.

FRANCHISE: right of voting at elections.

FRATERNITY: brotherhood.

FRAUD: criminal or dishonest trick to get money.

FREE TRADE: trade left to its natural course, without customs duties and taxes on goods (p. 122).

FREEHOLDER: outright owner of property.

FREEMAN: man who has the freedom of a city.

FRIENDLY SOCIETY: early sort of insurance society to help members save for sickness, old age, unemployment etc.

FRUGAL: careful, very sparing, especially of food.

FULLING: (textile) the process of washing and beating woollen cloth to clean and thicken it.

GAME LAWS: the laws about shooting and hunting wild animals and birds.

GARRISON: troops stationed in a town to defend it.

GENERAL STRIKE: strike in which working people in all industries take part.

GENERAL WARRANT: warrant issued for the arrest not of any named individual, but of all people belonging to a certain organisation or category.

GENTLEMAN: in the eighteenth century a man of a high social class who was not actually a member of the nobility.

GENTRY: the people who belonged to the next rank below the nobility.

GILDER: man who decorates in gold (p. 10).

GOVERNESS: female teacher usually of children in a private home and not in a school (p. 196).

GUERILLA WARFARE: irregular sort of fighting by scattered bands of soldiers acting independently (p. 184).

GUILD: society of members of the same trade – usually of masters rather than workmen.

HABEAS CORPUS: the law which says that a man must not be kept in prison without a definite charge being brought against him.

HEIR APPARENT: the next person in line for the throne.

HERBALIST: a dealer in herbs and plants for medicines.

HUMANITARIAN: a person who is concerned with the well-being of the whole of society.

HUSSAR: soldier of a light cavalry regiment.

HUSTINGS: platforms on which candidates for Parliament were nominated before 1872.

HYPOCRISY (HYPOCRITICAL): pretence of virtue or goodness.

ILLITERATE: unable to read or write.

IMPERIALISM: belief in the importance of the Empire (p. 169).

INDUSTRIAL REVOLUTION: the changes in the relations between employers and work-people which took place in the eighteenth and nineteenth centuries, particularly associated with new kinds of power. Ch III.

INDUSTRIALISATION: a change from a mainly agricultural way of life to one in which most people work at manufacturing goods.

INEFFABLE: too great for words.

INSPECTOR: man whose job is to see that the law is being carried out by examining institutions – schools, factories etc.

INSTITUTION: building or organisation set up for a particular purpose.

INTEREST: money paid in return for money lent or invested.

INVEST: put money into stocks and shares – to lend money for a profit.

JACOBITE: supporter of James II and his son the Young Pretender, particularly in the risings of 1715 and 1745.

JINGOISM: warlike, blustering patriotism.

JOURNALIST: person who writes for newspapers or magazines.

JOURNEYMAN: skilled worker who works for an employer.

JUDGEMENT: sentence of a court, can mean a judge's decision which is then taken as the correct interpretation of the law.

JUSTICES OF THE PEACE: magistrates.

KAFFIRS: African natives of South Africa.

KHAKI: dust colour used for the uniform of the British army in the South African war and since, so anything to do with the army.

KNIGHT: member of gentry or lower nobility who has the title "Sir".

LAITY: all people who are not the clergymen or church officials.

LEGAL: to do with the law, recognised by the law.

LIBEL: a published statement which can damage another person.

LUCRATIVE: profitable.

LUDDITE: member of a band of machine-breakers in the years 1811–1818 (p. 74).

MAGISTRATE: a man, usually not a professional lawyer, who presides over local courts, and administers justice and the law in his district.

MAINTENANCE: keeping up, paying for.

MALNUTRITION: undernourishment, having too little food.

MARSHAL: organise, arrange in order.

MERCENARY: interested only in money or reward.

MIDDLE PASSAGE: route taken to the West Indies by slave ships.

MILL: building fitted with machinery, originally for grinding corn, but gradually came to mean any factory.

MILLINER: hat maker; in the nineteenth century they were usually women who worked in their own homes or in sweated workshops.

MINORITY: a smaller group within a society – often a group of people having a different religion or nationality – like Jews or Irish immigrants.

MONOPOLY: exclusive possession or control of something.

MOSLEM: follower of Mohamet – one of the main world religions.

MUNICIPAL: to do with a town or city, or to do with local government in a town.

MUSKET: old-fashioned hand-gun, carried by infantry.

MUTINY: open revolt against officers by soldiers or sailors.

NATIONALISM: strong patriotic feeling.

NEGOTIATION: discussion aimed at reaching agreement by compromise.

NEUTRALITY: not helping either side in a war.

NIGGARDLY: stingy, mean, grudging.

NOBILITY: class of ruling families who pass on their titles and power from parents to children.

NON-CONFORMIST: some one who does not belong to or agree with the established church.

NON-DENOMINATIONAL: Christian teaching which does not follow the teaching of one particular sect.

OBSCENE: indecent, repulsive.

ORATOR: good public speaker.

ORIGINATOR: person who first thought of or started an idea or movement.

OUT-WORKER: worker employed by merchant or manufacturer, but who actually works in his own home.

PAGEANT: brilliant display, colourful procession.

PAMPHLET: small unbound booklet with paper covers.

PARISH: area having its own church.

PARLIAMENTARY PRIVILEGE: special rights of members of Parliament, including the right not to be arrested whilst they are members.

PASTURE: grassland used for grazing animals.

PAUPER: person with no money or means of livelihood of his own.

PEASANT: countryman, usually a small tenant farmer.

PEDLAR: travelling salesman who carries his pack of goods from door to door or around to fairs and markets.

PEELITE: a supporter of Peel in the Tory split after 1846 (p. 138).

PEER: member of the House of Lords.

PETITION: a written request from one or more people to the King or to Parliament.

PICKETING: practice in strikes of having Trade Union members standing outside the factory to persuade others not to go in to work.

PIECER: (textile) person who joins the threads together in a spinning factory.

PIETY: obedience to religious principles.

PIKE: long wooden weapon with iron or steel head, used by infantry before the bayonet was introduced.

PLAGUE: very infectious and deadly fever which spread through whole countries.

PLIMSOLL LINE: mark on the side of a merchant ship to show when it was too low in the water, and therefore overloaded.

POACHING: the taking of game in contravention of the game laws.

POLL: counting of voters at elections.

POOR RATES: rate paid by all property-owners to help support the poor.

PREDECESSOR: person who came before, or who held office before the present holder.

PREJUDICE: bias, unreasonable dislike of person or thing.

PRESTIGE: good reputation.

PROFANE: not sacred or biblical.

PROROGUE: end the meeting of Parliament.

PROPAGANDA: publicity in favour of something.

PROSECUTE: take legal proceedings against.

PROTECTIONIST: some one who believes that home industries should be protected by taxing foreign goods.

PROVINCIAL: to do with any part of a country outside the capital city.

PROVOCATEUR: an agent paid to persuade discontended people to take action, usually violent or illegal action, in order that they may be punished.

PRUDERY: excessive modesty.

PUBLIC OPINION: the general opinion in a country, as shown by its newspapers and other publications.

PUBLIC SCHOOL: an endowed school whose headmaster attends the Headmasters' Conference (p. 209).

QUARANTINE: period in which sick people have to stay on board ship or in a special hospital to prevent infectious illnesses being brought into a country.

RADICAL: going to the root of a question – so politicians who want reforms that call for considerable changes (p. 57).

RAW MATERIAL: materials out of which manufactured goods are made.

REACTIONARY: politics which are aimed at preventing change.

RECTOR: parson in a village.

REDRESS: set right.

REFORM: make better, improve.

REGENT: person appointed to rule in place of the King, usually if the king is very young or is ill.

RELIEF: help given to the very poor.

RELIGIOUS ORDER: group of monks or nuns who live according to agreed rules.

REMINISCENCE: book written by a person about his life and memories.

REPEAL: revoke, do away with. In Irish history, usually meaning the repeal of the Act of Union.

REPRESSION: keeping under, preventing from acting.

REPRIEVE: delay or abandonment of the death sentence.

REPUBLICAN: person who believes in a government without kings or queens, usually some form of democracy.

REVENUE: income, the money the government gets from taxes.

REVOLUTION: complete change, turning upside down.

RIDDLE: coarse wire sieve (p. 4).

RIDICULE: to make fun of.

ROSTRUM: a platform for public speaking.

ROTE: learning by heart, often without understanding.

SATIRE: making fun of something in order to improve it.

SEDITIOUS: likely to lead to rebellion, directed against the government.

SETTLEMENT: here means the system by which poor people were only allowed to get relief in the parish in which they had lived for a certain time (p. 24).

SHAREHOLDER: some one who has money invested in a business.

SLOGAN: motto, watchword.

SPECULATOR: some one who takes a risk in business, usually hoping for a bigger profit than usual.

SPEENHAMLAND SYSTEM: the system by which poor relief was given according to the price of bread (p. 24).

SPINNING-FLAT: the floor of the factory on which the spinning machines were (p. 206).

STRATEGIC: concerned with the long term direction of war.

SQUATTER: person who settles in a new country or on common land without a legal right to the land.

SQUIRE: country gentleman, usually the chief landowner in a district.

STOCKBROKER: man who buys and sells stocks and shares for a living.

SUBJECTION: being kept down, prevented from acting.

SUBSERVIENT: cringing, over-respectful, inferior.

SUPERSTITIOUS: believing in, and usually being afraid of, ghostly or supernatural forces.

SYLLABUS: list of subjects taught in a school.

TARIFF: duty or customs to be paid on imports or exports.

TALLY-MAN: some one who sells goods and collects the money in small installments.

TECHNIQUE: skill, method.

TEMPORISE: put off, try and avoid making a decision.

TEXTILE: to do with cloth, or the industries of cloth manufacture.

TITHE: tax of one-tenth in goods or money of the yearly production, which went to support the clergyman and the church (p. 13).

TOMMY SHOP: shop belonging to an employer, at which the workers had to spend part of their wages.

TRADE UNION: union of working people to improve wages and working conditions.

TRADES COUNCIL: meeting of representatives of all the Trade Unions in a town.

TRADITIONAL: according to custom.

TRANSPORTATION: the punishment of sending criminals to colonies overseas (p. 24).

TRIBUTE: money paid by one state to the state that controls it.

TRUCK: the system of paying workers in goods or in money to be spent at the company shop.

TRUSTEE: some one who looks after goods or money on behalf of a charity or public body.

TURBINE: specially constructed wheel which can be driven by water, air, steam or gas jets.

TURNPIKE: roads whose building was paid for by toll gates (p. 40).

TUTOR: private teacher, usually one who takes complete charge of a boy's education for a time.

UITLANDER: Afrikaans word for foreigner.

UNANIMOUS: all agreeing, no one voting against.

UNMERCENARY: not interested in money.

UNSTAMPED: (of the press) papers which did not pay the newspaper duty (p. 110).

UTILITARIAN: follower of the philosopher Jeremy Bentham (p. 81).

UTILITY: usefulness, profitability.

VETERAN: some one who has grown old in and has a long experience of a particular occupation, e.g. soldier.

VOLUNTARY SCHOOL: school set up by charitable or religious body, and not by school board or education committe (p. 213).

VOLUNTEER: some one who takes on a job or goes into the armed forces without being compelled to.

WATCH COMMITTEE: committee responsible for police force in a locality.

WORKHOUSE: house built by local authorities for paupers.

WORSTED: (textile) woollen yarn and cloth made from long-stapled wool. Usually finer than ordinary woollen stuff.

ZONE: well-defined area.

Index